James Bond and Philosophy

Popular Culture and Philosophy®

Series Editor: George A. Reisch

(Series Editor for this volume was William Irwin)

Popular Culture and Philosophy®

James Bond and Philosophy

Questions Are Forever

Edited by

JACOB M. HELD

and

JAMES B. SOUTH

OPEN COURT
Chicago and La Salle, Illinois

Volume 23 in the series, Popular Culture and Philosophy™

To order books from Open Court, call 1-800-815-2280, or visit our website at www.opencourtbooks.com.

Open Court Publishing Company is a division of Carus Publishing Company.

First printing 2006

Printed and bound in the United States of America.

Library of Congress Cataloging-in-Publication Data

James Bond and philosophy : questions are forever / edited by James B. South and Jacob M. Held.
    p. cm. — (Popular culture and philosophy ; v. 23)
    Summary: "A collection of philosophical essays about the fictional world of James Bond as seen in Ian Fleming's novels and the ongoing film series Issues addressed include existentialism and the good life, crime and punishment, gender politics, the cold war and nuclear proliferation, and human interrelation with technoogy" —Provided by publisher.
    Includes bibliographical references and index.
    ISBN-13: 978-0-8126-9607-3 (trade pbk. : alk. paper)
    ISBN-10: 0-8126-9607-7 (trade pbk. : alk. paper)
    1. Fleming, Ian, 1908-1964—Philosophy. 2. Fleming, Ian, 1908–1964—Characters—James Bond. 3. Bond, James (Fictitious character) 4. Spy stories, English—History and criticism. 5. Fleming, Ian, 1908–1964—Film and video adaptations. 6. James Bond films—History and criticism. 7. Philosophy in literature. 8. Philosophy in motion pictures. I. Held, Jacob M., 1977- II. South, James B., 1960-
PR6056.L4Z73 2006
823'.914—dc22

                       2006024448

*To my colleagues
in the Philosophy Department
at Marquette University*

—James B. South

To Wyatt and Lillian

—Daddy

Contents

SECTION I
No Mr. Bond, I Expect You to Die
Bond, Existentialism, and Death   1

SECTION II
Mr. Bond Is Indeed a Very Rare Breed
The Man Behind the Number   47

SECTION III
For England, James?
Bond, Politics, and Law   109

SECTION IV
Oh, Don't Be an Idiot, 007
Knowledge and Technology   155

SECTION V
Why Do Chinese Girls Taste Different from All Other Girls?
Multiculturalism, Women, and a More Sensitive Bond

Oh, Spare Me This Sentimental Rubbish

First, I would like to thank James South for suggesting this project, and then for allowing me to do the majority of work on it and thus gain valuable experience. I will take responsibility for all remaining errors and spare his reputation. I would also like to thank Bill Irwin for his support and insight in editing this volume, as well as a general "thank you" for editing this series and promoting the popularization of philosophy without diminishing its seriousness as a discipline. Thanks also to my wife who is always supportive, for some reason I haven't yet figured out. And to my mother and brother who put up with a young boy obsessed with James Bond who insisted that Bond and his feats were not impossible or ridiculous, but that he was simply very well trained, and if you're not going to take it seriously you can leave the room.

Jacob M. Held

My greatest debt is to my co-editor, Jake Held. Specifically, his enthusiasm for the project and conscientious work were essential for completion of this volume. More generally, my conversations with him have been philosophically rewarding, and I count myself fortunate to have collaborated with him over the last several years. My wife Kelly Wilson is largely responsible for re-introducing me to pleasures of the spy genre, so without her I never would have thought of doing a book like this. Also, my thanks to a group of friends—Betty, Bill, Cindy, Deb, Kate, Linda, Nancy, Nicky, and Sandy—who regularly remind me how much fun it is to talk about spies. Finally, I'd like to note my appreciation for support at Marquette University that Ms. Beth O'Sullivan and Ms. Lula Hopkins provide me on a daily basis. If it weren't for their patience, good humor, and efficiency, I would never have completed my work on this volume.

James B. South

Tell Me, Commander, How Far Does Your Expertise Extend into the Field of Philosophy?

Most people get introduced to James Bond early in life.[1] As a young boy, I was fascinated by him. He had the coolest gadgets, the wittiest comebacks, and when it came to getting the bad guy nobody did, and nobody does it better.[2] I would collect defunct electronics and other pieces of technical looking garbage so I could construct my own Q Branch in my attic.

How Sean Connery could inspire such rampant acts of geekdom still baffles me, but at least I was not alone. Many prepubescent secret agent wannabes were right alongside me. I would insist that my mother and brother keep quiet while watching Bond films; no laughing, take it seriously. (Yes, even *Moonraker*.)[3] I recall one instance where, during the beginning of *Goldfinger*, my brother commented how ridiculous Bond movies were simply because Bond saw an assailant approaching through a reflection in a woman's eye. I didn't see the problem. This is James Bond we are talking about.

I see my brother's point now and I see Bond a bit more clearly. I can say that I have outgrown my fannish interest in Bond, or rationalized it as a legitimate academic pursuit, at least for now. But my experience is not unique. Many of us grew up with Bond. After all, he has been around in film form since 1962 and is now a cultural icon. Bond is not merely one among many in the spy-thriller genre; he is a genre unto himself. His influence

---

[1] The bulk of what follows was written by Jacob Held; James South makes an occasional cameo appearance, and these are noted with a parenthetical (JS).
[2] James South (the forty-six-year-old co-editor) must at this point add a caveat: other spies in the 1960s were pretty darn cool as well, especially Napoleon Solo and his partner Illya Kuryakin of the TV series *The Man from U.N.C.L.E.*
[3] I am baffled that anyone could take *Moonraker* seriously. (JS)

has been profound. Action films seem to believe it obligatory to include advanced gadgetry and snarky one liners; both signature Bond. Mike Myers's Austin Powers trilogy, aside from being hilarious, trades almost entirely on the audience's knowledge concerning Bond the cultural icon. Most people can probably quote some line from a Bond movie, or at least recognize one once it has been quoted. "No Mr. Bond, I expect you to die." is as likely to be recognized as "To be or not to be." Indeed, more people probably know the movie in which the first is uttered than know the play from which the latter is drawn.

As with most people, my exposure to Bond began with the movies, and it was some time before I began to read Ian Fleming's books. But once I did I was in for quite a surprise. Fleming's Bond is very different from the Bond of the silver screen. Fleming's Bond isn't so confident or suave. He isn't a ladies man, rather he is described as cruel. He is frail, flawed, depressed, arguably an alcoholic and takes speed to help him perform his fantastic feats, that is, he is very, very human. This is a far cry from Sean Connery's portrayal of the super human, irresistible womanizer—or any subsequent portrayal for that matter. But whether one is looking at Fleming's Bond or Hollywood's version, Bond is a fascinating character. He's almost super human, yet flawed. Recall that he always gets captured. He is a complete womanizer in the worst sense: he is sleazy. Perhaps one of the worst moments occurs in the film *Diamonds are Forever* when he nonchalantly says to Tiffany Case that he doesn't much care about what she wears so long as the "cuffs and collars" match. What causes people to be drawn in by him, attached to his persona and to the fantasy he portrays? How many of us feel passionately that one or the other Bond actors provides the definitive portrayal?[4] And people take this seriously, perhaps too much so.[5]

---

[4] Timothy Dalton. Timothy Dalton—are you crazy? Sean Connery *is* James Bond. (JS)

[5] How did you react to the above footnote? JS: In Season Six of *Buffy the Vampire Slayer*, there is a humorous, yet serious discussion of this very question running throughout the season. The ultimate villain for that season preferred Sean Connery. That identification in turn has made me very worried about my own attraction to the Connery portrayal. That the Bond icon can be used in this way, as a method to reflect on someone's character, is some indication that the significance of Bond for popular culture is long overdue for the consideration it is given in this volume.

This phenomenon illustrates an important point about Bond: we are attached to him because we see ourselves in and through him. Bond exemplifies our hopes and dreams, a desire for a world where good always triumphs and where good and evil are clearly defined and easily recognizable. Perhaps this is why the movies do not accurately reproduce the books. In the books the line is not so clear between justice and revenge, good and evil, right and wrong. But in the movies we are given what we want, and what we need, namely, clarity and resolution.

Despite Bond's flaws, his status as a cultural icon, the themes of good and evil, and the degree to which we both identify with him and worry about that identification, make Bond an ideal vehicle for philosophical discussion. He provides the impetus for us to reflect upon ourselves, our values, and our world. He provokes us to ask ourselves what we believe, why we believe it, and if we should believe it.

The Bondscape is rife with important and thought provoking issues. There are the obvious issues pertaining to misogyny, objectification, feminism as well as cold war politics and nuclear proliferation. But the Bondscape is much lusher than some give it credit for. Through Bond we are confronted with humanity's intersection with technology: how we create it and it creates us. We are provoked into asking about the nature of a license to kill, the rule or law, governmental powers, and human rights. As a character study Bond provides an interesting window onto classical conceptions of the good life and themes in existential philosophy. The themes covered in this book range over a great deal of philosophy from existentialism to logic, law to eastern philosophy, and technology to phenomenology. There will be some areas not covered and some readers will find glaring omissions, but hopefully all will find present an introduction and discussion of major philosophical themes in a way that will both engage them as intellectuals and delight them as fans.

SECTION I

No Mr. Bond,
I Expect You to Die

Bond, Existentialism,
and Death

1

Being-Towards-Death and Taking Pleasure in Beauty: James Bond and Existentialism

BETH BUTTERFIELD

The film: *The World Is Not Enough*. The mission: protect the beautiful Elektra King from an anticipated attack. Bond's position: between the sheets, of course. In this scene, we find James in bed with Elektra, early enough in the film that we still believe her to be an innocent victim in need of James's protection. We've seen her cry as she describes the torture endured during her kidnapping, and we know that she has recently lost a "loved one," her father. Lying together between the silken sheets, Elektra notices James's wounded shoulder. In twenty films and nearly fifty years, it's one of the first times we've really seen James Bond get hurt. "Poor shoulder," she purrs, "it looks painful."

This scene reminds us that James's life as a double-0 is not all fun and games. Yes, the secret agent's life of international intrigue is full of excitement and adventure, traveling the world and sampling the best it has to offer. But the adventure comes at a price, and the life of danger can also sometimes be a life of suffering. Death lingers around every corner—not only the possibility that James himself will be killed, but also the possibility that he will lose someone he cares for. Caring for a woman is a dangerous thing in James's line of business. As he thinks to himself in the novel, *Doctor No*, "It had been a bad break coming across this girl. In combat, like it or not, a girl is your extra heart. The enemy has two targets against your one."[1]

---

[1] Ian Fleming, *Doctor No* (London: Coronet, 1988), p. 82.

Hardly a film goes by in which James doesn't lose a loved one—and often, the beautiful girl is murdered *simply because* of her association with him. Sleeping with James can be a perilous affair! Examples are easy to find—from his lover in the very first James Bond novel, *Casino Royale*, who turns out to be a double agent and commits suicide, to the beautiful Jill Masterson, suffocated by gold body paint in *Goldfinger*, to the wife of the media tycoon in *Tomorrow Never Dies*. We find the starkest example in *On Her Majesty's Secret Service*, when James's young wife is assassinated by Blofeld only moments after their wedding, as the newlyweds are driving off on their honeymoon.

With all of this in mind, we return to the bedroom. Elektra asks the injured James, "What do you do to survive?" And we must wonder this too—how is it that no matter what happens, at the end of every film we know that "James Bond will return"? How is it that he can put all of the loss, pain, and injustice in the world behind him, and move on? James answers the question in this way: "I take pleasure in great beauty." Brilliant! The beautiful women, the world's most beautiful and exotic locations, the martinis and fine wines—surrounding himself with beauty, indulging in sensual pleasures, helps James to survive.

Could it be that James Bond has really found an answer to the philosophical problem of human suffering in hedonism? Should we follow his example and indulge in sensual pleasures for the sake of our own emotional survival? Or could it be that Bond's hedonism is no more than an attempt to escape from reality? Is it perhaps the case that Bond, the courageous and hardened hero, loses himself in wine, women, and song simply so that he won't have to face life's harshest realities—namely, those of losing loved ones, and of being himself a murderer? What are we to take away from Bond's words of wisdom?

No, Mr. Bond, I Expect You to Die!

For James Bond, death is always right around the corner. As movie critic Anthony Lane puts it, Bond is "blessed with a license to kill and a refusal to die."[2] But the fact of the matter is that when he is on assignment, he is constantly facing the pos-

---

[2] Anthony Lane, "Mondo Bond: Forty Years of 007," *New Yorker* (4th November, 2002).

sibility of his own death. He is constantly aware that he could die at any moment, and there is no escaping this reality.

While Bond's situation may be slightly different from the everyday Joe's, his constant encounter with the possibility of his own death brings into high relief something that each one of us must face—as humans we are all mortal, and someday we are all going to die. We may not be forced to face this harsh reality on a daily basis like Bond, but it remains an inescapable fact of life.

In the nineteenth and twentieth centuries, a group of thinkers who came to be known as Existentialists asserted that the issue of our human mortality should be at the center of philosophical thought. They attempted to bring philosophy back down to earth and focus on questions that are central to human experience. And they were right to take up the issue of death as a philosophical puzzle—after all, how could something like death even be possible? How can it be that we live lives that feel so important, striving for decades to find understanding and meaning, building relationships, working to really achieve something, learning so much, developing ourselves, only to find that in the end, inevitably, *we will no longer exist?* How can it be that something as precious as life could actually come to an end? It's absurd. At one point or another, surely every person feels the absurdity of death—whether it is in the death of a parent, a sibling, a lover, a friend, a child, or even in the death of a total stranger. So one of the most important questions for the Existentialist philosophers is: How should the fact of our own impending deaths reflect upon our understanding of *life?* How should we live?

One philosopher in particular who explored this question was Martin Heidegger (1889–1976). In his book, *Being and Time*, Heidegger draws attention to the fact that humans experience death as a constant possibility, and he calls this constant awareness of mortality our state of "being-towards-death." Whether or not we admit it, we live our lives as "towards-death" everyday, always moving closer to the day when all that I am will no longer exist and I will be nothing. Heidegger writes as an atheist who holds out no hope for an afterlife—so death really is the end, ultimate nothingness.

Bond echoes Heidegger's notion of being-towards-death in the novel, *Live and Let Die.* He thinks to himself, "There's nothing to do about it. You start to die the moment you are born. The whole of life is cutting through the pack with death."[3]

Shaken? Perhaps, but Not Stirred

Of course, facing our own mortality can be pretty disturbing! Heidegger explains what you probably already know; confronting the possibility of our own deaths tends to produce a feeling of "angst," or anxiety. Angst is like fear except that whereas fear is in response to a particular scary thing, angst arises in reaction to nothingness itself. Our anxiety develops not only in response to the awareness that we too must die someday, but also in response to what this means for life—that in life, we are incredibly free. We are free to make choices about who we want to be and how we want to live.

Heidegger claims that this freedom itself is intimidating and that most people try to run away from it. He explains that we often do everything we can to distract ourselves from the thought of our own impending deaths and to avoid the responsibility we have to make something of our own lives. One of the most common strategies we use, according to Heidegger, is to try to lose ourselves (and our self-awareness) in the "busy-ness" of everyday life. We look to society and the fashions of the day to tell us how to live and to make our decisions for us. We give up our responsibility for creating our own lives, and as we focus all of our attention on trying to "fit in" and to keep up with the crowd we gradually forget ourselves.

Of course, for the Existentialists, this attempt to run away from anxiety is the wrong response and it comes at a price. The danger of losing ourselves in the world is that we forget that we are actually more than the pre-fab fashionable image we attempt to imitate—we forget that we are actually free. We lose the sense that it is possible to choose our own futures and consequently we lose the richest part of human experience.

Bond, by contrast, takes a much more Existentialist approach to life. We don't find Bond trying to lose himself in what society expects—he flouts that kind of life. He always sets himself

---

[3] Ian Fleming, *Live and Let Die* in *Casino Royale / Live and Let Die / Moonraker* (Harmondsworth: Penguin, 2003), p. 264.

apart. He seeks a life that is more exciting. He takes the Existentialist advice seriously; we shouldn't run away from anxiety in fear, we should face it courageously. We should bravely face the fact that we are ultimately responsible for what we make our lives into.

"Grow Up, 007." Is Our Beloved Seducer Simply Immature?

How does Bond react to a close shave with death? Just like a dry martini, he may occasionally be "shaken" by a particularly close call, but at a deeper level, he is never really "stirred." This leads us back to the question, how does Bond do it? How is he able to face death courageously? How does he deal with the anxiety in the face of mortality and in the face of freedom, which sends so many other people running? How does he survive? As we've seen he says that he survives by taking pleasure in great beauty. He embraces sensual pleasure and the aesthetic realm of existence. He immerses himself in the enjoyment of the best foods, wines, and women. The indulgences, which we see in the films, are even more pronounced in the novels—Bond takes such pleasure in the details of creating his own martinis and naming them after women, ordering the best caviar, making wine suggestions to the sommelier. He smokes seventy cigarettes a day and has them specially made with a particular blend. He is a true connoisseur.

Søren Kierkegaard (1813–1855) was another Existentialist philosopher who pondered the human experience of anxiety and the many ways we try to escape it. Kierkegaard gave particular attention to the sort of person he calls "the seducer," a Don Juan type living purely at the aesthetic level of existence. The seducer lives for sensation and feeling, and his main goal in life is to satisfy sensual desires. He pursues a life of intense pleasures, constantly seeking new thrills, and he occupies himself by creating elaborate strategies for his next conquest, relishing the rush of the pursuit. It's no stretch of the imagination to think that Kierkegaard might have seen James Bond as a perfect example of this personality type, the seducer extraordinaire!

Kierkegaard argues that this pleasure-seeking life-style can never bring true happiness or fulfillment. He believes that this hedonism is really just a front—it's the seducer's attempt to run away from anxiety. The seducer, according to Kierkegaard, is constantly trying to avoid facing his own freedom and responsibility. The seducer wants to lose himself; hiding under a load of distractions, beautiful distractions.

Unfortunately, this strategy is doomed to fail. The problem is that the pleasures the seducer experiences are only temporary—short and fleeting. They can't distract us from anxiety permanently. As soon as one pleasure is finished the seducer must start off in search of the next one—a process of endless searching which can produce its own anxiety. Finally, the seducer is in a sad position because as humans, Kierkegaard believes, we are capable of more than this. We are more than our animalistic sensual desires; we should aim for something higher.

Kierkegaard believes that the seducer, living at the aesthetic level of existence, is immature. At this stage, the seducer has no real sense of self, and cannot really know or love another person. In order to develop into a mature self, the seducer must move beyond this aesthetic level of consciousness, to develop a moral conscience, a sense of right and wrong. He must move into the moral sphere of existence, into an awareness of right and wrong. At this level, what becomes most important is commitment, especially in the form of an ultimate commitment to another person in marriage. The final step in personal development would be to move beyond even this moral realm of right and wrong, in a personal experience of religious faith, to live deeply and passionately in commitment to God.

If Kierkegaard were to look at Bond, he would most certainly echo the sentiments Q has voiced so many times: "Grow up, 007." Kierkegaard's diagnosis of Bond would be that he is no more than an immature boy, chasing after pleasure in order to hide from the anxieties of real life. And Kierkegaard's prescription for Bond might be to find a nice girl (perhaps Miss Moneypenny?), overcome his fear of commitment, and settle down. Develop a moral conscience, and finally, hope for a passionate religious conversion.

Is there any truth to this interpretation of Bond's hedonistic approach to life as mere immature escapism? Does it help us to understand his turn to aesthetic pleasure? And does it help us to judge whether or not James Bond's hedonism holds the answer for our own lives too?

There's no argument that Bond fits the description of a seducer, and he says himself that he turns to aesthetic pleasure in order to cope with (should we read, "escape from"?) the harsh realities of life. He also fits Kierkegaard's description in his distaste for boredom. According to Kierkegaard, the greatest danger for the seducer lies in boredom. What if, someday, the seductive pursuit is not as exciting as before? What if, someday, all the women seem to look alike? What if you find yourself simply going through the motions? The person who lives for pleasure is under constant pressure to do something even more exciting than before, or he will fall into boredom.

And James Bond shows us that he does in fact dread boredom most of all. In the novel *From Russia with Love*, he wakes up "disgusted to find that he was thoroughly bored with the prospect of the day ahead. . . . Boredom, and particularly the incredible circumstance of waking up bored, was the only vice Bond utterly condemned."[4] He craves adventure—he needs excitement so much that he can't handle the peace of ordinary, everyday life. (Could it be because without distraction, awareness of his underlying anxiety creeps in?) He needs to be on assignment. He says that the "soft life" of everyday, without an assignment, is "strangling" him, and that "he was a man of war and when, for a long period, there was no war, his spirit went into decline. . . . In his particular line of business, peace had reigned for nearly a year. And peace was killing him" (*From Russia with Love*, p. 78). Finally, in a twist on Euripides, who said that the gods make the people whom they wish to destroy "mad," Bond asserts, "Those whom the Gods wish to destroy, they first make bored" (*From Russia with Love*, p. 83).

But somehow wedding bells and church bells just don't seem to be on the horizon for James any time soon. And Kierkegaard's claim that the life of aesthetic pleasure can be no more than an attempt to escape, to hide from the realities of life, from anxiety and from real responsibility, seems to miss something. There seems to be more to the comfort Bond finds in sensual pleasures—we may hesitate to say more "maturity," but we can at least say more depth. Is there another way to understand Bond's experience?

---

[4] Ian Fleming, *From Russia with Love* (London: Coronet, 1957), p. 78.

Die Another Day

The Existentialist philosopher Friedrich Nietzsche (1844–1900) provides us with another possible interpretation. Nietzsche shares the belief that we experience anxiety at the prospect of our own death and of our responsibility to make something of our lives. But whereas Kierkegaard proposes that ultimately, religious faith is the answer, Nietzsche tells us that "God is dead." By this he means that "God" is no more than an idea that humans themselves have created, because at some point in history we needed it. However, Nietzsche believes that we now have outgrown the need for this imaginary figure, and it is time to put the idea of God and all that it entails to rest.

How should we react to the death of God? Nietzsche fears that some people will become lost in despair when they realize that there is no such thing as God, because they will become overwhelmed with a sense of the ultimate meaninglessness of existence. After all, if there's no such thing as God to give the world purpose, and no such thing as an afterlife, what is there to live for? If God is dead, then there's nothing outside of ourselves that could give meaning to our lives. And this is a scary prospect. Nietzsche worries that those who fall into despair will see no reason to go on. Their lives might fall into chaos and destruction, or they might even commit suicide.

The Existentialist novelist Albert Camus (1913–1960) explores this possibility in an essay called "The Myth of Sisyphus." Camus argues that while life is in fact meaningless, futile, and ultimately absurd, suicide is not the solution. To commit suicide would just be to give in, to surrender. Camus proposes, instead, that we should try to find a way to master the situation. By this he means that we should try to find a way to enjoy ourselves in spite of it all, to find a way to make the situation our own. We can create our own meaning.

And even when James Bond is face to face with the absurdity of life and death, he clearly does not consider suicide to be an option. In the film *From Russia with Love*, Bond is given a briefcase from Q Branch. What the film does not reveal is that in the novel, the briefcase has a secret compartment in the handle that includes a cyanide pill. Bond is instructed that if he should be taken captive, he should commit suicide. Later, in the film *Die Another Day*, when Bond has been taken hostage and held captive, he is criticized by M for not having taken his cyanide pill. He should have killed himself rather than risk the danger of talking under torture. But Bond explains that he got rid of it years ago—and it's true—in the novel *From Russia with Love*, when he first received it, he flushed the pill down the toilet (*From Russia with Love*, p. 92).

Nietzsche, like Camus and so many Existentialist thinkers, claims that it's up to each one of us to find our own individual truth and meaning in life, in subjective experience. For Kierkegaard, this can be found in a personal experience of faith and communion with God. But for atheist thinkers like Nietzsche and Camus, there is no God to turn to. We have to find a way to make our lives our own, and to give them our own individual purposes. This means, instead of turning to fads, fashions, and social norms to tell us what to believe and how to live, and instead of attempting to lose ourselves in the crowd, we must be courageous enough to take up the responsibility for making something of ourselves, and creative enough to find our own individual reasons to live. Nietzsche calls the person who is strong enough to do this an "overman."

Bond Beyond Good and Evil

Nietzsche goes on to explain that if God is dead, that means there is no absolute right and wrong in the world—there is no such thing as good or evil. In *The Genealogy of Morals*, Nietzsche explains that our moral ideas of right and wrong are also mere human creations, and this means that we are not actually obligated to take them seriously. There is no reason why they should govern our actions. It's possible to make choices in life that move beyond or outside of what traditional standards have taught us is right and wrong. According to Nietzsche, given the death of God, we are now "beyond good and evil," and it is our own responsibility to create the values we will live by.

To be "beyond good and evil" certainty seems to describe Bond's situation when he is on assignment, and he is granted permission to kill "whom he wants, when he wants, how he wants." His actions are beyond normal moral standards. But I would go even further and argue that at the heart of the whole Bond series we can find an expression of the idea that the whole world, in our time, has moved beyond good and evil.

In *Casino Royale*, the very first James Bond novel, setting the whole series into motion, we are at Bond's origin. We find out where he comes from, and we gain insight into his deepest motivations. In Chapter 20, called "The Nature of Evil," Bond has a very telling crisis of conscience. In this chapter, it seems as if the life of a double-0 is taking a toll on James. He talks about all of the killings and his own role as assassin, and he says that the problem is that "The villains and heroes get all mixed up."[5] He begins to have doubts and he worries: What if he is not actually working for the good guys? How would he know if he were on the wrong side? As a secret agent he is just a pawn. How can he know for sure that he is doing any good in the world? He can't.

At this point, Bond has moved beyond good and evil. He sees what Nietzsche described, that good and evil are not really absolute or objective in the world. In reality, the moral truth is not black and white, but many shades of gray. It is possible for good and evil to become confused.

In the midst of this moral crisis, Bond considers quitting MI6 altogether. But then a French agent named Mathis steps in and talks some sense to him. Mathis gives Bond this advice: He should come to understand evil in terms of something *personal*, rather than as an abstract principle. Bond considers this, and begins to think about what it would be like to kill out of personal revenge, rather than "for some high moral reason or for the sake of my country" (*Casino Royale*, p. 102). Mathis says, "Surround yourself with human beings, my dear James. They are easier to fight for than principles" (*Casino Royale*, p. 105).

So Bond finds an answer to his moral crisis, and decides to remain 007. From now on, he will make it *personal*. And consequently, in almost every film we find an example of Bond being motivated by some personal vendetta. By the end of this first novel he has found his meaning to go on—it will be a mission of revenge against SMERSH, which he holds responsible for his lover Vesper's death.

Nietzsche says that what is most important in life is to give "style" to your existence—to find a way to fit your life into an

---

[5] Ian Fleming, *Casino Royale* in *Casino Royale / Live and Let Die / Moonraker* (London: Penguin, 2003), p. 102.

"artistic plan" of your own creation.[6] The overman doesn't get lost in despair when he realizes that there's no such thing as absolute truth—rather, the overman continues to flourish, develop, thrive, and to keep moving forward. He creates his own meanings, and by doing so, gives his life a personal style. The overman embraces existence.

Bond does find a way to make the situation his own. He moves beyond the abstract old-fashioned ideas of good and evil, to find his own meaning in the situation. He creates his own purpose and his own values. From Nietzsche's perspective, we can also understand Bond's turn to aesthetic pleasure as a means of survival in a positive light. We come to see the hedonism as Bond's attempt to create his own meaningful existence in a world that is absurd.

James Bond as Existentialist Role Model? Or, Courage, Creativity, and a Sense of Humor

Who is James Bond, really? An underpaid civil servant, but when he is on assignment, he becomes superhuman in some way, with unlimited funds and unlimited power. As 007 he transcends the everyday and becomes a heroic individual. And as we watch him on the screen or read about him in the pages of a novel, we see someone who courageously confronts the harsh realities of death on a daily basis. While most of us don't have to face death at every turn as James does, it is still true that the possibility of death is always there for us. Whether the death of a loved one, a stranger, or ourselves, there's no escaping the fact that everything we care about, work towards, and love will someday come to an absurd end.

But as we have seen, the important lesson that the Existentialists draw from this encounter with our own mortality, our "being-towards-death," is not focused on death but rather on what we make of *life*. Looking back over Bond's adventures, has he found the answer to how we should live? Has he found a path of survival and meaning that could work for all of us? Is he to be admired as an Existentialist role model? The answer is threefold.

---

[6] See "One Thing Is Needful," in Friedrich Nietzsche, *The Gay Science*.

First, the Existentialists remind us that, while it is tempting to try to run away from our freedom and responsibility, hiding from ourselves is not the answer. Attempts to escape or avoid these realities can only be temporary. Sooner or later we will each come face to face with our own mortality, and at that moment we should be able to feel like we have really made something of our lives, as though we have really made our lives our own. It takes courage to keep ourselves from running away. To this end, we should be wary of all temptations to lose ourselves, whether it is in the "busy-ness" of everyday life, or in all the effort involved in "fitting in" and keeping up with the crowd, or even in indulgence in sensual pleasures. And in this respect, James Bond does in fact seem to be a good role model. He has the courage to face mortality and to take up his own freedom.

Second, the Existentialists have pointed out that it is up to each one of us, individually, to find our own personal "meaning of life." It is up to us to create our own values. This does not have to be as foreboding as it sounds—the truth is, when we stop running and hiding from ourselves we actually win our lives back. And in this respect as well, James Bond provides a good example of the Existentialist hero. He creatively finds his own meaning in life, and his own reasons to live. He makes the situation his own, and gives his life "style." James creates his meaning of life in "great beauty," sensual pleasure, and the personal vendetta.

However, when it comes to "creating your own moral values," we cannot follow James all the way. After all, on assignment, he is not a regular person living in society, but a double-0, licensed to kill. On assignment, James is beyond the reach of the law. But back home, he is the same as you and me, and for us everyday people, the laws of society do in fact serve a practical purpose. Nietzsche said that we should feel free to disregard all traditional moral norms, and in his nineteenth-century social setting those moral norms were by our standards quite repressive. One didn't have to go far to be beyond the rules of what was considered acceptable. But in our world today, to live in society, surely we must follow some rules. So while we can take Bond as a role model for creativity, as he finds his own personal source of meaning and reason to live, we shouldn't actually follow him all the way, and we must think of the greater consequences when we want to break the rules.

So we have seen that James Bond provides a good example of both Existentialist courage and Existentialist creativity. But finally we must ask, can he serve as a role model in a third respect, as the connoisseur of aesthetic pleasures? When James finds his meaning of life in "great beauty," sensual pleasure, and the personal vendetta, has he in fact found *the* meaning of life? Should we all follow his example, and look for our meaning in aesthetic pleasures too?

No, at this point we must part ways. For what has worked for Bond is not guaranteed to work for everyone. From the Existentialist perspective, it is up to each individual to find a meaning of life that is true for him or her *personally*—we each must create this meaning for ourselves. If we were to take Bond as an example and follow his lead, we would actually be giving up our responsibility, looking outside of ourselves for the answer, and this would go against the heart of Existentialism.

The Brighter Side of Existentialism

Over the years, Existentialism has gotten the reputation of being a philosophy that is dark, brooding, even pessimistic. And it's true that Existentialists give a great deal of attention to "darker" subjects that most people would rather avoid whenever possible, namely, our own mortality, the absurdity of death, and the absence of objective meaning in the world. But as we have seen, Existentialists have little interest in death itself—the emphasis is on life. How shall we live? How can we make our lives meaningful and worthwhile? And from this perspective, Existentialism can be understood as a very positive and life-affirming philosophical outlook. If we have the courage and creativity to embrace our freedom, it is possible to tune in to appreciating our lives, and to enjoying ourselves in the time that we have. And here, too, we can think of James Bond, after once again narrowly escaping death, "Bond sat for a while by the window and enjoyed being alive" (*Casino Royale*, p. 32).

2
How to Live (and How to Die)

MAHLETE-TSIGÉ GETACHEW

> But we must look at the question more closely. For it is not a trivial one: what is at stake is how we should live.
> —Plato, *Republic*, Book I

> Look at him. You'd think he was some sort of hero.
> —Agent Falco, *Die Another Day*

There is a fundamental sense in which all of us feel alive. We breathe, blink, think, read books and watch movies. But how often do we get that exhilarating affirmation of *being alive?* From the lush tropics of *Dr. No* to the ice-encased splendor of *Die Another Day*, it's obvious that James Bond, international connoisseur of whiskies and women, cars and cigars, is acquainted with thrill. His daily life seems to abound with pyrotechnics and excitement—and if none comes his way, James Bond simply creates some.

It's hard not to be impressed by this glamorous vision of how one could live; and yet, for all its appeal, few of us actually try to incorporate it *entirely* in our own lives. Perhaps this is because we think a good life is one where we have inner tranquility rather than serial adventures; or perhaps we think that happiness can be found in families and lasting relationships instead of in the brief and treacherous liaisons of espionage; or perhaps we think the point of living is to accumulate wealth or age (neither of which tend to be associated with deadly missions). In fact, there may be as many conceptions of 'the good life' as there are individuals. This is a problem when it comes to judging the quality of a life—our own, or someone else's. With all these conflicting ideas about 'successful living', it's difficult to assess what we're doing right and what we need to change.

Confronted by this ambiguity, Plato, the founder of Western philosophy, set out to answer the question, "How should we live?" But, in order to know how to live we must first know who or what we are.

Plato's Archetypes

Auric Goldfinger: You have been recognized, Mr. Bond.

Goldfinger

For Plato, we each have a *psyche*, an Ancient Greek word taken to mean 'personality' or 'soul'. Like much contemporary psychology, Plato argues that our *psyche* is made up of different elements or aspects. In Plato's theory these elements are Reason, Spirit, and Appetite. Reason is the element of the soul that desires knowledge and truth, and that makes us capable of activities like planning and solving problems. Spirit is the element of the soul that desires glory and honor, and that makes us capable of feelings like anger, jealousy, shame, and pride. Appetite is the most carnal element of the soul and is concerned with physical gratification through food, drink, sleep, money, and sex.

A quite basic part of living involves finding a balance between these three aspects of ourselves. If we were to try to do without even one of them, then our lives would probably be very dull and very, very short. Appetite ensures our physical survival, Spirit motivates us to engage with other people in a variety of ways, and Reason enables us to make the best of the present and look to the future. The three elements are all equal and necessary. But, to paraphrase George Orwell, some might be more equal than others. Plato certainly thinks so, and distinguishes between an element of the soul merely having a *function* and an element of the soul being in *control*. In *Republic*, his classic work about individuals and society, Plato delineates archetypal individuals, each ruled by a different aspect of the soul—archetypes that prefigure the central characters in the James Bond adventures by almost 2,500 years. The Tyrant is the man ruled by Appetite, and whom we would identify as the powerful villain whose greed threatens our civilization. The Guardian is the man ruled by Spirit, and whom we would identify as the daring 007. And the Philosopher-King is the man ruled by Reason, Bond's stern, ascetic boss, M.[1]

The poet Philip Larkin once wrote that "how we live is a measure of our nature." Because these individuals are archetypes, by considering their lives and lifestyles we should be able to see who is happiest and therefore which nature is worth emulating. Plato does exactly this and concludes that the happiest man is the Philosopher-King, the archetype that corresponds to M. One can imagine Bond receiving this news with a droll smile and a murmured flippancy; when we consider Bond's high-octane thrills, and the fabulous surroundings of someone like Scaramanga, and *especially* when we consider M's distinct and unremitting joylessness, Plato's answer seems somewhat . . . amiss . . . But philosophers, like spies, know that truth can be a surprising thing. So let's consider the lives of these archetypes, and judge their natures, and decide whether Plato is right or if we need to find another model of how we should live.

The Tyrant

KANANGA: Your power exists to serve me. It is mine to do with as I will.

—*Live and Let Die*

We begin with the Tyrant, the individual whom Plato thinks the most unhappy and who leads the worst life. The Tyrant is a man whose soul is ruled by a singular and dominant Appetite. This Appetite is often a desire for money or power, like Zorin in *A View to a Kill* seeking sole control of the microchip industry, or Stromberg in *The Spy Who Loved Me* trying to obliterate civilization so that he can establish an underwater kingdom. This ruling Appetite is so massively inordinate that it inspires a sort of

---

[1] Although I call the archetypes "men," Plato was remarkably contemporary in treating men and women equally in his theory of the archetypes. Plato sometimes calls the Philosopher-King "the Guardian" and the Guardian "the Auxiliary"; some modern commentators follow this practice but I prefer the names given above.

fanatical dedication in the Tyrant that disregards everything else, so that

> there's nothing, no taboo, no murder, however terrible, from which he'll shrink. His passion tyrannizes over him, a despot without restraint or law, and drives him into any venture that will profit itself and its gang, a gang collected partly from the evil company he keeps and partly from impulses within himself which these same evil practices have freed from restraint.[2]

Now, for those of us who are criminally inclined, this may not sound so bad. One could have a lot of fun with a gang of like-minded people, going around collaborating in misdeeds, happily sharing the illegal gains, and so on. This, after all, seems to be the spirit behind the nefarious SPECTRE organization (Special Executive for Counter-Intelligence, Terrorism, Revenge, and Extortion), and their various grand, and grandly diabolical, schemes. But Plato says even this limited community is impossible. For Tyrants,

> their companions are parasites in every way subservient to them . . . [They] put on the most extravagant act of friendship if it suits their purposes, though once that purpose is achieved their tune changes. . . . So tyrannical characters pass their lives without a friend in the world; they are always either master or slave, and never taste true friendship or freedom. (*Republic*, lines 575e–576a)

The primacy of this singular desire forfeits all normal human relations; instead of companions, the Tyrant has an obsession, and people are ruthlessly assessed by their usefulness—or otherwise—in helping the Tyrant attain his goal. The Tyrant, Plato says, tyrannizes over others but is also, in a way, enslaved by his own great desire. The sheer *scale* of his craving guarantees that his greed will never be satisfied, and so he is doomed. "His power will make him still more envious, untrustworthy, unjust, friendless, and godless, a refuge and home for every iniquity, and you can see that he's a source of misery above all to himself, but also to his neighbors" (*Republic*, lines 579e–580a).

But before this sorry end, Plato warns us that we can expect paranoia, pettiness, and a lingering insanity, for, "the master

---

[2] Plato, *The Republic* (Harmondsworth: Penguin, 1987), lines 574e–575a.

passion runs wild and takes madness into its service; any opinions or desires with a decent reputation and any feelings of shame still left are killed or thrown out, until all discipline is swept away and madness usurps its place" (*Republic*, lines 573a–b). This prospect does not faze the true Tyrant: "The distance between insanity and genius is measured only by success," Elliot Carver declares in *Tomorrow Never Dies*. "Caesar had his legions, Napoleon had his armies; I have my presses. Soon I'll have reached out to and influenced more people than anybody in the history of this planet save God Himself."

It seems Plato has made his point, and made it well: the villains of the James Bond adventures are men and women driven by a single-minded greed, megalomaniacs crumbling into pure mania. It would be easy to conclude that the Tyrant is unhappy and is living an inferior life. But is this actually *true?* Bond's grand foes possess a materially desirable lifestyle—a lifestyle made possible by their exceptional dedication. And not a single Tyrant shows interest in renouncing his life of crime despite the alleged misery it brings him. Admittedly, Blofeld requests a clean record in *On Her Majesty's Secret Service*; however, the possibility of any kind of *repentance* is ruled out by the fact that he uses global extortion and massively criminal methods to do so. Also undeniable is the evidence that Tyrants often seem to be enjoying themselves; Goldfinger and Blofeld, for example, demonstrate the sort of appreciation of witticisms that we might expect in Q and even in Bond. In fact, the more we consider it, the less unhappy the Tyrant seems.

Plato appears to be right when he says that the Tyrants are essentially alone in all that they do. Although this might seem a loss to the more conventional amongst us, to the Tyrant companionship means nothing anyway, and so no loss is felt. Abandoning the Tyrant to his solitude, then, let's consider a more socially-orientated archetype, and see if this is a lifestyle we can admire.

The Guardian

Q: Good to see you Mr. Bond. Things have been awfully dull around here. I hope we're going to see some gratuitous sex and violence.

—*Never Say Never Again*

While Plato is unrelenting in his criticisms of the Tyrant, he's a little gentler with the Guardian, the second-best type of individual. The soul of the Guardian is ruled by Spirit, the aspect of our character concerned with honor, glory, and the attainment of esteem through competition and prowess. Spirit is the part of our soul that makes us lively and motivates us to be brave and to outdo our peers. Spirited individuals, therefore, are courageous and dynamic, eager to assert their individuality, and keen to excel in physical and intellectual activity as a way of receiving recognition. And this category of proud, ambitious, action-orientated people is where we find James Bond. "Do you lose as gracefully as you win?" Emilio Largo asks Bond in *Never Say Never Again*. "I wouldn't know," Bond replies. "I've never lost."

Plato discerns that individuals with this sort of personality have great potential as warriors and protectors and so he sets them to be Guardians, defenders of the state—the role that puts their talents to the best use so long as they receive the glory they seek. And Plato obliges. Anyone who has distinguished themselves in bravery can, he says, expect the following legislation in their favor: "Add to your law a clause that would forbid anyone to refuse his kisses for the rest of the campaign . . . We will reward excellence with the best seat at the table, the first cut off the joint, and a never empty cup. In this way we shall honor the bravery of our men and women and improve their physique" (*Republic*, lines 468b–e).

Accordingly Bond's license to kill seems to come with a license to choose extravagantly beautiful women and assorted vintages of Dom Perignon to entertain him before, during, and after his missions. This all seems perfectly acceptable, but what Plato doesn't discuss, and what would have been obvious to his contemporaries and is obvious to us, is that the Spirited individual is not necessarily 'good'. Because honor and self-esteem are the goals of Spirit, slights and insults are taken very seriously indeed. Spirited individuals are vengeful and prone to a terrible anger. In the Ancient Greek tragedy *Medea*, the brave and headstrong princess is abandoned by her adulterous husband, Jason, whose life she had saved, and for whom she had sacrificed her royal heritage. Medea decides to take bloody revenge on him by slaughtering their children. Contemplating the horror of what she's about to do, she reasons with herself, "Do I want to make myself ridiculous by letting my enemies go unpunished? I must face the deed . . . I know what evil I am about to do, but my fury is stronger than my counsels of softness. Spirit, the root of man's worst acts!"[3]

While Bond doesn't perform quite these atrocities, he displays an unsettling preference for vengeance over national defense. More than once he has to be warned by M that he's on a delineated government task and not a personal vendetta. M is not the only person to express concern: even Bond's allies and enemies in the field question his motivation. "Is this about peace or revenge?" Chinese Agent Wai Lin asks him; Bond is evasive. Alec Trevelyan, opponent, traitor, and former double-0 colleague, gets an unequivocal answer. "For Queen and country?", Trevelyan wonders as Bond holds him upside-down, perilously suspended in mid-air. "No," Bond calmly replies, before letting Trevelyan plummet to his death, "For me."

This lack of commitment to his employer's principles is extended to the job itself: James Bond resigns, breaks rules, and inconveniences his colleagues in the most cavalier way imaginable. This would be inexcusable in a mediocre man, but Bond's audacity, his playful arrogance, and his insouciant charm somehow manage to make us—and Q, and Miss Moneypenny—forgive him, again and again. This public indulgence is something Plato knew about all too well. Plato's portrait of the Spirited man was based on Alcibiades, a famous Athenian warrior and statesman of the time. In Alcibiades we see the same amorality that we see in Bond, and how his talent brought him acceptance nonetheless. The historian Plutarch writes:

> The fame of his ancestors, his eloquence, his physical good looks and fitness, and his experience and prowess in war made the people of Athens tolerate and make allowances for everything else about him. They were constantly finding blatant euphemisms for his faults and attributing them to youthful high spirits and his determination to succeed.[4]

Like James Bond, Alcibiades was a smooth talker and a quick wit, a master of strategy who excelled at gambling, and a genius

---

[3] Euripides, *Medea,* translated by James Morwood (Oxford: Oxford University Press 1998), lines 1049–1080.
[4] Plutarch, "Alcibiades" from *Parallel Lives* (Oxford: Oxford University Press, 1998), Section 16.

of war who brought Athens unparalleled military successes and peace deals. But Alcibiades was not motivated by patriotism, or concerned with discretion, and he had no qualms about seducing the wives of kings (allies or enemies) or disrupting perfectly good diplomatic arrangements simply because he hadn't been involved in setting them up and wasn't receiving any personal glory from them. And so despite the victories he brought Athens, Alcibiades was exiled twice as a traitor and a threat to the people. A satirist of the time described the public attitude towards him as follows, "They miss him, hate him, want him to be with them . . . It's best not to keep a lion in the city. But if you do, pander to his moods."[5]

Why would the Athenians admire and make excuses for someone so contrary? Why do we admire James Bond and overlook his faults? Plato is silent on this point, but the answer, I believe, can be found in our moral culture. Anthropologists identify two major types of culture: guilt-culture, and shame-culture.[6] A guilt-culture is one where *guilt* is the worst state to be in, and a pure conscience is the most desirable thing. Many religions and deeply religious societies have a guilt-culture—for example, England and Germany in the Reformation, Catholicism in pre-Renaissance Italy. In contrast, a shame-culture is one where *shame* is the state one most hates and fears, and honor and glory are the highest goods.

Athens at the time of Plato and Alcibiades was a shame-culture: people were motivated to avoid shame and social disgrace, not to avoid guilt, and they were praised for their talents, not their virtues. Increasingly, modern Western society is following this pattern: we admire celebrities instead of saints, and we emulate famous people despite their moral paucity. As Andy Warhol put it, "In the future, everyone will be world-famous for fifteen minutes." We crave glory, not goodness. This trend towards stylish amorality seems to have begun in the 1920s; the decade that witnessed the decline of Victorian prudishness also saw the genesis of Spirited heroes like the Saint, charming rogue and witty law-breaker. In 1958, *Doctor No* was published, and

---

[5] Aristophanes, *Frogs* (in Plutarch), lines 1425 and 1432–33.
[6] E.R. Dodds, "From Shame-Culture to Guilt-Culture" in *The Greeks and the Irrational* (Berkeley: University of California Press, 1951).

by the time Warhol made his observation the Bond phenomenon had begun.

This ascendancy of shame-culture might seem unproblematic and maybe even quite attractive. Just as the Tyrant's material lifestyle appeals to our Appetite, the Guardian's bravado and celebrity appeals to our Spirit. But there's great individual and collective danger when Spirit is in charge: Spirit doesn't care for prudence, or for constraints, or for moderation. And sometimes Spirit will have its way—its sought-after revenge, its great achievement—no matter what the cost. In light of this, perhaps the Guardian cannot be the 'best' type of person. Similarly, perhaps a fame-obsessed society which encourages Guardian-types is not the 'best' type of society: we might be better off trying to build something a little more reasonable and a little more enduring.

The Philosopher-King

M: Oh, spare me this sentimental rubbish.

—*Licence to Kill*

Plato saves his praise for the soul and lifestyle of the Philosopher-King. This is the man or woman of thought whose soul is governed by Reason. Reason desires truth and knowledge, order and perfection. These are eternal and immutable things, unlike the goals of Spirit and Appetite, and so the goals of Reason are valuable goals with equally valuable rewards. It might seem difficult to imagine 'truth' and 'knowledge' bringing us more pleasure than widespread admiration or immense wealth. But Plato says it's a different *kind* of pleasure—a superior and enduring one, akin to serenity. He has a point: for all their glitter and promise, money, power, and competitive success do not guarantee a lasting happiness. Rather, they often seem to bring us even more turmoil and misery. Perhaps, then, we can find a more significant sort of pleasure in truth and ordered perfection.

Truth of the kind Plato has in mind is not easily come by: because it's eternal and immutable by nature, it requires us to try to think and act accordingly—that is, without change or compromise. The man of Reason has very exact and absolutely correct principles which he sticks to, no matter how he might feel about things, and no matter how unpopular these consequences might be. This sort of absolutism is exemplified by M telling Bond about the kidnap of Robert King's daughter: "Against every instinct in my heart, against every emotion as a mother, I told him not to pay the ransom." For Plato, the true Philosopher-King will eventually learn to not 'feel' about things, so that he can make perfectly rational decisions without emotional distraction. And there are plenty of occasions where M reprimands James Bond for being "too involved" and instructs him to see matters "coldly and objectively": informed of Blofeld's kidnap of Bond's fiancée, he retorts, "This department is not concerned with your personal problems."

Just as the man of Reason has the best sort of control over his life, Plato thinks he is also the best-equipped to govern others. "For, if philosophers have the capacity to grasp the eternal and immutable, while those who have no such capacity are not philosophers and are lost in multiplicity and change, which of the two should be in charge?" (*Republic*, line 484b) Thus we see the Philosopher-King reigning over Plato's ideal republic, and M, the Philosopher-King's counterpart, directing MI6. Plato isn't afraid to suggest that the Philosopher-King brings his thorough objectivity to the role of government, although this might result in some unpopular strictures and deeply troubling policies. For example, under the reign of the Philosopher-King:

> It would be a sin for mating or for anything else in a truly happy society to take place without regulation . . . A sacred marriage is one that produces the most beneficial results . . . We must, if we are to be consistent, and if we're to have a real pedigree herd, mate the best of our men with the best of our women as often as possible, and the inferior men with the inferior women as seldom as possible, and bring up only the offspring of the best. And no one but the Philosopher-Kings must know what is happening (*Republic*, lines 458c–459e).

Selective infanticide follows, for the edification of "the herd," and the surviving children are kept away from their parents and told lies about their origin so that they grow up with a blind loyalty to the republic. This isn't so different from the machinations of the Secret Service: double-0s are specially chosen from among the orphaned and the unmarried so that they have an absolute and unswerving loyalty to the state. Plato alludes to his citizens as if they are animals, and M alludes to his agents as numbers. James Bond is always "007" and never "Bond"; a resource and not a person; catalogued, functional, expendable. "If you think for one moment I don't have the balls to send a man to his death, you're wrong," M says quite coolly in *Goldeneye*. "I don't have any compunction about sending him to die."

Frightening as this portrait is, it's difficult to deny that the Philosopher-King possesses a clear-sightedness and stability which the Guardian and the Tyrant lack. Moreover, the Philosopher-King's laws and operations might fill us with horror, but they would also create a republic of enviably ordered and patriotic citizens. Perhaps Plato is merely being honest about what perfection costs, and instead of recoiling from his vision we need to consider it as he does—that is, from the cold perspective of eternity.

Immortality

Men are mere mortals who are not worth going
to the grave for.

—Song lyrics, "Diamonds Are Forever"

Plato's search for perfection is motivated by the intuition that the things that matter are the things that last. Consequently, any meaningful truth, or goodness, or beauty must be eternal and immutable, and therefore quite unlike the day-to-day transient and variable truth, goodness, and beauty that we see around us. So Plato calls what *he* is after the *Ideas* or Forms of Truth, Goodness, and Beauty. These Forms are perfectly abstract and beyond ordinary comprehension. But we have an inkling of them, a sort of sense that they exist, and Plato says this is because we see imperfect reflections of them around us which our soul somehow 'recognizes'.

We would be justified in wondering how plausible these perfect Forms are, and how useful they would be in the here and now. Aristotle, Plato's greatest student, expresses his skepticism thus, "And so we can say goodbye to the Forms. For they are twittering nonsense, and even if they exist, they are totally irrelevant."[7]

---

[7] Aristotle, *Analytica Posteriori*, my translation, lines 83a32–34.

Although Plato might be wrong about the Forms, he's right about the common intuition that there are ineffable 'things' beyond human ken that our souls can *just about* sense. In order for our souls to be aware of these timeless things, there must be, Plato reasons, a similarly timeless aspect to *us*. It can't be Appetite, because Appetite is linked to our material needs which are bound in time; and it can't be Spirit, because Spirit is to do with passion and esteem, which are essentially transient. Reason, then, is the part of our souls that's able to apprehend the timeless, and if Reason can do this it follows that Reason, like perfection, is timeless. This is a conclusion Plato happily accepts, asserting that Reason is the *essence* of our humanity, our immortal core, and Spirit and Appetite are just temporary add-ons that are a consequence of our 'embodiment'. We only care about possessions and status because we—woefully—have bodies and societies. But this misfortune can be overcome, says Plato, and *this* is the goal of his ideal social organization, the perfect republic.

In the perfect republic, ordinary relationships are denied in case they become a distraction: children are to be "held in common," with no child knowing its parent and no parent knowing its child; the citizens will "live and feed together, and have no private home or property" (*Republic*, lines 457d–458d). The family is completely dissolved, nothing is private and or can be possessed. The effect of these measures is to thoroughly eliminate any burgeoning sense of individuality so that it's easier for Reason to overrule Spirit and Appetite. The closer Reason gets to attaining its goal, the less distinctive we become. Plato has no problem with the idea that his Philosopher-Kings will become uniform with one another (*Republic*, lines 500b–d), like a row of brilliant, identical, flawless diamonds.

One senses that M would be happy with this description of himself, and that he would also wish this status for his secret agents. James Bond, in contrast, doesn't seem to mourn his corporeality, or regard embodiment as an affliction. In fact, Bond seems to have a perfectly splendid time checking into plush hotel suites with a variety of attractive women, and he orders his vodka martinis with a confident attention to detail that reveals that he knows what he likes, and he likes it very much. Bond and his Tyrannical nemeses, both ruled by the mortal aspects of their souls, often congratulate each other on their taste in comely assistants, exclusive weapons, and expensive champagnes. "There's no point in living if you can't feel alive," Elektra murmurs to Bond in *The World Is Not Enough*. If corporeality makes it possible for us to acquire expertise in physical pleasure, then embodiment doesn't seem such a terrible experience after all. M's disdain leaves Bond, and us, unaffected.

Corporeality also brings change and mortality, which Plato sees as less valuable than constancy and immortality. But this is not the only way of viewing things. Freud recounts a conversation with a young poet who was upset that all the beauty of nature, humanity, and human achievements, was "fated to extinction." Freud responded:

> What is painful may none the less be true. I could not see my way to dispute the transience of all things . . . But I did dispute the pessimistic poet's view that the transience of what is beautiful involves any loss in its worth. On the contrary, an increase! . . . Limitation in the possibility of an enjoyment raises the value of the enjoyment . . . A flower that blossoms only for a single night does not seem to us on that account less lovely.[8]

Maybe Bond reminds us of what it is to be mortal, and shows us how despite, or maybe even *because* of our mortality, we can truly live.

Mortality

The living's in the way we die.
—Song lyrics, "The Living Daylights"

If immortality and the eternal turned out to be difficult to grasp, mortality doesn't seem to be any easier. The problem is that we often *think* we know about mortality, and yet it doesn't take long for us to realize, uneasily, that we don't know about it at all. A strange thing happens to us as we watch Bond haul himself over a small aircraft in mid-flight, or dash over the backs of a drifting alligators: in addition to being *convinced* of his invulnerability, we find ourselves entertaining the rival and paradoxical thought

---

[8] Sigmund Freud, "On Transience" (1916) in *The Standard Edition of the Complete Works of Sigmund Freud: Volume 14* (London: Hogarth Press, 1953), p. 306.

that he is *mortal*. It's not just towards James Bond that we hold these contradictory ideas about invulnerability and mortality; there's a sense in which we think of *ourselves* as invulnerable while simultaneously knowing that we must die. Tolstoy describes this peculiar conflict in his short story *The Death of Ivan Ilych*, the account of one man's struggle to accept his mortality even as he dies.

> In the depth of his heart he knew he was dying, but not only was he not accustomed to the thought, he simply did not and could not grasp it. The syllogism he had learnt from Kiezewetter's Logic: 'Caius is a man, men are mortal, therefore Caius is mortal', had always seemed to him correct as applied to Caius, but certainly not as applied to himself . . . "Caius really was mortal, and it was right for him to die; but for me, little Vanya, Ivan Ilych, with all my thoughts and emotions, it's altogether a different matter . . . If I had to die like Caius I should have known it was so. An inner voice would have told me so, but there was nothing of the sort in me and I and all my friends felt that our case was quite different from that of Caius. And now here it is!" he said to himself. "It can't be. It's impossible! But here it is. How is this? How is one to understand it?"[9]

There's very little in European literature to match Tolstoy's harrowing account of Ivan Ilych's attempts to reconcile himself with his imminent death, and the twentieth-century German philosopher Martin Heidegger draws on the story to describe our basic inability to understand our own mortality. Explaining the role of social convention in this confusion, he writes: "In our everyday manner, death is . . . a mishap which is constantly occurring . . . [The public] talks of it in a 'fugitive' manner, either expressly or else in a way which is mostly inhibited, as if to say, 'One of these days one will die too, in the end; but right now it has nothing to do with us.'"[10] We are taught to regard death as an event, a distant and impersonal event, and to cultivate a sort of "indifferent tranquility" towards it. But death is *not* an event; it is an experience, and an experience of the most personal and intimate kind. Nor is it an experience that we can defer or afford to regard as

---

[9] Leo Tolstoy, *The Death of Ivan Ilych* (1886), translated by Louise and Aylmer Maude (Oxford: Oxford University Press 1935), pp. 44–45.

[10] Martin Heidegger, *Being and Time* (1927), translated by John Macquarrie and Edward Robinson (Oxford: Blackwell, 1962), Division II, Chapter 1, pp. 296–97.

distant, because "as soon as man comes to life, he is at once old enough to die." (*Being and Time*, p. 298) We are susceptible to death from the very beginning of our lives; we are "dying as long as [we] exist" (*Being and Time*, p. 295). For Heidegger, it's important that we acknowledge and understand these truths. Otherwise we're living in a state of delusion, which means that we cannot achieve fulfillment and self-realization, 'authentic' living, and like the pitiful Ivan Ilych we will not be prepared for death when our time to experience it is at hand.

So what is this personal and intimate experience? What do we know about it? We cannot know what death will be like because we have never died; all we can say is what death will *not* be like. It will not be like life, where we exist, and relate to others, and make choices. In death, we can no longer make choices; we can no longer have relationships with others; we can no longer *be*. In fact, death is "the possibility of the absolute impossibility" (*Being and Time*, p. 294). This is intolerable to most of us—something we cannot understand and do not want to consider. But consider it we must. And this is where Bond, courting danger and flouting death, comes in. In a culture where death is feared and misunderstood, Freud argues:

> It is an inevitable result of all this that we should seek in the world of fiction, in literature and in the theatre, compensation for what has been lost in life. There we still find people who know how to die—who, indeed, even manage to kill someone else. . . . For it is really too sad that in life it should be as it is in chess, where one false move may force us to resign the game, but with the difference that we can start no second game, no return-match. In the realm of fiction we find the plurality of lives we need.[11]

Films like *Moonraker* and *Octopussy* help us to get used to the idea that people die and that we *ourselves* only have one chance to live. We identify with Bond and Blofeld, the girls and the ill-fated henchmen, as they have lucky escapes or unlucky captures. And as we witness the consequences of their adventures, we begin to understand that we too will have our share of deliverances and final false moves.

---

[11] Sigmund Freud "Thoughts for the Times on War and Death" (1915) in *The Standard Edition of the Complete Works of Sigmund Freud: Volume 14* (London: Hogarth Press, 1953), p. 291.

Perhaps this makes for uncomfortable reading. But that's the point. And although this talk of 'considering death' may seem a pastime that will only darken our days and haunt our nights, to Freud and Heidegger it is absolutely *essential* if we are to understand our own humanity and have the insight that will allow us to truly *live*. Only in confronting death will we begin to comprehend life. Freud dismisses any residue of apprehension by showing us the need to be pragmatic. He states, "We recall the old saying: *Si vis pacem, para bellum*. If you want to preserve peace, arm for war. It would be in keeping with the times to alter it: *Si vis vitam, para mortem*. If you want to experience life, prepare yourself for death" ("War and Death," p. 300). And Heidegger reassures us that grasping our mortality in this way makes us lose both the public illusion that death is a distant event, and forces us to recognize just how *individual* death is and therefore how individual *we* are. In this way we become liberated from the social conventions that prevent us from achieving true self-realization. The anticipation of our end brings us "face-to-face with the possibility of being [ourselves]" (*Being and Time*, p. 311). It is only in *this* state that we can live in authenticity and truth, able to appreciate the singularity of every moment, and able to understand the real possibility of choice.

Risk

JAMES BOND: Me? I never take any risks.
—*You Only Live Twice*

And so we find ourselves asking, once again: how should we live? Plato seems to have been wrong about the value of immortality: acknowledging death shows us the incommensurable worth of life and our own individuality. The instinctive response to this is that we should preserve life with the utmost dedication. Or rather—preserve our *own* life, and, if necessary, treat the lives of others with disregard in the name of self-protection. Perhaps we could, like Blofeld and the other Tyrants, cultivate a self-fulfilling paranoia and dwell in impenetrable security and isolation, resisting all contact and all deviations from schedule, safe from everyone and everything (except impulsive British secret agents). This choice seems a fairly sure way of achieving *longevity*. But would we be truly *living*? Freud, wisely, says "No."

Life is impoverished, it loses its interest, when the highest stake in the game of living, life itself, may not be risked . . . We dare not contemplate a great many undertakings which are dangerous but in fact indispensable, such as attempts at artificial flight, expeditions to distant countries or experiments with explosives. . . . Yet the motto of the Hanseatic League ran: '*Navigare necesse est, vivere non necesse.*' ('It is necessary to sail the seas, it is not necessary to live.') ("War and Death," pp. 290–91)

Living, Freud is saying, with all its danger and variety, is more important than preserving the static *life*. And this willingness to play the highest stake is something we see in 007 again and again. To James Bond danger is an invitation, and risk is a pleasure. Where other heroes rely on strength, firepower, deceit, or superior intelligence to get out of a lethal situation, Bond's exploits are characterized by his *style*. Whether he is climbing onto a beach at night and peeling off his diving suit to reveal the impeccable evening dress beneath, or whether he is escaping machinegun-fire by slaloming down a mountain in a cello case (Stradivarius, naturally), the scale of the danger is matched only by the scale of his playful audacity. And it is this cool confidence that allows Bond to turn a threat into an opportunity— an opportunity to create dazzling moments of human achievement that endure despite the mortality of their creator.

Does this mean that we should live like Bond? Amoral and flippant, valuing choice over the consequences of that choice? Clearly not; we've seen that without the influence of Reason, the Guardian would be a liability to himself and to the people around him. But without the influence of Spirit, Plato's man of Reason would lead an impoverished life—too fixated on the eternal to recognize the marvelous potential of the now. Maybe we need Bond to remind us of what is possible; to leave our minds alert to our individuality, shaken but not stirred; to help us remember that we are mortal and unique, and so to find a balance between the man of action and the man of thought, between James Bond and philosophy.[12]

---

[12] I'm grateful to Julie Wainwright for her generosity with her film collection, and to Anna Armstrong and Kit Fan for their helpful comments on early drafts. My thanks also to Havi Carel for illuminating Freud and Heidegger to me, and to Roger Crisp and Nick Denyer for the inspirational conversations about Ancient Greece and living well. Dedicated to the memory of James Logue.

3

Six to Four Against: James Bond and the Hope for a Meaningful Life

JAMES B. SOUTH

Ian Fleming begins *Thunderball* with a memorable sentence: "It was one of those days when it seemed to James Bond that all life, as someone put it, was nothing but a heap of six to four against".[1]

While the idiom of 'six to four against' sounds a bit odd to the typical American ear, the meaning of the statement is clear enough—events and circumstances can make it less likely that we will achieve our goals. Indeed, phrased that way, the sentiment sounds banal. But I think the banality is merely apparent, and as an opening sentence it nicely prepares the reader for what promises to be a difficult challenge for Bond.

The challenge is not the adventure in which Bond travels to the Bahamas, seduces Domino, and confronts Emilio Largo. Instead, the challenge I want to look at is the one in which Bond must confront an overly optimistic, though widespread, philosophical view. That view holds that, in the words of a contemporary philosopher, "there is a harmonious fit between what is rational, what is good for us, and what is good for our society."[2] This philosophical vision has its origins in Plato and is the dominant strain of philosophical thought in the West. Indeed, one can say that this is the predominant promise of philosophy

---

[1] Ian Fleming, *Thunderball* (New York: Penguin, 2003), p. 1.

[2] Raymond Geuss, "Thucydides, Nietzsche, and Williams," in his *Outside Ethics* (Cambridge: Cambridge University Press, 2005), p. 224. This consensus philosophical view has come under challenge since the nineteenth century. Perhaps the first strong challenge came from Nietzsche.

as traditionally understood, and while individual philosophers in the tradition may have quibbled over just what the correct story about the harmonious fit might be, that there is such a fit remains the primary starting point on which most Western philosophy builds.

Obviously, that promise is also part of the allure of philosophy. Who wouldn't want to assume that everything, ultimately, makes sense? In what follows, I want to provide a reading of *Thunderball's* opening sentence that makes it representative of a significant challenge to this standard philosophical starting point about the meaning and purpose of human life.

Stupid, Ignorant Bastard

Why does Bond think life is a heap of six to four against? Fleming tells us that the reason for the belief is that Bond is "ashamed of himself," and he makes clear that this psychological state is a rare one for Bond to experience. The shame, in turn, seems dependent on a chain of events. First, Bond has a hangover along with the resulting physiological miseries that typically accompany a hangover. But while a hangover might cause one to be ashamed, it is a result of another action, most obviously his decision to drink an eleventh whiskey and soda the previous night. On top of the eleventh drink, Bond had agreed to play one more rubber of bridge. But he "played the rubber like a fool," and ended up losing a hundred pounds, "important money."

The hangover brings to mind a series of cognitive failures on Bond's part, and the failures bring shame. At the same time, though, what caused those failures of judgment? What explains the decision to have the eleventh drink? Why did he play the rubber like a fool? Bond traces the root of the problem to boredom: "It all came from having nothing to do." Yet even that is not the whole story as he has been at headquarters for more than a month doing paperwork, answering phones calls from station agents, and the like. So, it would be more accurate to say that the problem is that Bond has not had the right kind of work to do, presumably the field work befitting a highly trained British Secret Service agent.

Let's pause here for a bit and think more about the source of Bond's shame. Why is Bond ashamed and not, say, guilt-ridden or merely remorseful for the hangover, the bad bridge play, and the eleventh whiskey? The philosopher Bernard Williams has argued that shame is best understood as an emotion that grounds identity.[3] The idea here is that someone can learn much about herself, perhaps very central aspects of herself, through what kinds of actions she takes to be shameful. But how is shame structured as a psychological state? Williams states, "What arouses shame . . . is something that typically elicits from others contempt or derision or avoidance. This may equally be an act or omission, but it need not be: it may be some failing or defect. It will lower the agent's self-respect and diminish him in his own eyes. His reaction . . . is a wish to hide or disappear, and this is one thing that links shame as, minimally, embarrassment with shame as social or personal reduction. More positively, shame may be expressed in attempts to reconstruct or improve oneself" (Williams, p. 90). Bond's self-condemnation as a "stupid, ignorant bastard" and his looking at himself in the mirror and despising "the face that stared sullenly back at him" are clear examples of personal reduction, and Bond is diminished in his own eyes. But what in his actions—the hangover, the decision to play another rubber, playing that rubber like a fool—would elicit from others contempt or derision or avoidance? And is the shame Bond is experiencing merely embarrassment or is he going to use his shame in an attempt to reconstruct or improve himself?

Take it Easy, Mr. Bond

As if on cue, the direct phone from headquarters rings and Bond is summoned to the office. The reader expects that Bond is about to receive some dangerous assignment, but that expectation is quickly dashed. Instead, Bond has been called to a meeting with M in which M expresses concern about a recent report of Bond's fitness:

> Unfortunately, his mode of life is not such as is likely to allow him to remain in this happy state. Despite many previous warnings, he

---

[3] Bernard Williams, *Shame and Necessity* (Berkeley: University of California Press, 1993), p. 75–103. The account of shame I use in this paper is taken from Williams's book.

admits to smoking sixty cigarettes a day. These are of a Balkan mixture with a higher nicotine content than the cheaper varieties. When not engaged upon strenuous duty, the officer's average daily consumption of alcohol is in the region of half a bottle of spirits of between sixty and seventy proof. . . . He is not responsive to the suggestion that over-indulgence is no remedy for the tensions inherent in his professional calling and can only result in the creation of a toxic state which could finally have the effect of reducing his fitness as an officer. (*Thunderball*, p. 3)

Bond shrugs off the medical report, but M is having none of that:

> "It's no laughing matter." M tapped his forefinger on the desk for emphasis. "Mark my words. There is no way to health except the natural way. All your troubles"—Bond opened his mouth to protest, but M held up his hand—"the deep-seated toxaemia revealed by your Medical, are the result of a basically unnatural way of life." (*Thunderball*, pp. 4–5)

M's criticism is that Bond lives an "unnatural way of life." Given the philosophical tradition's emphasis on living according to nature, however 'nature' might be understood, M is essentially telling Bond to become 'philosophical' in the traditional sense of that term. And I think it's telling that the person making this judgment is M, Bond's boss, of course, but also clearly an authority figure in the sense that Bond would be especially sensitive to his judgment. That it is M making this claim reinforces the sense of shame that Bond experienced upon looking at himself in the mirror.

M proceeds to order Bond to spend a couple of weeks at a spa specializing in healthful food, drink, and exercise. And it is crucial to the argument I'm making that Bond does indeed change as a result of his time at the Spa. He begins to eat healthy food and cuts out smoking and drinking. Since leaving the Spa, Bond "had never felt so well in his life. His energy had doubled. Even the paperwork he had always found an intolerable drudgery was now almost a pleasure" (*Thunderball*, p. 63). When his housekeeper, May, complains about the healthy foods Bond is eating, he exercises "infinite patience and good humour" while explaining to her the benefits of his new diet: "And anyway, look how wonderfully well I am. I feel absolutely a new man since I took to eating the right things and gave up drink and so on. I sleep twice as well. I've got twice as much energy. No headaches. No muscle pains. No hangovers" (*Thunderball*, p. 66). The reference to hangovers recalls the book's initial scene. The proximate cause of Bond's shame in that scene, the hangover, won't bother him again. The more remote cause, his having nothing to do, is gone as well since he now finds that paperwork almost makes him happy.

Bond is not only a new man due to his newfound healthy habits, but his character has also undergone a transformation. That is, all these changes have a salutary effect not only on his health, but also on his character. He has developed an infinite patience and good humor. In the past, May's disapproval would have warranted a sharp retort: he would have told her "to go to Hell" (*Thunderball*, p. 65). No longer does Bond respond that way. We certainly do think that patience and good humor are preferable to a quick temper and a dismissive profanity. It would seem, then, that at this point in the novel we have a transformed James Bond, not only a healthy but a happy James Bond.

And what is the ultimate source of this transformation? At one point, while thinking about what he is eating based on his newfound knowledge of nutrition, Bond "couldn't understand why no one had told him these things before" (*Thunderball*, p. 63). Bond's experience of shame at the beginning of the novel along with the contempt directed his way by M, have provoked him to change. This reconstructed and improved Bond, a Bond who has an understanding of nutrition, has started eating according to nature, and his interactions with others manifest a new outlook of patience and good humor. This new Bond has managed to discover the traditional philosophic truth: that knowledge of the world will tell us what is good for us.

Big Fleas Have Little Fleas

The reader is no doubt intrigued at this point in the novel to find out how this new James Bond will respond to the dangers of his job as a secret agent. As Bond finishes talking with May, his direct phone to headquarters rings again, and he is called to the office. SPECTRE has stolen an airplane with two atomic weapons aboard, and M has an assignment for him. From that point, Bond is off the paperwork rotation and back in the field. But the Bond that goes back into the field turns out not to be the new Bond, and we should think about why that must be the case.

As I mentioned earlier, the predominant tradition of Western philosophy holds that "the universe or history or the structure of human reason can, when properly understood, yield a pattern that makes sense of human life and aspirations" (Williams, p. 163). But what if there is no such pattern? There exists a counter tradition in Western philosophy that tries to show that there is no pattern that can help us make sense of our lives. The reasons given for the need to abandon such a hope can vary, but one very common way of thinking about the world as being inhospitable to human interests is to talk in terms of 'disenchantment.' John Diggins has expressed quite well the sense of disenchantment I want to explore:

> What, specifically, is modernism? As a way of reacting to the modern world, modernism is the consciousness of what once was presumed to be present and is now seen as missing. It might be considered as a series of felt absences, the gap between what we know is not and what we desire to be: knowledge without truth, power without authority, society without spirit, self without identity, politics without virtue, existence without purpose, history without meaning.[4]

Stated so succinctly, Diggins presents a very bleak picture of human possibility in the modern world, and one sensibly wants to object that surely matters are not *that* grim. It's important to recognize, though, that the bleakness is dependent upon the now apparently broken promise of philosophy. Philosophy had promised that human happiness could be had, with diligent work, by accommodating some pattern. But whether that pattern is identified with the universe or human history or the structure of human reason, it would be a universally applicable pattern—all humans could, in principle, achieve a life that makes sense. Yet the history of the twentieth century calls that

---

[4] John P. Diggins, *The Promise of Pragmatism: Modernism and the Crisis of Knowledge and Authority.* (Chicago: University of Chicago Press, 1994), p. 8.

universal hope into real question. For example, the very technology that makes for great medical advances is also the technology that allows us to build gas chambers. The human ability to build complex routes of transportation is also the ability that permitted and enabled us to kill millions of people in gas chambers. Returning to *Thunderball*, one can say that the same human ingenuity that can create the British intelligence agency for which Bond works is also the ingenuity that can create SPECTRE.

Consider the painfully bureaucratic language of SPECTRE.'s note announcing their reason for stealing the plane with its atomic weapons:

> Failure to accept these conditions within seven days from 5 pm GMT on 3 June 1959—i.e. not later than 5 pm on 10 June, 1959—will have the following consequences. Immediately after that date a piece of property belonging to the Western Powers, valued at not less than the aforesaid £100,000,000, will be destroyed. There will be loss of life. If, within 48 hours after this warning, willingness to accept our terms is still not communicated, there will ensue, without further warning, the destruction of a major city situated in an undesignated country of the world. There will be very great loss of life. (*Thunderball*, pp. 70–71)

Seriously, what could be a 'proper' reaction to a world that can produce people willing to write that memo and perform the actions standing behind it?

Life's Too Short

It's worth noting that as M briefs him on the crisis, Bond begins to chain smoke. At one point, calling attention to what is happening as Bond lights another cigarette, Fleming describes it as "his sinful third in one hour" (*Thunderball*, p. 77). Of course, this return to chain smoking might just be a reversion to a bad habit in a time of stress, but that "sinful" gives the reader pause, suggesting a kind of willful wrong-doing on Bond's part. We are not given enough information about Bond's internal thoughts at this point to judge how volitional the reversion to chain smoking is, yet Fleming has certainly made the reader wonder just what the point of describing smoking as "sinful" might be. Is Bond's smoking sinful because smoking is intrinsically sinful, or is it the quantity (three in one hour) that makes it sinful, or is it rather what the smoking represents, the old Bond, that is best described as "sinful"? There's an additional disquieting possibility—it may not be sinful at all. That is, it may appear sinful given an optimistic acceptance of the promise of philosophy, a view that shapes the creation of the new Bond. That story would hold that Bond will have no one to blame but himself if smoking causes him harm. But in the larger context of the stolen plane and weapons, and the very real threat it represents, smoking can hardly be considered a sin. In short, Fleming's use of 'sinful' here appears ironic, especially as we progress to the next scene.

Having received his instructions from M, who is himself uncharacteristically breaking an oath of secrecy in telling Bond about the stolen plane, Bond is almost assassinated as he leaves headquarters. When he finally gets back home, he has had it with his new life and philosophically optimistic attitude. He tells May: "You were right. I can't do my work on carrot juice. I've got to be off in an hour and I need some proper food. Be an angel and make me your kind of scrambled eggs—four eggs. Four rashers of that American hickory-smoked bacon if we've got any left, hot buttered toast—your kind, not wholemeal—and a big pot of coffee, double strength. And bring in the drink tray." When May wonders what happened, Bond replies, "Nothing, May. It just occurred to me that life's too short. Plenty of time to watch the calories when one goes to heaven" (*Thunderball*, p. 84). This dismissive profanity, along with Bond's reversion to his old unnatural eating and drinking appetites, signals the end of the new Bond both in terms of health and in terms of moral character. As a result, we never get to see the "new" Bond in espionage action. But that is for the best, no doubt, since a Bond who held to the optimistic philosophical orientation would be likely to fail in the face of those who don't.

Swimming the Gauntlet

Still, it might be objected that Bond's thought that occurs as a result of everything that has transpired is as apparently banal as the one that opens the novel. How can a truism as shallow as "life's too short" cause Bond to abandon the natural healthy way of life he's adopted and that has made him a new man? Note, too, the way Bond talks about his "work." It's his work that is incompatible with a healthy, happy life lived according to nature.

Now, no one who returns home after a journey is exactly the same on return. Bond may be back to his 'old' ways, but he cannot be the same Bond who was ashamed at his hangover. Let's call the Bond who has returned to his old ways the 'new/old' Bond. The new/old Bond has the habits and skills of the old Bond, but a realization that resulted from the failure of the new Bond to be adequate to his work. In his conversation with May, Bond may claim that 'nothing' happened to cause him to abandon the new Bond, but we need to consider carefully that 'nothing'. After all, he has learned of SPECTRE's plot and been the target of an assassination attempt. Those are two pretty substantial 'somethings'. On the surface, then, Bond's claim is nonsense. At a different level, though, Bond is no doubt correct. What has caused him to abandon the old Bond in search of another Bond is the 'nothing' that represents precisely those experiences 'missing' in Diggins's description of the modern condition. Bond has come to feel the absences, the absences manifest in the demands and plans of SPECTRE. Now, though, the new/old Bond faces a difficult problem. How is he to act? He cannot act like the new Bond, since that would be inadequate to his work. At the same time, though, he cannot just revert to the old Bond's ways. He has to come up with a new way of thinking about his work.

One particularly persuasive account of the human predicament in such a situation was given by the twentieth-century philosopher Theodor Adorno. Here is Geuss's summary of Adorno's view:

> Adorno held that advanced societies in the modern world were closed, total institutions that were radically implicated in evil. In such societies, no action could be, as it were, fully innocent, and consequently demands that philosophy be connected with any kind of injunction to perform specific actions are themselves both forms of repression and an incitement to evil.[5]

---

[5] Raymond Geuss has set forth concisely a range of options available to those who might want to take seriously the problem of the bleakness of human possibility. See his essay "Outside Ethics," in *Outside Ethics*. I have dealt in more detail with the problems modern society poses for philosophical hope in my essay "Of Batcaves and Clocktowers: Living Damaged Lives in Gotham City," in Jorge Gracia and William Irwin, eds., *Philosophy and the Interpretation of Popular Culture*.

If our choices are all implicated in evil, what can guide them? Adorno's suggestion is that "Any attempt on the part of the individual to consider what he or she as an individual ought to do is a completely pointless exercise," and all we can really do is try to " maintain shreds of our subjectivity and spontaneity" and "to cultivate reflection" relative to our complicity with evil. (Geuss, p. 56).

A philosopher might be able to follow this advice, but not a man of action such as James Bond. It is, after all, just a bit too continental for a subject of the Queen of England. The new/old Bond will necd a more practical approach to proceeding against SPECTRE. I think it's no accident that the closest friend Bond has is the American CIA agent Felix Leiter. This friendship is not simply a representation of the special relationship between the UK and the USA during the Cold War. Rather, it shows a practical, anti-theoretical streak in Bond, and I think that Fleming wants us to take the new/old Bond as a model for action under the conditions that Bond has come to recognize.

After all, the new/old Bond does not retire from the British Secret Service, but continues his 'work'. Is that simply complicity in evil? Partly, no doubt, at least formally speaking. Nonetheless, it's not easy to see his actions in defeating Largo and SPECTRE. as evil simply speaking. He saves a tremendous number of lives. Rather, I think the important lesson we learn from the new/old Bond is that worry about the morality of particular actions is a dead-end street for him. In accord with Adorno's deep pessimism and Diggins's account of the absences felt in modern life, there are no universal resources available for guiding his actions. Instead, it is the acceptance of his 'work' that determines what he should do in any situation. Many of those actions, obviously, are outside the pale of conventional morality and ethics. By this time, that should not be excessively troubling for us since, if Adorno is correct, the conventional morality harbored within itself such events as the Nazi Holocaust.

Time for Decision

I think it's more useful to view the new/old Bond as working within the confines of necessity that comes with that sense of identity shaped by the need to avoid shame. If the world is only at best partially intelligible, then as Williams states, "in itself it is not necessarily well adjusted to ethical aspirations" (Williams, p. 164). But then what can guide our lives if the world cannot, and how can we judge Bond's actions? Here, the notion of "thick" ethical concepts can be useful.[6] Thick concepts, on Williams's view, are more descriptive than the contrasting, and more abstract, "thin" concepts. So, for example, the thick concept 'treachery' carries a much stronger negative evaluation than the thinner concept 'deceit'. As a moment's reflection shows, though, it's impossible to go from thin concepts to thick ones, since it doesn't make enough sense to say that treachery is wrong because it is a form of deceit. So thick concepts cannot be fully justified by thinner ones, and that lack of justification means that there will always be a gap between our conviction about thin concepts and our conviction about thick ones. In fact, thinking about the distinction between types of evaluative concepts provokes the idea that thick concepts such as 'treachery' do most of the work in guiding our actions precisely because they provide a richer ethical experience than thinner concepts do. At the same time, though, inasmuch as those thick concepts cannot be fully justified, ethical conviction can appear as little more than wishful thinking.

In *Thunderball*, once Bond abandons the effort to make the world fit his thin ethical aspirations, he becomes free to use thick ethical concepts again. Thus, in thinking about ways to deal with Largo and SPECTRE, he is better prepared to do what he must in accord with his work. But now we have one more quandary, since Bond cannot thereby be an ethical guide for us and it becomes difficult to see how we can make a judgment about Bond's actions. In order to get around these sorts of worries, Williams offers the metaphor of an "ethical federation" in which "thicker" ethical concepts hold good at more local levels while "thinner" concepts hold good at more general levels. Bond's work clearly goes on at a very local level indeed, but at the same time it is not our local level. Only secret service agents know and can accept ethically what must be done in fighting the evils perpetrated by villainous people and organizations. This means that we're not in a position to judge accurately the

---

[6] Williams has written often of the distinction between "thick" and "thin" ethical concepts. Here I'm relying on a discussion in his "Modernity and Ethical Life," in Williams, *In the Beginning Was the Deed* (Princeton: Princeton University Press, 2005), pp. 40–51.

morality of a spy like Bond, though we are in a position to judge that Bond is not living a life that the philosophical tradition would deem happy. At the same time, it's clear that Bond's knowledge and acceptance of the local necessities of being a spy take quite a toll on him. Bond's local world necessitates that he act in certain ways, but those ways are not well suited to Bond's flourishing in a more general sense.

I suggested before that Fleming wants us to take the new / old Bond as a model. We can now see how Bond could function as a model. He is not a model for our everyday actions at a local level, nor is he a model for action at a general level in the sense that we cannot generate universal guidelines for action from observing how he acts. Rather Fleming's Bond serves as a philosophical model. What makes *Thunderball* philosophically interesting is that in it Bond is given a glimpse of a different sort of life that promises a fit between reason, personal good, and social good, but he ends up rejecting the proffered alternative.

To be a spy in Fleming's universe is to be doomed to the explicit realization that there is no clear fit between what's good for the spy, what's good for a human being, and what's good for society. If, as I hold, there is no such fit between the happiness of a person and what is good for society, then Fleming's Bond has provided us with an insight that has eluded most philosophers: the odds of our living a happy life are six to four against.

SECTION II

Mr. Bond Is Indeed a Very Rare Breed

The Man Behind the Number

4

Bond and Phenomenology: Shaken, Not Stirred

SUZIE GIBSON

"Shaken, not stirred"—this is James Bond's preferred way to drink a martini. The familiar, oft-repeated phrase tells us many things about Ian Fleming's hero—some obvious, some obscure. For instance, Bond's choice of drink reveals that he not only enjoys strong alcohol, but the sort consumed in high society. The martini connotes the glamour, sophistication, and wealth of the fashionable and privileged. Bond's partiality for this drink, and indeed his strict instructions concerning its preparation, suggest that he is no slouch when it comes to fashion.

Bond is the epitome of cool. His reconnaissance activities often require that he rub shoulders with the extravagant and elite. Although he is adept, even triumphant in this role, he is not a full-time member of the martini-drinking class. His work, which is his *raison d'être,* is far too important for that. Yet it's not simply a matter of national and patriotic duty over-riding excessive and indulgent desires—it's a matter of international security! What's more, Bond would never dream of becoming a member of any social group, glamorous or otherwise, because he is far too cool and sophisticated for that.

Bond is a loner, which agrees with his secret life and work as a spy. Being a licensed-to-kill member of the British Secret Service, he lives, acts, thinks—and drinks—outside the fray of social climbers and glamorous wannabes. From this vantage point, he is untouchable. He is also, perhaps, invincible. The injunction—"shaken, not stirred"—enunciates a cool sensibility that is the result of a carefully developed, fostered, and cultivated intelligence. Bond's experiential understanding and pleasure in all things fine discloses his one weakness or strength (depending on which way you look at it): he is a consummate materialist. As a materialist, he acts on his nerves, relies on his instincts, and makes decisions according to empirical evidence and sensory data. His manner of living and spying is deeply phenomenological.

Phenomenology is concerned with the study of phenomena, with observable matter. Spy and phenomenologist unite in their desire to fathom the world of experience. Bond is a super-spy because he applies all of his sensory abilities to the work of surveillance. His perception of the world is therefore far richer than his comrades and foes in arms. Bond is a sensualist who is very much in touch with the observable world and, as such, he has the insight to delve into the invisible realm of latent dangers, concealed plots, and terrible intentions.

The phenomenology of Maurice Merleau-Ponty (1906–1961) provides a rich, philosophical dimension to Fleming's hero. Yet it is not simply a case of Merleau-Ponty informing and enriching Bond, it is also a case of Bond fleshing out the ideas and contours of his very particular philosophy. There is, in Merleau-Ponty's words, a "reversibility"[1] of influences, interests, and connections between the British secret agent and the French philosopher. For example, Bond enacts Merleau-Ponty's fervent belief in the unity of mind and matter in battle scenes where success is dependent upon the interaction of thought and action. Bond is a thinking action hero whose intellect and thought processes are fleshed out in grand feats of physical activity and in discreet acts of sophisticated indulgence.

Bond effectively illustrates Merleau-Ponty's conviction that no thing exists or operates independently from other things because everything (including nothing) is connected. Even the activity of philosophical enquiry itself involves the interaction of mind and matter since the very process of asking the big questions (and the small questions) to do with the what, how, when, where, and why of existence requires both intellectual and physical exertion. The mental life of the questioning individual is an expression of his or her physical life and vice-versa. However, this doesn't mean that Merleau-Ponty valued the inter-

---

[1] Maurice Merleau-Ponty, *The Visible and the Invisible* (Evanston: Northwestern University Press, 1992), p. 144.

nal, subjective life of the individual over and above the external, objective world. Such an approach is more in keeping with the existentialist philosophy of his colleague and drinking buddy, Jean-Paul Sartre (1905–1980). Instead, Merleau-Ponty was interested in understanding the *relationship between* the physical subject and the physical world. He is fascinated by the *process* through which we come to perceive, question, and experience the world. In this way, the perceiving-subject and world of perception are equally important to his task to fathom both the visible and invisible structures underpinning existence.

Although phenomenology is concerned with the study of perceptible matter, Merleau-Ponty thought, along with his predecessor, Edmund Husserl (1859–1938), that not all things could be perceived. Husserl certainly took this idea very seriously by turning his phenomenology into a non-empirical (or non-experience based) study of the mind. For him, perception was not limited to the sensory faculties of sight, sound, smell, and touch; it also included mathematical equations, cognitive states, moods, and abstract concepts. Basically, Husserl was interested in exploring the realm of the invisible. In spirit, Merleau-Ponty takes up Husserl's fascination in the non-observable world of the mind, but unlike Husserl he did not try to turn his philosophy into a method of scientific enquiry. For Merleau-Ponty, Husserl's abstract mind-states were not mere instances of insular life; they were also expressions of a broader existence and consciousness. Merleau-Ponty is concerned with the *interaction* of mind and matter, not the workings of the mind in isolation from the manifest world. The field of the visible, manifest world and the field of the invisible, hidden world are of the same substance, material and matter; only that the latter is not as available as the former to sensory perception.

The visible and the invisible are intertwined in the secret work of James Bond. These two interlocking realms and planes of existence are part and parcel of the work of a spy. Yet Bond's ability to distinguish the unseen from the seen is not only crucial to his profession; it is absolutely integral to his success, power, and endurance. Bond is very much a flesh and blood hero who is entwined in the sensible, empirical world of sensation and experience. He is so immersed in what he sees that he has the ability to see what others can't. Bond is a super-spy because he is super-sensible. From the humble egg that must be

"speckled brown" and boiled no more and no less than "three
and a third minutes,"[2] to the not so humble vintage of "Mouton
Rothschild '53,"[3] Bond is exceptionally acute and meticulous in
his tastes and knowledge of the world. Fleming's invention not
only illustrates Merleau-Ponty's phenomenology, he enacts it.
Just as the complex nature of perception fuels the thought and
philosophy of Merleau-Ponty, so too is perception, in all its myriad forms, essential to the work and life of Bond. And what a
life it is! Bond embraces all that life has to offer, especially when
it comes to material delights.

A Man of Style, a Man of Substance

Bond is certainly aware and willing to reveal his predilection for
material pleasures. In fact, he can be quite apologetic about it—
"'you must forgive me . . . I take ridiculous pleasure in what I
eat and drink. It comes partly from being a bachelor, but mostly
from a habit of taking a lot of trouble over details.'"[4] Bond's
ostensible apology to the *femme fatale* in Fleming's *Casino
Royale* is significant on many levels. As Fleming's debut fiction,
it is important that Bond's personality, likes, and dislikes be dis-
closed. This revelation has the dual effect of introducing
Fleming's invention and consolidating it for future publication.
Yet Bond's words do more than disclose and cement character—
they also provide a telling connection between his professional
life and general *modus operandi*. Bond associates his meticulous knowledge of good food and drink with the care and attention he puts into his work. Fleming's secret agent certainly does
take "a lot of trouble over details," and this has proved to be critical in not only saving his life but also perhaps more importantly
considering Bond's healthy libido, the life of his leading lady.
There is a fluency expressed here between Bond's attitude
toward consumable items and his work. Willingly or unwillingly,
we are drawn, along with his love interest (or sexual curiosity),
Vesper Lynd, within the very personal horizon of his *manner*
and *style* in the world. [5]

---

[2] Ian Fleming, *From Russia, with Love* (London: Pan, 1963), p. 80.
[3] Ian Fleming, *On Her Majesty's Secret Service* (London: Pan, 1965) p. 25.
[4] Ian Fleming, *Casino Royale* (London: Pan, 1965), p. 61.
[5] In this scene between Bond and his leading lady, he asks if he can borrow her first

According to Merleau-Ponty, one's style and manner of conduct is not an affectation that conceals a deeper nature, or a superficial appendage that detracts from a "true" self. Rather, it is *the* means through which we interpret and access the world. A body's (any-body's) particular style of vision, manner of hearing, touch and smell, brings the phenomenal, object world, within the borders of our sensory experience. Our manner and style of perception both filters and shapes our understanding and knowledge of the things we hear, see, smell, and touch.

Merleau-Ponty's understanding of style departs from the Platonic tradition of opposing art and reality, appearance and truth. As an external representation of self, style is not a mere outward semblance of an interior and more authentic self. No, it is a manifest expression of self-hood. Yet Plato (around 428–around 348 B.C.E.) would argue otherwise and as such he is remembered for his dismissal of art, fine and otherwise, and his exaltation of philosophy. According to Plato, philosophy, unlike every other profession (politics included) was concerned with the truth.[6] Suffice to say, Merleau-Ponty did not subscribe to Plato's mistrust of representation because he believed that philosophy, along with poetry, literature, painting, and so forth, provided an alternative means of interpreting and understanding the world. Philosophy did not deserve to be placed over and above other art forms and endeavours, because it is like any other human activity, just as fallible and mortal as its practitioner.

It goes without saying, but I will say it nonetheless, Plato would have dismissed Fleming's novels not only for their fiction, but also for their glamorous take on the seedy under-world of spying. In such a world, a bullet can annihilate complexity, and intelligence has nothing to do with a relentless process of philosophical enquiry. In general, Plato would have been scathing of Bond's mass appeal and rise to fame as a global entertainment industry. Indeed, Bond's very popular and particular style has

---

name 'Vesper' to describe his "special martini" (p. 59). And so the "three measures of Gordon's, one of vodka" and a "half measure of Kina Littet" shaken "very well until it's ice-cold" and served with a "large slice of lemon peel" (p. 51) is almost named 'The Vesper' but only on the condition that Vesper Lynd is given the benefit of tasting this concoction. Suffice to say, the opportunity never arises.

[6] Plato's denigration of art and elevation of philosophy is discussed in *The Dialogues of Plato*, especially Book X of "The Republic," in The Great Books of the Western World Series (Chicago: University of Chicago Press, 1952).

been detached, transposed, transported, and translated into a
variety of texts and contexts. Over the last fifty years or so, the
very singular style that is Bond has undergone adaptation, repetition, appropriation, imitation, and caricature. (With this in
mind, perhaps Plato's mistrust of art as an infinitely duplicitous
enterprise wasn't so paranoid after all.) There is an abundance
of written and cinematic material that has borrowed and capi-
talized upon the particular habits and idiosyncrasies of the
world's most famous spy. Many of these texts take the form of
film adaptations and versions of Fleming's hero; others take the
form of parodic derivations and variations on his character, such
as the ridiculous Austin Powers. However, the variety, kind, and
volume of responses to Bond's cool manner in no way diminish
or detract from his particular style. In fact, the plethora of rep-
resentations and variations on Bond only further enshrine,
renew, and preserve his style within the annals of past and contemporary cultural history. In the spirit of Aristotle's affirmation
of art (which is a welcome relief to Plato's dour attitude) Oscar
Wilde's aphorism "imitation is the highest form of flattery" is not
only relevant here; it is an understatement.

One's style and manner of perception is an essential part of
our dwelling in the world. The "self", in Merleau-Ponty's usage
is fundamentally a physical, corporeal, and sensory phenomenon. And the perceived world is also a physical, corporeal, sensory phenomenon. Perception is the interaction between the
physical body and the physical world. But this does not mean
that in order to perceive the world, the perceiving individual or
subject is detached or in any way separate from the world or
object perceived. No such division exists in his philosophy. For
Merleau-Ponty, the perceiver as a body, man, woman, or in this
case, spy, is not a subject who can "soar over" (*The Visible and
the Invisible*, p. 27) the world as inanimate matter, brute material, or in this case, an environment full of communist villains,
Russian agents, and sexy women. Subject and object, body and
world, spy and environment are two sides of the same coin. And
the "coin" in Merleau-Ponty's thinking is the *flesh,* a concept
central to his phenomenology.

The flesh plays a vital role in Merleau-Ponty's theory of
reversible communication between subject and world. The flesh
could be imagined as a coin that has two sides or two faces—
or in the case of *Casino Royale*—it could be imagined as a mir-

ror which not only reflects vision, it also *enables* vision. In this book, we are given our first glimpse of Bond's now famous body through a mirror: "he paused for a moment and examined himself levelly in the mirror. His grey-blue eyes looked calmly back with a hint of ironical inquiry . . ." (*Casino Royale*, p. 56). Through the mediation of a mirror, Bond's body is revealed. His very particular style of vision, which is described as "ironical," not only gives him the power to interpret his image, it also gives him the authority to direct our vision of him. Bond's body is conveyed through the involvement of four agencies: a mirror, his vision, the reader's vision, and ultimately, his creator's vision. The complex nature of perception is enacted in and through these four overlapping and intertwining perspectives and agencies. The mirror both reveals and reverses Bond's image. It is also operates as a means through which he is brought into the field of vision.

The interlocking of vision between perceiver and perceived, subject and object operates like a mirror that emits countless reflections. Merleau-Ponty believed that "there is a fundamental narcissism of all vision" (*The Visible and the Invisible*, p. 139) because much like the effect of a mirror reflection, perception is reversed and turned back upon the subject who sees. This process of vision is not linear but reversible in that the subject who sees is reflected in the perceived world. In this way, the opposition between subject and object, perceiver and world is blurred and dismantled. The world for Merleau-Ponty is perception, and perception involves the integration of subject and world, perceiver and perceived.

Merleau-Ponty's theory of the over-lapping relationship between subject and object, seer and seen radically departs from his philosophical forebears, notably René Descartes (1596–1650), whose famous or infamous dictum, "I think, therefore I am" announced (among other things) the division between mind and body. Merleau-Ponty believed this opposition to be false. Thinking did come before existence and existence did not come before thinking—both were interlocking and reversible. For Merleau-Ponty, the very act of seeing, hearing, touching, and smelling involved the subject within his or her sensory environment. And the sensory environment was not an impassive object that awaited discovery, but another life form that was just as animate and vital as the perceiving subject.

Descartes's opposition between the mind and the body is dismantled by Merleau-Ponty's concept of the flesh. Much like the connecting powers of a mirror reflection, the flesh lives between and connects mind and body, subject and object, seer and seen. It is an invisible medium of communication that brings these two faces or forms of life into contact: "the thickness of flesh between seer and the thing is constitutive for the thing of its visibility as for the seer of his corporeality; it is not an obstacle between them, it is the means of communication" (*The Visible and the Invisible*, p. 35). The mind and the body, subject and object, seer and world, come from the same matter, material or core substance—they are all of the *flesh*.

In the Field of the Visible and Invisible

The flesh is the invisible that upholds and makes possible the visible world. Being a secret agent, Bond works within the field of the invisible so that he can protect the visible, conventional, and everyday world from odious forces and ferocious schemes. He is skilled in surveillance because he is entrenched and immersed in the world of vision. In fact, he is so attuned to the visible that he can also fathom what lies beneath or beyond the manifest world.

In order to be an effective spy, Bond is both visible and invisible. He is visible because his cases demand that he operate openly to make contact with the underworld of villains, counter-agents and megalomaniacs, and he is also invisible because his identity as 007 of the British Secret Service, must be concealed for as long as possible in order to protect his cover and life. Visibility and invisibility intertwine in the dangerous work and world of James Bond.

For Merleau-Ponty, the fields of the visible and invisible intertwine, overlap, and cross over in that each is co-dependent on the other for existence and sustenance. By working as a secret agent, Bond chooses to throw himself within the field of these two inter-connected planes of existence. It is, though, not a question of being either "in" or "out" of these fields—it is rather a question of levels or degrees of involvement. Suffice to say, Bond is "up close and personal" with the seen and the unseen. In fact, he draws his strength from being in the field of blazing gun battles, dangerous women, lethal situations, and cruel men. Without the interaction and intersection of this world upon his astute consciousness and primed body, he would be nothing—he certainly wouldn't be the James Bond we have come to know and love.

Bond's uncommon, even perverse delight in skirting the edges of life and death reveals his predilection for the invisible, unknown realm of concealed peril over and above the knowable, visible realm of comfort, safety, and security. As Fleming writes: "he was a man of war, when, for a long period, there was no war, his spirit went into decline" (*From Russia with Love*, p. 78). Because his extraordinary adventures have led him into the murky waters of savage experience, his powers of perception have been sharpened and refined all the more. Bond's experience and knowledge of the world is far richer and more abundant than any other mortal's and as such he is not just human, he is super-human. To paraphrase Merleau-Ponty, Bond is a wild being, a brute being—he is primordial flesh.

Flesh Touching Flesh: Spy and Gun

The flesh could be considered a misleading term because it does not denote excess girth and it does not always refer to anything *corporeal* for that matter. Rather, it is very much connected to Merleau-Ponty's very specific understanding of style. As he writes, the flesh is "a sort of incarnate principle that brings a style of being wherever there is a fragment being" (*The Visible and the Invisible*, p. 139). In other words, the flesh is an "incarnate principle" that allows a "style of being" to come into existence. Where style is an outward, visible expression of self-hood, the flesh is an interior (Merleau-Ponty also names it primordial) invisible force that allows one's style to come into appearance. Our style of perception or our mode of interaction with the sensible world is mediated, carried, and filtered through the flesh. The body-as-world and the world-as-body are both flesh and are brought into being through an incarnate flesh. The flesh is an invisible element that upholds and supports the visible world. The physical world and the human body alike are matter. They are flesh touching flesh through the mediation of an invisible flesh. Perception involves the body-as-world and world-as-body interacting, overlapping, and intertwining. The flesh is the juncture, or point of intersection that both enables and characterizes their relationship. The end of one body and the beginning of another is the *chiasm* or the center of being where all perception begins and ends. This center of being that radiates outward and brings all things, all beings into the world and into contact is the flesh.[7]

Auric Goldfinger's villainy, and indeed his fatal flaw, is that he cannot bear to touch the flesh of another human being. As Fleming writes: "Goldfinger pressed Bond's hand briefly and pushed it away from him. It was another mannerism of the millionaire subconsciously afraid of 'the touch' . . . it was up to him to keep close to Goldfinger!"[8] Dr. No is another Bond antagonist whose withdrawal from the world of matter is an indication of truncated experience. His self-imposed and ultimately false detachment from society is dramatically and violently expressed through his near-impenetrable island fortress and by hands that are not flesh and blood but "articulated steel pincers."[9] Bond's enemies are doomed at the outset because they believe that they can remove themselves from the mortal world of sensation and experience. But the flesh cannot be dismissed. Goldfinger's and Dr. No's plans for world domination inevitably fail because they cannot "soar above" or go beyond the world of flesh because they too are of the flesh. Their mixture of greed and naïveté leads to their eventual annihilation at the hands of a man who enjoys the flesh and embraces its power.

For Merleau-Ponty, the flesh is everything: it encompasses all things and is in all things. It is both of the world and not of the world. It is both of the visible and of the invisible. This complex and layered process of interaction between the physical body and the physical world is both an indication and expression of the all-consuming flesh.

Fleming's spy is very much a flesh and blood hero whose desires are precisely of the fleshy kind. But as already suggested, his love of good food, drink, and beautiful women (not

---

[7] French feminist philosopher Luce Irigaray argued in *An Ethics of Sexual Difference* (New York: Cornell University Press, 1993) that the flesh in Merleau-Ponty is in fact the womb. As a receptacle and vehicle through which life is both born and borne into the world, the womb inaugurates and carries the responsibility of existence. The maternal figure is therefore flesh in the carnal sense, and of the flesh in Merleau-Ponty's incarnate sense.

[8] Ian Fleming, *Goldfinger* (London: Ebenezer Baylis and Son, 1959), p. 146.

[9] Ian Fleming, *Doctor No* (London: Morrison and Gibb Ltd., 1958), p.158.

necessarily in that order) do not impede his powers of perception—on the contrary—they enhance and enrich his sensory abilities. There is of course something very sexy about the style and body of James Bond, which does not have to do with his obvious good looks and charm but with the fact that he exudes a deep and intense sensuality. For example, "He pulled a chair up to the window . . . letting the scented air, a compound of sea and trees, breathe over his body, naked save for the underpants. He drank the bourbon down in two long draughts and felt its friendly bite at the back of his throat."[10]

Bond is very conscious of his body as an instrument of perception, as a professional vehicle of defense and, moreover, as sensual matter: "he explored his present physical sensations. He felt dry, and uncomfortable gravel under his evening shoes, the bad, harsh taste in his mouth and the slight sweat under his arms . . ." (*Man with the Golden Gun*, p. 9). As the British Secret Service's weapon of defense and, as his own man, Bond's body serves at least two masters (and many desires). In the words of French agent Mathis of *Casino Royale*, he is to both country and fellow agents "a wonderful machine" (*Casino Royale*, p. 147). But Bond's body is "much more than an instrument or a means" of perception and a "wonderful machine" of violent energy, it is his *only* means of "expression in the world." [11] Moreover, without the mediation of the flesh, his style, manner of conduct and talent for spying would mean and come to nothing. In this way, the flesh is perhaps the ultimate weapon in Bond's artillery since it is the means through which his intentions, which are often violent but sometimes tender, are realized. The flesh is an elemental force that mediates all experience, all perception and action.

What is further efficacious about the flesh is that it dissolves the opposition between Bond's professional detachment from the world as a spy, and his immersion in the world as a red-blooded male. Bond's two ostensibly different styles and attitudes to the world are conjoined in and through the flesh. The flesh is therefore an elemental principle that undercuts an oppo-

---

[10] Ian Fleming, *The Man with the Golden Gun* (London: Cox and Wyman, 1965), pp. 66–67.
[11] Maurice Merleau-Ponty, *The Primacy of Perception* (Evanston: Northwestern University Press, 1978), p. 5.

sitional logic and structure. As a sensualist spy, Bond thrives on conflict and straddles difference like an ardent lover. Bond likes to be "an actor and spectator" all at once by taking "part in other men's dramas and decisions" (*Casino Royale*, p. 48). Bond is an effective spy because he's a sensualist, not the other way around. And because of this, everything he encounters does not operate in opposition but in accordance to his fluid and adaptable identity. Even his gun, an instrument of death, operates neither as an appendage nor as an attachment, but as an extension of his "living and upright body" (*The Visible and the Invisible*, p. 138). As Fleming writes, "Bond went into his bedroom and took out his two guns and looked at them. Neither was a part of him as the Beretta had been—an extension of his right hand" (*Doctor No*, p. 84). Fleming is certainly aware of the "Freudian thesis . . . that the pistol, whether in the hands of an amateur or of a professional gunman, has significance for the owner as a symbol of virility—an extension of the male organ" (*Man with the Golden Gun*, p. 34). But for Bond, the gun doesn't so much operate as a "symbol of virility" as it works as a natural, direct extension of his body. The relationship between Bond and his gun is not symbolic but indexical in that the connection between them is organic and unfettered. Both hand and gun are flesh and are connected in and through the flesh.

The flesh, in Merleau-Ponty's understanding, extends and enlarges experience, since it is through and because of the flesh that we are on intimate terms with our bodies and the carnal world in general. As an instrument of perception or as a means of communication, the flesh opens up and enlarges perception. Like the devastating reach of Bond's gun, the flesh closes the gap between self and other, individual and world, hero and villain. As Merleau-Ponty writes, the "thickening" powers of the flesh "far from rivaling that of the world, is on the contrary the sole means I have to go unto the heart of the things, by making myself a world and by making them flesh" (*Visible and the Invisible*, p. 135). Bond's gun provides another means by which to immerse him in the world—the gun is his way of touching the world.

Bond is a razor sharp "wonderful machine" whose finely tuned attitudes and preferences are centralized, anchored, and rooted in his fallible, yet by no means, sensual body. If according to Merleau-Ponty, the body is the origin and the end, alpha and omega of all knowledge, then Bond's instincts and highly sensitized body is an impossible machine to reckon with. Bond's acute awareness of his corporeal parameters and his strong sense of what he cannot see, of what mortal perceptions cannot fathom, makes him near immortal. He is a super-spy because he sees and feels what others can't.

Carnal Life: Shaken, Not Stirred

Bond is carnal life, shaken, not stirred. The style and manner in which he drinks a martini is an expression of his wild nature that is at once savage and cultivated, raw and sophisticated, untamed and cultured. The elemental, constituent parts of the dry martini—gin, vodka, and a hint of vermouth—are as agitated, disturbed, and unevenly mixed as the heady and highly intoxicating character of Bond. Even Bond's steely eyes express a wild nature with the mixture of blue and grey. The direction, "shaken, not stirred" is but a fragment line and an orphan phrase that provides us with a clue to a whole way of being that is large, intense, and deeply sensual. Bond embraces all that is flesh and the flesh embraces all that is Bond. Bond is so much *of* the world and *in* the world that he is a world unto himself. He is invincible, untouchable, and incomparable. Yet this does not mean of course, that he is above and beyond the finite, humble pleasures of the flesh. For him, it is precisely in the details of experience that the hidden, invisible face of epic life can be felt. Fleming closes most (if not all) of his fictions with the sexual union of Bond and his "extra heart" (*Doctor No*, p. 110) and the extra heart is none other than the gorgeous Honeychile Ryder of *Doctor No*:

> Bond's eyes were fierce blue slits. He got up and went down on one knee beside her. He picked up her hand and looked into it. At the base of the thumb the Mound of Venus swelled luxuriously. Bond bent his head down into the warm soft hand and bit softly into the swelling. He felt her other hand in his hair. He bit harder. The hand he was holding curled round his mouth. She was panting. (*Doctor No*, p. 247)

Fleming's love scene captures the wild nature and sensuality of the super-spy. Bond may live for action and danger but he also lives very much for bodily pleasures in the here and now. Bond sees and experiences the world as a sensualist and carnal being. His adventures have taken him deeply into the heart of a world, unfettered and untamed by convention and rule. He cannot return from the dark and invisible quarters of such a sphere to the conventional reality (and morality) of civilian life because he knows and has seen too much. The "Mound of Venus" which swells so "luxuriously" and beautifully is for Bond the visible and invisible irresistible flesh that draws him in every time. His only choice (oh but what a choice!) is to bite down softly and then more firmly in order to make sure that he remains in the heart and in the flesh of experience.

5

He Who Eats Meat Wins: Appetite, Power, and Nietzsche in the Novels of Ian Fleming

SUE MATHESON

In the twentieth century, popularized versions of Nietzsche's *Übermensch*[1] proved to be remarkably resilient, in part because of their Darwinian emphasis on muscular strength as the mark of power and excellence. As a rule, it seems the *Übermensch* appears to be a Super-animal, whose will to power is embodied by his physical perfection.

One of the most disturbing and memorable expressions of the twentieth century's conflation of primitive masculinity and the concept of the Overman is found in Ian Fleming's best-selling series of 007 novels. *From Russia with Love* is a particularly good example of Fleming's interest in the popular notion of the Overman. The novel begins by offering its reader an unrelentingly detailed description of the massage of Donovan Grant, SMERSH operative *Granit*, the chief Executioner of SMERSH, and Russian *Übermensch*. Possessing "the finest body" that his masseuse has ever seen, Grant occupies the top position of the murder *apparat* of the MGB and is concerned only with acquiring "absolute supremacy" in his field of work.[2] However, in spite of his magnificent physicality, arguably some would say because of it, Grant is a repellant figure, a cold blooded "reptilian" killer whose animality suggests the vices of the masculine primitive

---

[1] *Übermensch* can be translated as "superman" or "overman." Given the association of "superman" with the comic book hero it seems more appropriate to use the term "overman." This term also more clearly expresses Nietzsche's sense of the *Übermensch* as one who is beyond all others, morally speaking.

[2] Ian Fleming, *From Russia with Love* (London: Pan, 1959), p. 10.

(*From Russia with Love*, p. 10). His wide nostrils, in particular, have a "pigginess" about them and his "embryo tail of golden down above the cleft of the buttocks" is "somehow bestial" (*From Russia with Love*, p. 10).

Less than thirty pages later, a picture of James Bond, handed around a boardroom table at SMERSH Headquarters, introduces the notion of a more sympathetic sort of Cold War warrior. Unlike Grant, Bond is a super-spy who embodies the virtues of the masculine primitive. Looking at Bond's photograph, General G notes "Decision, authority, ruthlessness—these qualities he could see" (*From Russia with Love*, p. 45). Yet, whatever their differences, Grant and Bond both share what E. Anthony Rotundo terms "the same primordial instincts for survival" and pattern of male behavior in popular literature in which one finds the evaluation of men according to their physical strength and energy, the view of man as the master animal who could draw on primitive instincts when reason would not work, and the popularity of the metaphor in which a man's life was a competitive jungle struggle.[3] Nowhere is this pattern of behavior more celebrated than in Hollywood's flamboyant and sensational adaptations of Fleming's novels in which British Super-Agent 007, Man-the-Master-Animal, is played by Sean Connery, Roger Moore, George Lazenby, Timothy Dalton, Pierce Brosnan, or Daniel Craig. Whether he's being chased in a high-speed motorboat, playing golf for astronomical stakes at an exclusive country club, or making love to a beautiful enemy agent, James Bond on the big screen relies on his luck, charm, lightning quick reflexes, good taste, sexual prowess, and, above all, his animal instincts to save Britain (and the rest of the world) from the forces of evil.

Needless to say, Friedrich Nietzsche would have found the popularization of the Overman as Man-the-Master-Animal in Albert Broccoli's Hollywood block-busters simply appalling. Nietzsche's Overman is an individual, motivated by his or her will to power, who expresses that drive intellectually rather than physically. An independent, creative, and original thinker, the

---

[3] E. Anthony Rotundo, "Learning About Manhood: Gender Ideals and the Middle-Class Family in Nineteenth-century America," in *Manliness and Morality: Middle-class Masculinity in Britain and North America 1800–1940,* edited by J.A. Mangan and James Walvin (New York: St. Martin's Press, 1989), pp. 40–41.

Overman frees himself from all values, except those that he deems valid, and as a result, becomes what Nietzsche deems an example of true humanity, a morally responsible individual who, by becoming so, takes over the function of a recently deceased God. The Overman's ability to transcend his limited and limiting human condition is the result of using his will, not his muscles, to reconfigure his moral and religious realities.

Fleming's own portrayals of the Overman as Man-the-Master-Animal are a far cry from the celebration of the masculine primitive that one finds in the 007 movies. Unlike Broccoli's celebration of the type, Fleming's treatment of the barbarian aristocrat forms an intelligent, well-read, and, at times, acerbic critique of the value placed on the popular conflation of Man-the-Master-Animal and Nietzsche's Overman by his reading public.

Who's Who: The Master Animals in Fleming's Zoo

The emphasis that Ian Fleming places on primitive masculinity in the James Bond saga is enormous. Most of the major players in the Cold War are masculine primitives, and their "vigour and strength of body . . . and personality" (Rotundo, p. 41) are expressed in terms of animal imagery. As Meir Sternberg remarks, at times, Bond's world seems to resemble "a human zoo."[4] The master criminals of the Cold War are the master animals, variously described as fish, sharks, eels, snakes, octopuses, spiders, worms, toads, pigs, apes, mongooses, wolves, dogs, hawks, scorpions, and bulls. All Fleming's master criminals are charismatic. In particular, Blofeld, a very big fish indeed, exudes such "powerful animal magnetism" that "in primitive tribes you will find that any man singled out by nature in this fashion will also have been chosen by the tribe to be their chief."[5]

As Blofeld's animal magnetism suggests, Fleming's Cold War is an exercise in Social Darwinism played out on a global scale. The Cold War players' animal identities inform the reader that

---

[4] Meir Sternberg, "Knight Meets Dragon in the James Bond Saga: Realism and Reality Models," in *Style* 17: 2 (Spring 1983), pp. 142–180.

[5] Ian Fleming, *Thunderball* (London: Pan, 1963), p. 47.

Fleming's master animals are really the wolves who, Nietzsche would say, make it their business to prey upon the sheep. Bond and his place in the "private jungle" of the Cold War can be confusing at times, because, like the villains, he is also a master animal (*Thunderball*, p. 47). Bond himself believes that he is "playing at Red Indians," but he is not awarded the role of either the Noble Savage or the Great White Hunter.[6] Rather, Fleming assigns him the identity of the largest and the most dangerous predator of all the jungle animals—the big cat: the tiger or the panther. Throughout the series, Bond is a master animal—even in the unlikely setting of Shrublands. In the health clinic, lying on the massage table, he waits for "the authoritative voice and the quick steps of the naked feet of his prey" (*Thunderball*, p. 40). As Irma Bunt warns Blofeld in *You Only Live Twice*, one must be careful when dealing with 007: "This animal is dangerous."[7]

These master animals are awarded the position of the Overman because of the principle of natural selection at work in Fleming's "private jungle."[8] In Fleming's novels, the action of the Cold War functions like a food chain and as the top predator, the Overman, who overcomes others, occupies the most privileged position. The strong survive and the weak get eaten—literally. The Robber, for example, feeds Felix Leiter to the sharks at the Ourobouros Worm and Bait Factory in *Live and Let Die* and announces his superiority by delivering the leftovers to Bond's motel room with the following note: "HE DISAGREED WITH SOMETHING THAT ATE HIM."[9] Mr. Big attempts to feed Bond and Solitaire to the "carnivorous fish," but is himself eaten by a shark (*Live and Let Die*, p. 147); Dr. No is curious about the amount of time it will take an army of "black crabs" to pull Honeychile Ryder to pieces; Bond, the more dangerous animal, he reserves for a giant squid.[10] Scaramanga in *The Man with the Golden Gun* reserves Bond for the crocodiles:

---

[6] Ian Fleming, *Casino Royale* (London: Pan, 1955), p. 141.

[7] Ian Fleming, *You Only Live Twice* (London: Pan, 1965), p. 171.

[8] Ian Fleming, *The Spy Who Loved Me* (London: Coronet, 1989), p. 170.

[9] Ian Fleming, *Live and Let Die* (New York: Signet, 1954), p. 198. This note and Fleming's notion of the survival of secret agents being a process of natural selection in which the largest and hungriest predator wins reappears in the film *Licence to Kill* when Franz Sanchez feeds Felix Leiter to sharks.

[10] Ian Fleming, *Doctor No* (London: Pan, 1956), p. 147.

"those crocs have a big appetite. Ruby'll be the main dish but they'll need a desert [sic]."[11]

In fact, Fleming's emphasis on the food chain is so central to his critique of the Overman that he devoted an entire novel to exploring the notion that countries, like armies and individuals, must fill their stomachs to dominate others. In *On Her Majesty's Secret Service*, Bond thwarts Blofeld's nefarious plot to mount "Biological Warfare" against Great Britain by discovering the villain has created "the biggest outbreak of fowl pest affecting turkeys in the history of England" just before Christmas, and more importantly is about to return ten young naive women to the United Kingdom, whom he has hypnotized and who are "all from the danger spots" of British agriculture.[12] Bond realizes that the ensuing chaos caused by Blofeld's protégées spraying Swine Fever and unleashing Colorado Beetle at local agricultural shows would cause the pound sterling to "literally go through the floor—and the country with it" (*On Her Majesty's Secret Service*, p. 237).

Natural competition in Fleming's novels is much more than a matter of satisfying natural appetites. Competitive struggle not only expresses the individual's will to gain political power but also reveals the drive underpinning capitalism itself. Free enterprise is couched, like the Cold War, as a matter of predators and prey. In *Moonraker,* for example, at Blades Drax evokes the principle of natural competition as well and reveals his identity as a master animal when inviting M. and Bond to a game of bridge: "'are *the lambs ready for the slaughter* and *the geese for the plucking?*' He grinned and in *wolfish* pantomime drew a finger across his throat"[13]. Overseas, Bond discovers that the law of the jungle also applies in America. In *Diamonds Are Forever,* he spends some of his free time in a Las Vegas casino, a crass, middle-class version of Blades, built on the principle of "'The Gilded Mousetrap School . . . whose main purpose was to channel the customer-mouse into the central gambling trap where he wanted the cheese or not."[14] At the slot machines in the central trap, Bond encounters women who remind him of "Dr. Pavlov's

---

[11] Ian Fleming, *The Man With The Golden Gun* (London: Coronet, 1989), p. 110.

[12] Ian Fleming, *On Her Majesty's Secret Service* (London: Cape, 1963), p. 23.

[13] Ian Fleming, *Moonraker* (London: Pan, 1956), p. 43; italics mine.

[14] Ian Fleming, *Diamonds Are Forever* (London: Coronet, 1988), p. 115.

dogs, the saliva drooling down from their jaws at the treacherous bell that brought no dinner," "tough lynx-eyed pit-bosses with guns at their waists," and a man who is "a tiger watching the tethered donkey and yet sensing danger" (*Diamonds Are Forever*, pp. 116, 117, 124).

Dining Determines Dominance

Naturally, dining is an important activity; in Fleming's novels, what and how one eats signifies whether the diner is dominant. In *The James Bond Dossier*, Kingsley Amis remarks that Fleming's detailed descriptions of meals generate "a sympathetic warmth, a close and ready identification with the people who do the eating and drinking."[15] Notably, since those who do the eating and drinking survive the competitive struggle of Fleming's food chain, Bond's "armchair observers" who salivate "enviously," are identifying with the forksmen's strength and virility—and their abilities to transcend the condition of the average human being.[16]

As Fleming playfully points out, Overmen are deeply committed carnivores. After all, meat is the most powerful of foods and its consumption ensures the consumer's strength. The more primitive the stuff of his meals it seems the more dominant the Overman is in the 007 novels. As M's subordinate, Bond has many of the same preferences at the table as his commanding officer but is not offered and does not eat marrow. "Placed upright in a spotless lace napkin on the silver plate" with "an ornate silver marrow-scoop beside it" (*Moonraker*, p. 42), M's marrow bone is one of only half a dozen available to diners at the club and has been reserved especially for him. At the pinnacle of his profession, M eats not only the flesh of animals but also the very marrow from their bones. Bond himself may sit down to *poulet supremes, poulard à la crèmes,* and asparagus with béarnaise sauce in polite company, but when he is in the field, he eats red meat—and large quantities of it. Before avenging Felix in *Live and Let Die*, for instance, Bond deliberately orders "the biggest steak, rare . . . he had ever seen," "a quarter

---

[15] Kingsley Amis, *The James Bond Dossier* (London: Cape, 1965), p. 103.
[16] O.F. Snelling, *007 James Bond: A Report* (New York: Signet, 1965), p. 25.

of a pint of Old Grand-Dad," "two cups of very strong coffee" and then begins "to feel more sanguine" (*Live and Let Die*, p. 101).

Power-eating, however, is not as important as a man's ability to master and curb his appetites. Fleming's treatment of dominance, the overcoming of others, becomes delightfully tongue-in-cheek when he displaces Nietzsche's concept of the will to power with the notion of will power. After all, if dieting is a matter of overcoming and transfiguring one's self, then one's will must be powerful indeed if one does not eat. Because Fleming's master animals are all voracious predators, the question of will power regarding food becomes an important indicator of character. Darko Kerim, for instance, does not really care what other people eat, but he "can't stand sad eaters and drinkers" (*From Russia with Love*, p. 110). Unfortunately, because he cannot control his own appetites, Darko does not last long as the Head of British Secret Service in Istanbul. In *From Russia with Love*, as in all the Bond novels, success in espionage is primarily a matter of self restraint. In *Thunderball*, M sends Bond off to a Sussex health club (Shrublands) for an exercise in self-overcoming. Guilty of overindulging his appetites, Bond is expected to "make a complete return to his previous exceptionally high state of physical fitness" (*Thunderball*, p. 11). The importance of will power, in particular the controlling of one's appetite, is the key to dominance and therefore success, as Blofeld is well aware. Self-discipline is the basis of professional and successful conduct in any espionage organization. "There is no discipline in SPECTRE except self-discipline," Blofeld remarks before punishing a subordinate who has indulged his carnal appetites, "We are a dedicated fraternity whose strength lies entirely in the strength of each member. Weakness in one member is the death-watch beetle in the total structure" (*Thunderball*, p. 56).

Because the weak cannot diet well, Bond's sojourn at Shrublands is highly instructive, demystifying the importance that Fleming places on Bond's stomach. Throughout Bond's adventures, Fleming assigns appetites, instincts, and intuition to the stomach. As in Shakespeare's *Coriolanus*, the stomach, not the heart or the head, governs the state of man: gut responses of fear and intuition ultimately determine the well-being of the secret agent. In the novel *Doctor No*, for example, Bond's body recognizes the danger that the giant centipede represents before his brain does—once the danger is past, Bond's reaction is to vomit. In *Thunderball,* the "crawling sensation" that Bond knows so well, the signal that he has "made a dangerous and silly mistake," is located explicitly in "the pit of his stomach" (*Thunderball,* p. 27).

At Shrublands, Bond's will power is amazing: he does not cheat once, not even at The Thatched Barn where "large plates of sugar cakes" are placed on the table uninvited" (*Thunderball,* p. 36). As his diet shrinks his stomach, restricts his appetites, and to some degree changes his tastes, Bond begins to worry that he is losing his "cdgc" (*Thunderball,* p. 37). He appears to be losing the individuality that makes him such an effective Overman for the British government. Bond is beginning to look forward to drinking tea, which he had formerly despised as "that flat, soft, time-wasting opium of the masses" (*Thunderball,* p. 36). Even more, he fears that his personality, his "masculine animal nature" is changing: that is he is in the process of becoming "a soft, dreaming, kindly idealist who would naturally leave the service and become instead a prison visitor, interest himself in youth clubs, march with the H-bomb marchers, eat nut cutlets, and try and change the world for the better" (*Thunderball,* p. 37). Bond, however, is, at base, a carnivore. Although the H-cure draws his "teeth," three primitive "obsessions" from his "former life" do not leave him: Bond still craves meat, "a large dish of Spaghetti Bolognese," and "the . . . body of Patricia Fearing," before finding the "ways and means *to wring the guts* out of Count Lippe" (*Thunderball,* pp. 37–38; italics mine).

Willpower and Appetite: Apollonian versus Dionysian Diners

Because of Fleming's emphasis on appetite and will-power, Overmen generally fall into one of two basic categories in the Bond series. Like gourmets, there are the Apollonian eaters who are capable of controlling their appetites and who generally consume fine foods and drink good wines in moderation, and then there are the Dionysians who are incapable of self-control and are characterized by their gluttony and their greed. M. is probably the best example of the gourmet in the series. Although he indulges an occasional weakness for marrow, his meals at Blades are described as "meager" (*Man with the Golden*

Gun, p. 28). Ordering a whole bottle of wine instead of his usual half carafe is so unusual for M that Porterfield, Blades' headwaiter who prides himself as "something of an amateur psychologist" knows "something hit Sir Miles hard this morning and no mistake" (*Man with the Golden Gun,* p. 29).

"Not a gourmet" (*On Her Majesty's Secret Service,* p. 27), Bond is not as self-disciplined as M would like him to be and enjoys satisfying his appetites, but he is, by no means, a glutton. In *Goldfinger,* there is enough of the "puritan" in him to find the "slice of life" which Mr. Du Pont obligingly stuffs down his throat highly distasteful. What approaches a religious experience in Mr. Du Pont's estimation, Bond considers "a hoggish display"; and he is so "disgusted" by eating stone crabs "like a pig" that "the idea of ever having another meal like this or indeed any other meal with Mr. Du Pont" revolts him.[17] This disgust is generated by what the reader of Nietzsche's *Thus Spoke Zarathustra* would recognize as the difference between the average human being and the man who has control of his mind and body. According to Nietzsche's Zarathustra, those involved in the process of self-overcoming are as like the ordinary human being, as that human being is like a worm. The average man, Zarathustra says, is still an extremely primitive creature—often "more ape than any ape"[18]. Ascending the evolutionary ladder, Bond satisfies his cravings for smoked salmon and lamb chops in *Moonraker,* but it is the quality of food at the table, not its quantity that counts. In *On Her Majesty's Secret Service,* Bond finds himself in France "fed to the teeth with the sucker-traps for gormandizing tourists . . . he had had their 'Specialities du Chef—generally a rich sauce of cream and wine and a few button mushrooms concealing poor quality meat or fish" (*On Her Majesty's Secret Service,* p. 27). To efface his "dyspeptic memories" and to prepare himself for a night of high-stakes gambling he frequents one of his favorite restaurants in France, "a modest establishment" and eats a gourmet meal before returning to the Casino with "Turbot poche, sauce mousseline, and half the best roast partridge he had eaten in his life, under his belt" (*On Her Majesty's Secret Service,* pp. 28–29).

---

[17] Ian Fleming, *Goldfinger,* (New York: Signet, 1959), p. 20.
[18] Friedrich Nietzsche, "Thus Spoke Zarathustra," in *The Portable Nietzsche* (New York: Viking, 1954), p. 124.

A true Dionysian like Giuseppe Petacchi, however, has no qualms about swallowing that "high and easy" life. In fact, Petacchi would probably be unable to wait for the waiter to tie the bib around his neck before sticking his nose in the trough at "Bill's On The Beach" (*Thunderball,* p. 17). He is so gluttonous that Blofeld's No. 4 is "almost put off by the greed" with which "the fish" gobbles "the bait" that he inches toward it (p. 84). In a world where only the strong and the strong-willed survive, the Italian airman's greed for "flashy, exciting, expensive things" is a fatal flaw (p. 84); instead of having his appetites satisfied, "the fish," predictably, becomes fish food himself. Another "greedy fish" (*Moonraker,* p. 33), Sir Hugo Drax, a flamboyant and committed Nazi, is arguably Fleming's most acerbic and successful parody of the popular notion of the Overman as Master Animal. Cribbing from Nietzsche, Bond wonders how Drax, who is a "hairy ape" could possibly fancy himself "a law unto himself, so far above the common herd and their puny canons of behaviour that he could spit in the face of public opinion" (pp. 46, 61).

Among these professionals, gluttony is a reliable indicator of one's place on the evolutionary ladder in a world where the greedy do not survive. In other words, Overmen who overconsume inevitably become victims of their own appetites. Watching the races at Saratoga in *Diamonds Are Forever,* for example, Bond evaluates the nature of the criminals dining with Shy Smile's owner, who like Du Pont in *Goldfinger* is eating soft-shelled crabs. How these men eat enables Bond to determine how dangerous they are. Rosy Budd "forks down frankfurters and sauerkraut and drinks beer out of a stein. Pissaro who looks like "a gangster in a horror comic" concentrates on his food, "occasionally glancing across at this companion's plate as if he might reach across and fork something off for himself " before spooning a mound of ice cream "rapidly up into his small mouth" (*Diamonds Are Forever,* p. 82). Comparing Budd and Pissaro to "cold, dedicated, chess-playing Russians; brilliant, neurotic Germans; silent, deadly anonymous men from Central Europe; the people in his own Service—the double-firsts, the gay soldiers of fortune," Bond decides, on the basis of their insatiable appetites and poor table manners, that these American gangsters are "just teenage pillow-fantasies" (pp. 82–83).

Curiously, in the 007 series, an Overman's drive to dominate is also often expressed in the terms of his sexual appetites. In general, women are regarded as foodstuffs that satisfy men's sexual appetites. Both Le Chiffre and Mr. Big, for example, "consume" women in large quantities. Other characters with a sweet tooth for the feminine include Largo, Peter Franks, Seraffimo Spang, and Sluggsy Jones. Bond himself can be included in this group: as far as he is concerned, women are "for recreation" (*Casino Royale*, p. 32). When Mathis informs him that his Number Two is feminine, Bond replies, "What the hell do they want to send me a woman for? . . . Do they think this is a bloody picnic?" (p. 32).

Mania and Megalomaniacs: Living by the Wolf's Laws

Fleming goes to great lengths to link appetite and power, but one cannot be mistaken for the other. As a top predator, Bond suffers from occasional manias for smoked salmon but at no time does he question or disobey M's authority. Unlike Bond, all of Fleming's master criminals, from Le Chiffre in *Casino Royale* onwards, are subject to the drive that creates "all great men"— what Dr. No aptly describes as "a mania for power" (*Doctor No*, p. 131). Megalomaniacs, they envision a world far more frightening than the simple Darwinist could imagine, for they all profess Nietzsche's "hard" truth that "men of prey with their force of will and desire for power still intact" are designed to live off the "weak."[19] "I am by nature and predilection a wolf, and I live by the wolf's laws," Mr. Big, who also borrows Nietzsche's vocabulary from *Thus Spoke Zarathustra*, tells Bond, "Naturally the sheep describe such a person as a criminal" (*Live and Let Die*, p. 145).

Fleming's beasts of prey evoke Nietzsche's "blond beast" which "lustfully prowls after booty and victory" (*Genealogy of Morals*, pp. 40–41). The men who have chosen Blofeld as their leader all have the "eyes of the wolves and hawks that prey on the herd" (*Thunderball*, p. 51); Bond sums up Count Lippe as a

---

[19] Friedrich Nietzsche, *On The Genealogy of Morals; Ecce Homo* (New York: Vintage, 1969), p 40.

man with a "yellow streak" who preys on those weaker than himself—he lives off women (p. 32). Moreover, when one examines the nationalities of Bond's allies and adversaries, Fleming appears to have taken a leaf out of *The Genealogy of Morals*. According to Nietzsche, "the animal which must out again, must return to the wilderness," emerges in Roman, Arabian, Germanic, and Japanese characters (pp. 40–41). Emilio Largo, Darko Kerim, Hugo Drax, and Tiger Tanaka, who are respectively Italian, Turkish, German, and Japanese, aristocrats by nature and breeding, are all illustrations of the popular concept of Nietzsche's elite barbarian. They are, in final analysis, all master animals—muscular or secular versions of Nietzsche's Overman.[20]

In *You Only Live Twice*, Dikko Henderson's lecture on the nature of the barbarian—"scratch a Russian and you'll find a Tartar . . . a Japanese and you'll find a samurai"—includes the American Wild West and the "knights in shining armour at King Arthur's court" (*You Only Live Twice*, p. 57). According to Henderson, the basic layer of every human being, however civilized, is the animal, and in light of the evidence, he appears to be absolutely correct. Fleming's Cold War illustrates, in part, Nietzsche's belief that it is "ultimately, an exploitative drive for self-aggrandizement rather than a mere struggle for existence, which directs the evolutionary process, that is, the will to power rather than the 'mere' will to life."[21]

When reading the Bond canon, it is tempting to believe that Fleming is using Bond to reinforce the popular attitude of the British towards Nietzschean philosophy—that Nietzsche was "very wicked" and for his sins was punished "by madness."[22] After all, Fleming's villains are very wicked indeed—and all are undeniably insane. However, they are not punished for their crimes by madness. Rather they are driven mad, as Zarathustra predicts men will be in *Thus Spoke Zarathustra*, by their inabilities to restrain "the spirit of revenge" which is "a great folly" in

---

[20] In *A View to Kill*, Max Zorin's megalomania, the result of Nazi eugenic experiments, is arguably Hollywood's best example of the madness that is a trademark of the Master-Animal as Overman in the Fleming novels.

[21] Patrick Bridgewater, *Nietzsche in Anglosaxony: A Study of Nietzsche's Impact on English and American Literature* (Leicester: Leicester University Press, 1972), p. 228.

[22] Edward Thomas, "Nietzsche." *The Bookman* (June 1909), p. 140.

the will ("Zarathustra," p. 252). Blofeld is probably the most colorful example of this sort of madness, strolling about in his Garden of Death while planning to get even with his enemies and garbed in the regalia of a seventeenth-century Samurai.

Bond is an ironic agent of retribution in Fleming's novels, for he punishes the madmen, not only by killing them, but also by psycho-analyzing their characters. His unsympathetic diagnosis of Drax, for example, reduces the German aristocrat to three short and very unromantic phrases: "galloping paranoia. Delusions of jealousy and persecution. Megalomaniac hatred and desire for revenge" (*Moonraker*, p. 163). Likewise, Bond assesses Dr. No as "a maniac," (*Doctor No*, p. 131), gambles on Mr. Big's "mania for exactitude and efficiency" (*Live and Let Die*, p. 148), and informs Blofeld and Irma Bunt that they are "both mad as hatters" (*You Only Live Twice*, p. 172). Bond's diagnoses of his enemies are ironic, because he himself is a part of the "evolutionary" process of overcoming in which they are involved. A large part of 007 is the beast of which Nietzsche speaks. Like Fleming's villains, Bond also despises the "herd"; in fact, he became a 00, because the "dangerous" assignments are the only ones that he enjoys (*Doctor No*, p. 18).

Unlike his adversaries, however, 007 has his will to power under control. Although he succumbs to a "mania" for smoked salmon in *Moonraker* (p. 7), Bond prefers to be a "Scottish Peasant" and not a knight (*Man with the Golden Gun*, p. 170). Ascending the evolutionary ladder by overcoming his will to power, as well as his stomach, he achieves Zarathustra's "self-overcoming."[23] Transfiguring himself, he transforms the master animal's potential for "evil" into the potential for "good": there is little doubt that Bond belongs on what could be described as the side of the angels—hanging "crucified" from a wire fence after successfully running Dr. No's gauntlet, Bond, ironically, is accorded the status of a Christ figure (*Doctor No*, p. 161). In the jungle world of the Cold War, however, the meek do not inherit the earth. Only the master animals like Bond enjoy the fruits of victory—the elite lifestyle of Nietzsche's barbarian aristocrat: as we all know, there are moments of "great luxury in the life of a secret agent" (*Thunderball*, p. 3).

---

[23] R.J. Hollingdale, *Nietzsche* (London: Routledge, 1973), p. 92.

Towards the conclusion of *Casino Royale*, Fleming presents his reader with the question: is it indeed a good thing, as Theodore Roosevelt believed, to make the wolf rise in a man's heart? (*Casino Royale*, p. 140) Overall, the answer is probably not. The master animal may ascend the evolutionary ladder but his primitive nature, expressed by his appetites, is something that must always be restrained for the good of others. As the narrator points out, the hidden layer of Bond's basic nature reveals itself when his features relax. In sleep, his face returns to type: the anti-social face of a predator, it is "a taciturn mask—ironical, brutal, and cold" (*Casino Royale*, p. 13). As Bond himself discovers, in the Cold War, secularized Overmen are found on both sides of the Iron Curtain, and the values embodied by primitive masculinity do not ensure, as they seemed to in earlier times, the survival of the society which the hero protects, for "the villains and heroes get all mixed up" (p. 143). Even patriotism cannot solve this problem, Bond says, for "this country-right-or-wrong business is getting a little out-of-date . . . History is moving pretty quickly these days and the heroes and villains keep on changing parts" (p. 143).

In *The Spy Who Loved Me*, Stonor best sums up the character of the muscular Overman and gives Vivienne Michel some sound advice: "the top gangsters," he says, "the top FBI operatives, the top spies and the top counterspies are cold-hearted, cold-blooded, ruthless, tough, killers"; he advises her to "keep away from all these men" (p. 170). Ironically, Hollywood has ignored these warnings about the Master Animal and romanticized 007, his appetites, and his drives: Bond, in the popular imagination, has become what Fleming, who termed the character, in private, a "cardboard booby," did not intend him to be—a gender ideal.[24] Gender ideals are closely related to the broader values of the culture in which they develop, because they represent a series of cultural choices out of the enormous range of qualities possible for a man or a woman. Judging by the enduring popularity of Secret Agent 007, primitive masculinity, so ably displayed by the master animals in Fleming's novels, is something that we have chosen to continue to value

---

[24] John Pearson, *The Life of Ian Fleming: Creator of James Bond* (London: Cape, 1966), p. 303.

even after the Iron Curtain collapsed. Nonetheless, the message that the James Bond novels carry is disturbing: a collection of instincts and appetites, man is little better than an animal. He would be, in Nietzsche's view, an ape. By valuing Bond's primitive masculinity, we are, it seems, reinforcing the notion that we are still driven to a great extent by our stomachs. In the final analysis, the concept of human nature underpinning Fleming's Cold War asks a question that Nietzsche himself posed: is it better to out-monster the monster or to be quietly devoured?[25]

---

[25] I would like to thank Dr. Jim Gough, Department of Humanities and Social Sciences, Red Deer College, for his insights regarding Nietzsche's use of irony in *Thus Spoke Zarathustra.*

6

James Bond: A Nietzschean for the Cold War

ISHAY LANDA

Although James Bond is one of the greatest of all popular icons and Friedrich Nietzsche is the arch-patron of elitism, Ian Fleming's secret agent is one of the most notable expressions of a Nietzschean heroic model.

What ultimately unites the Bondian perspective with the Nietzschean one is their joint opposition to mass-society and the attempt to bolster a neo-aristocratic, elitist alternative. Bond's 'Nietzscheanism' manifests itself quite palpably and consistently throughout Fleming's stories. To be sure, 007 faces a series of arch-villains who flaunt an unmistakable Nietzschean credo; his foes are, more or less explicitly, wicked specimen of the *Übermensch* (the famous term Nietzsche used to refer to his hypothetical individual of the future, whose self-mastery, heroism, and amoral daring would triumph over the meekness and mediocrity of the present individual, chained by the inhibitions of Judeo-Christian, "slave morality"). And thus, at least superficially, Bond appears to be rather an *anti*-Nietzschean, barricading the advances of political and moral nihilism.

Yet this outward rejection of Nietzscheanism is in fact profoundly Nietzschean, inasmuch as it seeks to defend not democracy but elitism, to cement hierarchy rather than promote equality. Fleming is Nietzsche's enemy in the national sense, inasmuch as Nietzsche was associated with German fascism; however, as far as class politics is concerned, in defending global capitalism, they are brothers in arms.

Bond as an Aristocratic Bourgeois

In the modern age of the masses, the bourgeoisie was driven to validate its social supremacy by developing a neo aristocratic discourse, a mode of behavior and a cultural demeanor which hark back to the epoch preceding the American and the French revolutions, when the old nobilities were still calling all the shots, more or less unhampered by popular, democratic intervention.[1]

A major task of Nietzschean heroism was to impart something of that flair and glamour formerly associated with the aristocracy upon the rather uninspiring bourgeoisie. One way to achieve this was to depict the neo-aristocratic individual as possessing an acute artistic and sensory sensibility. If the pea under the twenty mattresses could identify the princess of the classic legend, a similar process can authenticate the natural aristocrat in the modern one. In such terms, we can understand the social logic in operation behind James Bond's exquisite culinary demands condensed in the famous 'shaken, not stirred' phrase. Or in the meticulous details of one of his breakfasts:

> The single egg, in the dark blue egg cup with a gold ring round the top, was boiled for three and a third minutes. . . . Then there were two thick slices of deep yellow Jersey butter and three squat glass jars containing Tiptree 'Little Scarlet' strawberry jam; Cooper's Vintage Oxford marmalade and Norwegian Heather Honey from Fortnum's. The coffee pot and the silver on the tray were Queen Anne, and the China was Minton, of the same dark blue and gold and white as the egg-cup.[2]

A breakfast such as this confirms Bond's elevation above the vulgar. The slightest nuance matters to Bond since he is a natural aristocrat. Such hedonism is consistent with the claim of Nietzsche's prophet, Zarathustra, that "The best belongs to me and mine; and if we are not given it, we take it: the best food, the purest sky, the most robust thoughts, the fairest women!"[3] Bond's hedonism, moreover, is thoroughly disciplined, thus not

---

[1] John Carey has contended that "In response to the revolt of the masses, intellectuals generated the idea of a natural aristocracy, consisting of intellectuals" Carey, *The Intellectuals and the Masses: Pride and Prejudice among the Literary Intelligentsia, 1880–1939* (London: Faber and Faber, 1992), p. 71.

[2] Ian Fleming, *From Russia with Love* (London: Hodder and Stoughton, 1988), pp. 80–81.

[3] Friedrich Nietzsche, *Thus Spoke Zarathustra* (Harmondsworth: Penguin, 1969), p. 296.

conflicting with Nietzsche's contention that the "'predominance of suffering over pleasure' or the opposite (hedonism): these two doctrines are already signposts to nihilism."[4]

Bond's heroic way of life consists precisely of a fine balance between pain and pleasure. He does not indulge in gastronomic or sensual pleasures for their own sake and certainly does not shirk suffering. Rather, he seeks to combine pleasure and pain in order to enhance life, intensify the quality of his experiences. Bond is not the usual moneyed and dissipated hedonist, but a *puritanical one*, a hedonist with a purpose. He exemplifies what Nietzsche extolled as a "fusion of a Stoic and a frivolous appearance of happiness, characteristic of noble cultures" (*Will to Power*, p. 41). Nor is Bond a libertine, for "the libertinage . . . should not be confused with the will to power (—which is the counterprinciple)" (*Will to Power*, p. 75). In Bond, as Anthony Burgess observed, the "gusto is controlled: the banquet of the senses is a reward for dangerous work performed on behalf of a free world."[5] The eclipse of noble culture, according to Nietzsche, reveals itself in the aimless and cowardly self-indulgence of the rich who are characterized precisely by shunning anything resembling "dangerous work": "Our time, with its aspiration to remedy and prevent accidental distresses and to wage preventive war against disagreeable possibilities, is a time of the *poor*. Our "rich"—are poorest of all. The true purpose of all riches is forgotten" (*Will to Power*, p. 41). Accordingly, after sharing a luxurious, "purposeless" meal with a millionaire, Bond cannot but feel disgust. "Bond thought, I asked for the easy life, the rich life. How do I like it? How do I like eating like a pig . . . ? Suddenly the idea of ever having another meal like this, or indeed any other meal with Mr. DuPont, revolted him. . . . It was the puritan in him that couldn't take it."[6]

The Competitive Way of Life

Perhaps the single most important point of ideological convergence between Bond and Nietzscheanism, concerns Bond's

---

[4] Friedrich Nietzsche, *The Will to Power* (New York: Vintage, 1968), p. 23.
[5] Anthony Burgess, "The James Bond Novels: An Introduction" (1988), in *Thunderball* (London: Hodder and Stoughton, 1989), p.6.
[6] Ian Fleming, *Goldfinger* (London: Hodder and Stoughton, 1989), p. 22.

unquenchable competitive drive.[7] Nietzsche proclaimed that the distinguishing feature of ancient Greek greatness was the construction of society and state around "the finest Hellenic principle, competition."[8] Modern, "emasculated" humanity, cowardly shunning the benison of struggle and favoring instead the timorous harmony of Christian fraternizing, was encouraged to embrace competition in all spheres of life, spiritual as well as material. Not confined to spiritual excellence, competition is rather a general economic propeller, "the permanent basis of life in the Hellenic state."

Such celebration of competition, however, should not be taken at face value. In truth, far from being universal, competition was by definition restricted to the handful of members of the elite, "the geniuses," while sternly excluding the rest, the vile herd. Consider the following affirmation: "In order for there to be a broad, deep, fertile soil for the development of art, the overwhelming majority has to be slavishly subjected to life's necessity in the service of the minority. . . . At their expense, through their extra work, that privileged class is to be removed from the struggle for existence, in order to produce and satisfy a new world of necessities."[9] By definition, therefore, the "finest principle" of competition excludes the "overwhelming majority" of the people.

Competition serves to identify the abler and nobler individuals since "the greater and more eminent a Greek man is, the brighter the flame of ambition to erupt from him, consuming everyone who runs with him on the same track" ("Homer on Competition," p. 190). That Nietzsche employed a metaphor from the world of sports is by no means accidental. Rather, he regarded the Greek concern with athletic-triumph as epitomizing the healthy agonistic, competitive drive of their culture. [10] James

---

[7] On James Bond as a "competitive hero" typical of the modern thriller see Jerry Palmer's excellent analysis, *Thrillers: Genesis and Structure of a Popular Genre* (London: Edward Arnold, 1978), especially Part One, 'Heroes and Villains,' pp. 5–54.

[8] Friedrich Nietzsche, "Homer on Competition," in *On the Genealogy of Morality* (New York: Cambridge University Press, 2000), p. 194.

[9] Friedrich Nietzsche, "The Greek State," in *On the Genealogy of Morality*, pp. 178–79.

[10] For the connection between Nietzsche's thought and sports see the following essays, published in *International Studies in Philosophy* XXX: 3 (1998): Lawrence J. Hatab, "The Drama of Agonistic Embodiment: Nietzschean Reflections on the Meaning of Sports," pp. 97–107; Steven G. Crowell, "Sport as Spectacle and as Play: Nietzschean Reflections," pp. 109–122; Richard Schacht, "Nietzsche and Sport," pp. 123–130.

Bond could be seen as a modern embodiment of the agonistic spirit, of Nietzsche's assertion that "the cruelty of victory is the pinnacle of life's jubilation" ("Homer on Competition," p. 188).

Bond is, to start with, an athlete of sorts, not so much as regards physical prowess, but in his fascination with games. Golf, a test of shooting skills or, most frequently, diverse card and gambling games: they all provide him with an opportunity to indulge his competitive appetite. Meticulously described, and greatly entertaining to read, the sheer pleasure-value of Bond's myriad "games" should not allow us to overlook their deadly seriousness. Winning, for Bond, is a necessity; his entire personality and sense of self-esteem are constructed around his sense of invincibility. To lose spells complete ruin. Thus, in *Casino Royale*, Bond loses—that is, momentarily *thinks* he has lost—a game of baccarat:

> Bond sat silent and frozen with defeat. . . . What now? . . . Back to the telephone call to London, and then tomorrow the plane home, the taxi up to Regent's Park, the walk up the stairs and along the corridor, and M's cold face across the table, his forced sympathy, his "better luck next time" and, of course, there couldn't be one, not another chance like this.[11]

Such depictions of the psychological effects of competition show how misguided is the conventional, sanguine reading of Nietzsche as a defender of individual integrity in face of mass-inauthenticity. For the celebration of competition which Nietzsche promoted and James Bond practices, actually ratifies society as the last arbiter as regards individual value. As Bond painfully realizes upon losing, his essence is not some internal, authentic core, which he can protect from social scrutiny. On the contrary, what he *is*, a winner or a loser, is what he can gain through competition.

What counts is only what one is willing to deposit beside the roulette wheel, literally to put into circulation, for only that can accrue surplus value. It is no coincidence that gambling scenes are so central in the Bond stories. 007 provides, in that sense, the literal enactment of Zarathustra's proclamation that "The devotion of the greatest is to encounter risk and danger and

---

[11] Ian Fleming, *Casino Royale* (London: Hodder and Stoughton, 1988), pp. 83–84.

play dice with death" (*Zarathustra*, p. 138). It's precisely the relative unimportance of the skill-factor and the comparative significance of pure luck involved in gambling games, that make them all the more suitable for conveying the Calvinist logic of the ideology of competition, a logic predicated on the notion of "*predestination*," of a person's fate being decided in advance.

Here luck is never, in fact, *pure* luck. "Fortune as luck" and "fortune as money" are bound together in unfathomable, yet divinely ordained ways. As Calvin put it: "For all are not created in equal condition; rather eternal life is fore-ordained for some, eternal damnation for others."[12] This means that the dice are *metaphysically loaded;* whether one is predestined for salvation or for damnation, can only be found out by entering competition to see which way the dice fall. The will of God manifests itself through the apparent contingencies and fluctuations of market transactions. It is hence that the casino becomes of all places the perfect arena for enacting the drama of competition. And it is hence that Bond is absolutely devastated after losing a "mere" game of cards. His desolation reflects the shocking realization that he is after all not one of the elect, but bound for damnation; or, in Nietzschean terms: not an *Übermensch* but merely human-all-too-human.

This is why those moments in which the possibility of defeat is contemplated, let alone materialized, can only be striking exceptions in Bond's gaming experiences. As a rule, these scenes rather convey the exhilaration of competition and the gratification of victory, the thrilling adventure offered by the "risk society." For all the fatality of defeat, Bond never shrinks from conflict or suspends it until no peaceful alternative remains open. On the contrary, being "a man of war . . . peace was killing him" (*From Russia with Love*, p. 78). Bond must necessarily war, not primarily because there is a good moral reason to do so, but because of his natural need "to live dangerously." He therefore looks for trouble and plunges himself head-on into the heat of battle. Fighting for the cause of justice though he is, Bond is nonetheless almost invariably the

---

[12] John Calvin, *Institutes of the Christian Religion* (Philadelphia: Westminster, 1960), p. 926.

aggressor, the one to draw first blood; hence the ritual movie scene where Bond gallantly enters the casino to search and provoke the villain, who is at that stage usually unsuspecting and ignorant of his rival's identity and intentions. As Nietzsche stated, the "mature man has, above all, weapons: he attacks" (*Will to Power*, p. 385).

The Common Man Fighting the *Übermensch*?

Bond's fundamental Nietzscheanism, however, is nowhere openly manifested. Rather, it is ideologically encrypted, to the point where Bond is routinely presented as a true champion of herd morality against the rapacity of overman-like arch-villains. The many bigger-than-life villains in the Bond stories are unmistakable caricatures of the *Übermensch*, obsessed with the conquest of absolute power and showing complete disregard for the conventional norms and inhibitions of herd-morality. This is the case of Mr. Big, Goldfinger, Dr. No, Hugo Drax, and Ernst Stavro Blofeld, to name but the most formidable ones. Hugo Drax, "a sort of superman,"[13] is further described in the following terms:

> Why should . . . this remarkable man cheat at cards? . . . Did he think that he was so much a law unto himself, so far above the common herd and their puny canons of behaviour that he could spit in the face of public opinion? . . . Spit in their faces. That just about described his manner at Blades. The combination of superiority and scorn. As if he was dealing with human muck so far beneath contempt that there was no need to put up even a pretence of decent behaviour in its company. (*Moonraker*, pp. 61–62)

Indeed, this seems to be a clear enough statement in refutation of Nietzschean, elitist hubris, accompanied by a defense of democratic "public opinion" and the values of the "human muck," of common humanity. Yet, on closer inspection, many ironies reveal themselves at the heart of such 'anti-Nietzscheanism'. For one thing, what is the nature of the "human muck" Bond is willing to protect? These are, in truth, the very cream of the British upper-classes, who enjoy exclusive

---

[13] Ian Fleming, *Moonraker* (London: Hodder and Stoughton, 1989), p. 15.

membership at Blades, "the most famous private card club in the world" (*Moonraker*, p. 24). Blades is not exactly the corner pub where "the common herd," as usually conceived, would gather to have its evening beer. Far from representing some democratic alternative to Nietzschean elitism, it is itself a temple of exclusivity, superiority, and distinction. Thus, it is not Drax's contempt for his fellow human beings as such which unsettles Bond. The true outrage about Drax's "superior manners" is rather the way he dares to mishandle the refined people of Blades as "human muck," giving them a taste of the same treatment they accord everybody else. Which brings us directly to the second significant variation on the Nietzschean theme, concerning Drax's social origins: Drax is a self-made-millionaire, a plebeian success-story of a man rising from the ranks to the heights of British society. Whereas Bond sees in him a "bullying, boorish, loud-mouthed vulgarian" (*Moonraker*, p. 32), the vile masses are delighted:

> And all the time he went on getting richer and the people simply loved it. It was the Arabian Nights. It lit up their lives. If a wounded soldier from Liverpool could get there in five years, why shouldn't they or their sons? It sounded almost as easy as winning a gigantic football pool. (*Moonraker*, p. 18)

Drax is therefore an *Übermensch* of the people, a working class hero, challenging the established order. In view of the pernicious example he sets, it is all the more vital to check his meteoric rise to glory, lest many more vulgar *Übermensch* present themselves at the gates of Blades. It is, hence, *in the service of hierarchy*, and *with Nietzsche*, not against him, that a maverick *Übermensch* like Drax must be exposed and ousted as a false, illegitimate, mad *Übermensch*, a traitor to England, in fact a Nazi impostor plotting to eradicate London. If Drax is the Nietzschean as a plebeian Nazi, the Chinese Dr. No is likewise a perverse and destructive *Übermensch*, rising to defy authority. He craves absolute power and rejects Bond's charges of lunacy with Nietzschean aloofness:

> Mania, my dear Mister Bond, is as priceless as genius. Dissipation of energy, fragmentation of vision, loss of momentum, the lack of follow-through—these are the vices of the herd. . . . I do not possess these vices. I am, as you correctly say, a maniac—a maniac,

Mister Bond, with a mania for power. That . . . is the meaning of my life. That is why I am here. That is why you are here. That is why here exists.[14]

As against such deranged will to power, Bond utters a refutation of key Nietzschean tenets. To start with, he argues against Dr. No's ambition to have overcome common humanity by reminding him that, whatever his achievements and eccentricities, he remains inexorably a mere human: "you are still a man who sleeps and eats and defecates like the rest of us" (*Doctor No*, p. 130). Still more remarkably, Bond goes as far as advancing, in the name of the community, a philosophical negation of the very concept of power. "Other people beside you have murdered in secret and got away with it. A greater power than they possess is exerted upon them by the community. . . . I tell you, your search for power is an illusion because power itself is an illusion" (*Doctor No*, p. 132). Yet, Dr. No clings to his Nietzschean perspective: "So is beauty, Mister Bond. So is art, so is money, so is death. And so, probably, is life. These concepts are relative. Your play upon words does not shake me. I know philosophy, I know ethics, and I know logic—better than you do, I daresay" (*Doctor No*, p. 132). The Doctor embodies the entire gamut of ugly traits which can be gathered under the title of "evil Nietzscheanism": he is an immoral atheist, who can summarily dismiss the threat of a punishment in the next world: "Mister Bond, I do not admit the existence of hell" (*Doctor No*, p. 148); a cynical sadist, he endorses the Nazi experimentation with human beings; most significant, perhaps, is his nihilistic refutation of all hierarchy: "I changed my name to Julius No— the Julius after my father and the No for my rejection of him and of all authority" (*Doctor No*, p. 134).

Mr. Big in *Live and Let Die* is a racial rebel, a black giant standing for "negro emancipation." And he is, no doubt, a thorough Nietzschean:

It is unfortunate for you, Mister Bond, and for this girl, that you have encountered the first of the great negro criminals. I use a vulgar word, Mister Bond, because it is the one you, as a form of policeman, would yourself use. But I prefer to regard myself as one

---

[14] Ian Fleming, *Doctor No* (London: Hodder and Stoughton, 1988), p. 131.

who has the ability and the mental and nervous equipment to make his own laws and act according to them rather than accept the laws that suit the lowest denominator of the people . . . I am by nature and predilection a wolf and I live by wolf's laws, naturally the sheep describe such a person as a "criminal" . . . The fact that . . . I survive and indeed enjoy limitless success against countless millions of sheep, is attributable . . . to an infinite capacity for taking pains. Not dull, plodding pains, but artistic, subtle pains.[15]

Strangely, yet most instructively, for all his alleged "manias" the typical Nietzschean villain is in many respects but a negative duplicate of Bond himself. The following could perfectly have been said of Bond's gambling fascination: "What's he trying to prove with it? That he can beat everyone at everything? He seems to put so much passion into his cards—as if it wasn't a game at all, but some sort of trial of strength" (Moonraker, p. 40). Yet the reference is not to Bond but to Hugo Drax. What is more, Nietzscheanism, however evil, exercises an enormous appeal for Bond. For all the enmity, he cannot but admire the greatness of his adversaries, for instance that of Mr. Big: Bond "shivered at the beauty of it all, at this fabulous petrified ballet . . . His eyes came back to the . . . great zombie face and into the wide yellow eyes with awe, almost with reverence" (*Live and Let Die*, pp. 217–18). In such passages, the paradoxical ideology of the Bond stories clearly manifests itself. Bond's own obsessions are conveniently displaced onto his enemies: 007 remains the good Nietzschean, whereas Drax, Mr. Big, Dr. No and Co. are the evil Nietzscheans.

Working Undercover

But why should Bond be the anti-Nietzschean Nietzschean rather than dispense with such intricate maneuvers and proudly brandish his Nietzscheanism? Bond's ambivalent perspective reflects the historical context in which the novels were written: Following the triumph over world fascism, the Western world was ideologically driven to assume a double identity, whereby its structural Nietzscheanism—revolving around competition, elitism, and contempt for mass democracy—had to go under-

---

[15] Ian Fleming, *Live and Let Die* (London: Hodder and Stoughton, 1988), p. 225.

cover, and a formal refutation of at least the most notorious Nietzschean creeds was espoused.

The secret of Bond's double standard is such division between the good, and unspoken, Nietzscheanism of the West, and the evil, explicit one, of old-Germany, still sprouting mischief, and the Communists. This displacement of evil Nietzscheanism towards the Cold War adversary was of major significance in the attempt to deal with the disturbing social Darwinist heritage of the West. So now, Soviet agents such as Kronsteen were presented as machine-like, beyond-good-and-evil, social Darwinists "not interested in human beings—not even in his own children. Nor did the categories of 'good' and 'bad' have a place in his vocabulary" (*From Russia with Love*, p. 53). His partner, Rosa Klebb, is no less of an evil Nietzschean: "In her, the herd instinct would also be dead. Her urge for power demanded that she should be a wolf and not a sheep" (*From Russia with Love*, p. 54). Bond, on the other hand, becomes an icon of the crusade against totalitarianism, and Anthony Burgess could therefore have commended him for fighting "on behalf of a free world." More often than not, however, Bond was fighting to keep the world free not for, but *from* democracy. If Bond manifested nothing but disdain at social-democracy at home, democracy *as such* was discarded when turning to the so-called Third World; as in the case of Turkey, called on during one of the campaigns for a free world. Fleming refrained from letting Bond himself condemn the idea of Turkish democracy. Instead, he permitted local friends of Bond, insiders to native "mentality," to convey the message, while Bond quietly acquiesces. It was left to Darko Kerim, a Turkish friend of England and a "remarkable fellow" (M's judgment), to teach the reader something about Turkish democracy:

> Kerim harangued the waiter. He sat back smiling at Bond. "That is the only way to treat these damned people. They love to be cursed and kicked. It is all they understand. It is in the blood. All this pretence of democracy is killing them. They want some sultans and wars and rape and fun. Poor brutes, in their striped suits and bowler hats. They are miserable. You've only got to look at them." (*From Russia with Love*, p. 110)

It would be a mistake to dismiss such political content as part of half-humorous jingoism by a diehard British conservative.

Rather more ominously, it reflects the very consensual approach of the Western political elites towards Second and Third World democracy, the way the free world shakes itself free of democracy, when party politics forms an obstacle to its economic prerogatives.

The most symptomatic case of the split between good and evil Nietzscheanism is the showdown between James Bond and his greatest adversary, Ernst Stavro Blofeld, in the novel *You Only Live Twice*. Of all Bond's foes, Blofeld is the only one who explicitly mentions Nietzsche as a source of inspiration. To Bond's accusation that he is mad, he aloofly replies: "So was Frederick the Great, so was Nietzsche, so was Van Gogh. We are in good, in illustrious company, Mister Bond."[16] 007, by contrast, is belittled by Blofeld as a member of the common throng: "On the other hand, what are you? You are a common thug, a blunt instrument wielded by dolts in high places" (*You Only Live Twice*, p. 171). To extract from its context the direct confrontation between Bond and Blofeld, which constitutes the last part of the story, is to remain with what appears a militant anti-Nietzschean message. Giving the ultimate performance in the role of the evil *Übermensch*, Blofeld makes for Japan and embarks on a profoundly Nietzschean scheme: he creates a garden of death, where desperate Japanese youths who regard themselves failures can commit suicide. There is no material gain in store for him; the naked, philosophical issue is here at stake. "It is the concept that matters," Blofeld insists: "If my bridge, my waterfall, yields a crop of only perhaps ten people a year, it is simply a matter of statistics. The basic idea will be kept alive" (*You Only Live Twice*, p. 154). Just Like Nietzsche—encouraging the weak and sickly to remove themselves from life[17]—Blofeld regards his garden a vital service for the preservation of culture. "And so, Mister Bond, I came to devise this

---

[16] Ian Fleming, *You Only Live Twice* (London: Hodder and Stoughton, 1988), p. 171.

[17] As in the following example: "Problem: with what means could one attain to a severe form of really contagious nihilism: such as teaches and practices voluntary death with scientific conscientiousness (—and *not* a feeble, vegetable existence in expectation of a false afterlife—)? One cannot sufficiently condemn Christianity for having devaluated the value of such a great purifying nihilistic movement, . . . through the hope of resurrection . . . , through continual deterrence from the *deed of nihilism*, which is suicide—" (*Will to Power*, p. 143); see also, Friedrich Nietzsche, *Twilight of the Idols / The Anti-Christ* (Harmondsworth: Penguin, 1990), p. 99.

useful and essentially humane project—the offer of free death to those who seek release from the burden of being alive . . . . What you saw done was only helping a weak man to his seat on the boat across the Styx" (*You Only Live Twice*, pp. 173–74).

Bond, reflecting bitterly and ironically on Blofeld's project, does not fail to realize its anti-democratic significance: "perhaps, one day, they would get a Minister of Self Destruction appointed in the Diet! Then the great days of the Black Dragon *Kÿan* would come again to save the Country of the Rising Sun from the creeping paralysis of *demokorasu!*" (*You Only Live Twice*, p. 153).

Yet what are the values which Bond himself appeals to in his defense of democracy against the assaults of the devilish *Übermensch?* These are conveyed via Bond's conversations with his two buddies in Tokyo who can say openly, mischievously, and with impunity what Bond secretly thinks. The recurrent motif of Bond's "lessons" is that Japanese elitism—conservative, ruthless, and deferential—must substitute for the permissive mushiness of Welfare England.

The unsentimental Australian, Dikko Henderson, explains to Bond the advantages of the Japanese way of doing things, in which absolute commitment to one's superiors is decisive. This allegedly "Japanese style" immediately calls to mind, however, the fascist notion of the leader as ultimate point of reference. Significantly, Henderson goes on to equate the central authority principle with the mode of decision-making prevalent in big capitalist corporations. He tells Bond, "Got it? It's not really as mysterious as it sounds. Much the same routine as operates in big corporations, like ICI or Shell, or in the services, except with them the ladder stops at the Board of Directives or the Chiefs of Staff" (*You Only Live Twice*, p. 43). When Bond objects that: "It doesn't sound very *demokorasu*," Henderson, as if he were the Turkish Darko Kerim in disguise, promptly replies:

> For God's sake, get it into your head that the Japanese are a separate human species. . . . Just because people play baseball and wear bowler hats doesn't mean they're quote civilized people unquote. . . . I fornicate upon thy *demokorasu* . . . I stand for government by an *élite* . . . And voting graded by each individual's rating in that *élite*. And one tenth of a vote for my government if you don't agree with me! (*You Only Live Twice*, p. 43).

Henderson's boisterous defense of elitism is mitigated by having him utter these scandalous truths under the effects of *Sake*. The Japanese agent Tiger Tanaka, by comparison, is decidedly sober when expounding his own, remarkably similar, social theories. Tanaka, educated in Oxford, learnedly compares Japanese vigor with the sickness of American mass-society, which "has become . . . more and more unattractive except to the lower grades of the human species to whom bad but plentiful food . . . and the 'quick buck', often dishonestly earned, or earned in exchange for minimal labour or skills, are the *summum bonum*" (*You Only Live Twice*, p. 59). Bond, being a consummate gourmet who certainly does not belong to those inferior rabble for whom "bad but plentiful food" is such a blessing, must nevertheless disagree when Tanaka begins to batter American plebeianism. He champions the honor of his Trans-Atlantic cousins, yet introduces a telling distinction between genuine, aristocratic Americans, and the riff-raff of the working-class immigrants:

> I've got a lot of American friends who don't equate with what you're saying. Presumably you're talking of the lower level GIs—second-generation Americans who are basically Irish or Germans or Czechs or Poles who probably ought to be working in the fields or coalmines of their countries of origins instead of swaggering around a conquered country under the blessed coverlet of the Stars and Stripes with too much money to spend. (*You Only Live Twice*, p. 60)

Thus, despite the immensity of the cultural gulf which reputedly separates them, both Japanese and Englishman are united in their frustration about the comfortable life run by the workers worldwide. Tanaka has nothing but contempt for the British "so-called aristocracy," the demise of the British elite, and he thus makes Bond a tempting, and highly instructive, offer. He suggests that, by defeating Blofeld, Bond will vouch for the abiding worth of the British elite. He says, "And, for your information, those are very similar to the words I addressed to my Prime Minister. And do you know what he said? He said, all right, Mr. Tanaka. Put this Commander Bond to the test. If he succeeds, I will agree that there is still an *élite* in Britain" (*You Only Live Twice*, p. 78).

Thus, Bond's *anti-Nietzschean* and *anti-elitist* mission is formulated in terms which are decidedly *Nietzschean* and *elitist*; the fight against Blofeld's "evil Nietzscheanism" is undertaken under the latent premises of "good Nietzscheanism." Fleming's ideological split, reflecting the duplicity in Western, Cold War ideology, reveals the narratives as spy-stories in more sense than one: James Bond is a secret agent in the service of Nietzscheanism.

7

Bond as Chivalric, Comic Hero

CHARLES TALIAFERRO and MICHEL Le GALL

James Bond is complicated. In Ian Fleming's books, Bond morphs from being just slightly above average in stealth and intelligence (*Casino Royale*) to almost a superhero (*Thunderball*). And in the Bond novels written by others after the death of Fleming in 1964, 007 changes from someone who is virtually a Christian in sentiment and prayer (see especially John Gardner's novel *Win, Lose, or Die*), to being a pure action figure with a penchant for Asian philosophy (see any of the Raymond Benson books). Add the films to this large gallery of Bond portraits, and you have such a diverse depiction of Bond that almost any praise or criticism of him can find *some* justification book or film.

One of the more famous objections to the Bond genre was advanced by Paul Johnson in a review of the book *Doctor No* in the *New Statesman* in 1958. Johnson charged that *Doctor No* was "the nastiest book" he had ever read. "There are three basic ingredients in *Doctor No*, all unhealthy, all thoroughly English: The sadism of a schoolboy bully, the mechanical, two-dimensional sex longings of a frustrated adolescent, and the crude snob-cravings of a suburban adult." [1]

This is completely wide of the mark in the case of *Doctor No*, but more importantly, it seems to be false of nearly all the many Bond books and films that have seen the light of print or celluloid since Johnson's comment nearly fifty years ago. While

---

[1] Paul Johnson, "Sex, Snobbery, and Sadism," *New Statesman* (5th April, 1958), p. 431.

Johnson's judgment and tone—that of a disapproving headmaster—may not be widely shared today, it is still alive. James Chapman, in his authoritative study *Licence To Thrill: A Cultural History of the James Bond Films*, singles out Johnson's critique as an exemplary representation of the sustained critique of Bond films. Explaining just why Johnson's depiction of Bond is wrong will help us come up with a more accurate portrait of Bond. We'll find that the character Bond is best seen within a worldview and a set of values that blends ancient Greek philosophy and medieval romance. Bond displays practical wisdom, courage, and other virtues that comprise a chivalric, comic hero.

The Greek and Medieval Background to 007

You might think that Ancient and Medieval philosophy would be quite foreign territory to the "virtues" of a James Bond. What might Bond have in common with Socrates, for example? For one, both of them were soldiers and applaud soldierly virtues (see Xenophon's *Memories of Socrates*). Socrates served in the Athenian army in the Peloponnesian War and distinguished himself in battle, bravely saving a friend without assistance from others and demonstrating an uncommon coolness in the heat of battle (Plato's *Symposium*, lines 220, 221).

We sometimes underplay the military background and interests of the earliest philosophers, but Plato expresses a preference for land warfare rather than naval engagements in *Laws* Book Four, and Aristotle praises the courage of a citizen-soldier in the *Nichomachean Ethics*; Aristotle even aligns masculine beauty with fitness for battle (*Rhetoric,* line 1361b). Socrates may not have had Bond's reputation for rakish, romantic adventures, but he too was famous for eating and drinking, well but not to excess. For Socrates, the right customs for eating and drinking (as for sex as well) were part of living wisely (this is underlined in Xenophon's *Memories*). There's also another philosophical element in the Bond character that reflects a Platonic tradition from the ancients on through the Medievals: optimism. Plato's work may be read as a critical response to the Greek tragic poets whose "heroes" wind up utterly destroyed. The Platonic or Socratic hero ultimately overcomes conflicting desires and even the obstacle of physical death. Medieval Christian philosophers (like Augustine and Boetheus) transformed and carried on elements of this optimism, which formed some of the background to the chivalrous tradition we will address shortly. Before that, let's look at Johnson's first objection.

The Sadism of a Schoolboy Bully?

We see Bond as a soldier who (like Socrates) fights for honor and fights with bravery (see especially the books *Role of Honor* and *For Special Services* by John Gardner). Bond's ethics of engagement is sorely tested in the short story "For Your Eyes Only" when Bond is asked by M to assassinate von Hammerstein in Vermont (M does this implicitly, without issuing an explicit order). A former Gestapo agent, von Hammerstein went to the Caribbean after the war where he thrived through murder, extortion, and blackmail. He also had two friends of M's killed in cold blood—an elderly couple, the Havelocks—and threatened their daughter in an effort to compel her to sell some land. Von Hammerstein had settled temporarily near the Canadian boarder in Vermont, and M had exhausted all efforts at bringing them to justice. With great reluctance Bond took on the case but while his principle motivation is loyalty to M, it was also because the execution seemed the only possible way to bring von Hammerstein to justice and prevent more murder. (Incidentally, Bond does not kill him; he is killed by Judy Havelock in her private act to avenge the murder of her parents.) We are not suggesting that Socrates, Plato, and Aristotle would approve of Bond's mission, but in that mission and virtually all the others, Bond is moved by a concern for justice and protecting the innocent.

In response to Johnson's first objection, it must be admitted that the books and films often portray Bond as taking a mixture of pleasure and disgust in killing the villain. Perhaps we are intended (in the film and book) to enjoy Dr. No's sliding down a pipe into a vat of heavy water in his laboratory in Crab Key. In terms of the films, only in *On Her Majesty's Secret Service* do we not get to "enjoy" the demise of the main "bad guy." But none of these scenes quite reach the more lurid pleasure offered in, say, the classic, Clint Eastwood *Dirty Harry* movies. Certainly some villains meet rather spectacular ends. Consider, for example, the opening scene in *For Your Eyes Only* when Bond drops Blofeld down a smoke stack, wheelchair and all. But this scene and others resemble cartoon or fantasy violence in which persons can fall thousands of feet without a parachute and survive (as Jaws does in the film *The Spy Who Loved Me*), not boyhood, sadistic bullying.

We know of no case where Bond kills a person or an animal out of mere spite or hubris. There are occasions when M, and the readers and viewers, may express reservations as to whether revenge is a key motive. While this concern arises in the short story "For Your Eyes Only," it is the central concern of the film *Licence to Kill* where Bond is bent on destroying Franz Sanchez. But here any desire for personal retribution or revenge for Sanchez's mutilation of Bond's friend Leiter is channeled through his service of justice. In addition to smuggling, and beating his female companion Lupe Lamora, Sanchez is, after all, a murderer.

The issue of sadism is perhaps best addressed through the depiction of torture. Bond is subject to systematic, sustained torture in many of the books but only a few movies. *Die Another Day* has scenes of Bond being tortured in the course of an interrogation in North Korea, but it is in the literature that one encounters a more philosophical reflection on the nature of torture as a way of removing the barriers—and perhaps the differences—between the torturer and the victim. In *Colonel Sun*, written by Fleming's friend Kingsley Amis in 1968, the colonel invokes the Marquis de Sade to explain how the infliction of pain can bring about an almost mystical transformation of consciousness, merging the torturer and victim. There is also a hint that physical pain might bring about personal transcendence and purgation in *Broken Claw* (by John Gardner).

But one must consider which character is commending the torture and the outcome of the applied philosophy of torture. Colonel Sun repudiates de Sade (just before he dies). The Colonel tells Bond:

> I want to tell you now that what I said to you earlier was quite wrong. De Sade misled me. Or I didn't read him properly. I didn't feel like a god when I was torturing you back there. I felt sick and guilty and ashamed. I behaved in an evil and childish way. It's ridiculous and meaningless, but I want to apologize. Can you forgive me? [2]

---

[2] Robert Markham (pen name of Kingsley Amis), *Colonel Sun*, (New York: Bantam, 1968), p. 186.

Johnson may be right that the Bond genre contains some schoolboy bullying, but none of that seems to be endorsed by any book or film. In fact, as we become more acquainted with the mettle of Bond's character and mind, even in *Doctor No*, we discover a person that is far gentler, almost domestic, rather than a classic bully. Consider this passage from *Doctor No*:

> His mind drifted into a world of tennis courts and lily ponds and kings and queens, of London, of people being photographed with pigeons on their heads in Trafalgar Square, or of the forsythia that would soon be blazing on the bypass roundabouts, of May, the treasured housekeeper in his flat off the King's Road, getting up to brew herself a cup of tea . . . of the first tube trains beginning to run, shaking the ground beneath his cool, dark bedroom. Of the douce weather of England: the soft airs, the heat waves, the cold spells—the only country where you can take a walk every day of the year.[3]

A recurring theme throughout the novels—and occasionally the movies—is Bond's revisiting of a tranquil past, perhaps even before his parents were killed (see Bond during Christmas in *Win, Lose or Die*, or Bond's visit to his wife's grave in the movie *For Your Eyes Only*) or of an ideal time that was hinted at but not fully realized in the last scenes in the Caribbean in the book *Casino Royale* (compare the end of that book with *High Time To Kill*; these are pacific scenes of sensuality, sun, swimming, eating, drinking, conversation, and recollection. Think of the ending of *On Her Majesty's Secret Service*: Bond's weeping over his wife's body, saying "We have all the time in the world." This is the lament of someone who prizes a haven or home, not a bully. (The end of *Seafire* by John Gardner is very similar to *On Her Majesty's Secret Service*; Bond mourns the death of his lover Flicka von Grusse.)

The Mechanical, Two-Dimensional Sex Longings of a Frustrated Adolescent?

No discussion of Bond would be complete without addressing— or undressing—the subject of sex and taking up the question of

---

[3] Ian Fleming, *Doctor No* (London: Cape, 1961), p. 182.

sexism. But, at least in matters of the bedroom, the criteria of sexual success or failure are not entirely exact. What may seem to one couple as adolescent and mechanical may seem to another to be youthful and ecstatic. Yet, if consent and mutual satisfaction are the measure of success—not to speak of prowess—then Bond seems to be doing very, very well indeed. He is insulted by M in the film *Goldeneye* for being a sexist. And while in the film *A View to a Kill*, Bond bakes quiche, he is not a "new male." Fleming's choice of names for several female characters (Pussy Galore, Mary Goodnight, Kissy Suzuki, and so on) is not particularly amusing, and is grating by contemporary standards. Still, he admires talent in women (the films *Moonraker, The World Is Not Enough*, for example, and the book *High Time to Kill*) and at times Bond teams up with a woman as an equal partner in fighting evil (most recently the films *Tomorrow Never Dies* and *Die Another Day*). In all the films and books, he seeks to save and protect women from evil.

As we noted at the beginning, the Bond literature and films are so broad that there is probably fodder for almost any critique. One passage about sex in the book *The Spy Who Loved Me* penned by Ian Fleming himself is, however, disturbing. The book, so very different from the movie, is told in the first person by a young woman Vivienne Michel in Vermont. Fleming wrote the novel in the form of a memoir from Vivienne's viewpoint in which she retells her encounter with Bond. She has been held hostage by two criminals. Bond comes on the scene by accident, overcomes the heavies, and sleeps with the main character who proffers this theory of the female psyche and sex:

> All women love semi-rape. They love to be taken. It was his sweet brutality against my bruised body that had made his act of love so piercingly wonderful. That and the coinciding of nerves so completely relaxed after the removal of tension and danger, the warmth of gratitude, and a woman's natural feeling for her hero.[4]

Does this passage constitute a tacit endorsement of rape or sexual assault?

Before answering this question, one must bear in mind several mitigating factors or circumstances:

---

[4] Ian Fleming, *The Spy Who Loved Me*, (London: Cape, 1960), p. 154.

1. Bond did not rape Vivienne, nor does he rape or engage in nonconsensual sex with any character in any film or book. When Vivienne refers to the bruises on her body, these were inflicted by the criminals, not Bond.
2. This "philosophy" of love articulated by Vivienne is never explicitly endorsed by Bond; nor, given the narrative conceit of this novel, is Bond even aware that Vivienne holds these views.
3. The beginning of *The Spy Who Loved Me* contains an overview of Vivienne's past romantic attachments in which she was not appropriately loved and desired. One way to read her line about loving "to be taken" is that she desires to be with a man who has an overwhelming, irresistible desire for her.

That much can be said in defense of the passage. In the final analysis, however, we believe that the passage is, in fact, profoundly regrettable and revolting. Yet nowhere is Bond presented as having an irresistible desire for a woman that might lead him to force himself on a woman without her consent. And so the passage stands as a blemish on the portrait of Bond in that novel. But, as we noted, Vivienne's views on "semi-rape" are not presented as affirmed by either Bond or Fleming (though, as the author, Fleming is hardly an innocent bystander!). While the passage remains inappropriate, it is still possible to read Vivienne's statement as a dazed response to being loved by a man who has rescued her from violent death; and not as a serious statement of sexual ethics.

Bond's approach to sex has little to do with overcoming initial resistance; rather, it often implies a kind of "moral redemption." To make progress in filling out this portrait, consider the medieval understanding of the knight in courtly love literature and the accompanying cultural view of women in the medieval period. This courtly tradition is highly problematic from the standpoint of a contemporary philosophy or ethics of eros and gender, but we will suggest that the Bond books and films employ the courtly tradition with irony and comedy, rather than serious advocacy.

The medieval era produced a broad literature on the ideal conduct of the knight, the nature of women, the sanctity of marriage and the evolving authority of the Church. Some of it appeared as codes of conduct, others were tales such as Benoît de St. Maure's *Roman de Troie.* While recognizing that noble women—and not all women were noble in class or character—were not the main focus of a knight's endeavors, women were nevertheless cast as both a catalyst and object of good intentions, and sometimes evil ones—the profoundly disturbing dichotomy of the mother and the whore.

The rise of knightly conduct in tandem with a sharper theological view of marriage and women came about, according to the late French historian Georges Duby, as part of the Church's effort to assert a broader authority over twelfth century society.[5] It also entailed an effort to redirect the energy and violence of the knightly class for the benefit of the Church. The Crusades were, one might argue, part of that effort.

The special role accorded to noble women in knightly tradition paralleled in some fashion the rise of the cult of the Virgin Mary (Mariology). For some, Mariology traces its origins to the preaching and writings of Bernard of Clairvaux (died 1153) who saw in the mother of the Christ child a female figure to whom monks and men of religion could constructively direct their masculine devotional energies, not to speak of their desires. By the Renaissance, the knightly tradition of jousting gave way to jostling in the Doge's court and knightly manners became those of the courtier—best exemplified by Castiglione.

The Bond literature develops these chivalric and courtly traditions—stirring in an appropriate dose of Mariology—to emerge with a rather surprising depiction of sex as an act of redemption which delivers the damsel in distress from the clutches of an evil overlord. The result is a comic affirmation of the good of *eros* in overcoming evil. The theme of redemptive sex is made rather explicit in the early Bond films, notably *Dr. No*, *Goldfinger*, and *Thunderball.* In each of these films the heroines—Honey Ryder, Jill Masterson, Pussy Galore, and Domino—are saved from evil by Bond. In turn they play a discreet but important role in assisting Bond in his ultimate triumph over evil. Pussy Galore, for example, agrees to substitute a non-lethal gas in operation Grand Slam thereby foiling Goldfinger's

---

[5] For these and other perspectives on the varied roles of medieval women see, Georges Duby, *Le chevalier, la femme at le prêtre*, (Paris: Hachette, 1981); or his three-volume study, *Dames du XIIe siècle* (Paris: Gallimard, 1995), especially Volume 3, subtitled *Ève et les prêtres.*

attempted assault on Fort Knox. When Bond is asked how he succeeded in convincing Miss Galore to effect the substitution, he replies coyly: "I appealed to her maternal instinct."

Before the intervention of Bond, however, these women are depicted as being of questionable virtue despite their denial of having sex with the evil protagonist. Nevertheless, the novels and the films exhibit a clear literary topos for the role of women which follows a course of development from whore to mother: from enslavement to seduction, sex, and ultimately the redemption of these "lost women" along with the absolution of their sin and guilt from association with the criminal mastermind.

There is also a variation on this chivalric theme, that of avenging the death of the knight's "bride." In several of the Bond films and novels, a central female character or member of her family is killed early on and Bond is called in to avenge her death; witness his avenging of Jill and Tilly Masterson's death in *Goldfinger*, or the avenged murder of Sir Timothy Havelock on behalf of his daughter, Judy,[6] in "For Your Eyes Only."

These themes are sustained throughout most of the novels and movies and they remain intact, especially in the movies, even when the level of action and technological feats reaches an almost ridiculous fever pitch. Chivalrous sex is a sustainable theme which is almost independent of the noise and action.

Is this view of chivalrous sex defensible? Clearly the mother-whore dichotomy is morally repugnant. And the idea that Bondian *eros* is redemptive may well seem less than mature, if not adolescent. However, there's also something comic and life-affirming in depicting *eros* as a positive element in the redemption of men and women. Later in this chapter, we'll highlight the comic element of the Bond character—which allows us to treat the chivalrous sex with irony and humor rather than advocacy. In the end, it's the comedy—the ultimate, sheer impossibility of Bond actually pulling off all his knightly rescues—that best answers Johnson's charge. There is a comic, ironic edge that makes Bond an ideal, youthful—not essentially adolescent—optimistic character. But before we get to the comic aspect, let's consider Johnson's charge of snobbery.

---

[6] "Judy" in the short story; "Melina" in the film *For Your Eyes Only*

The Crude Snob-Cravings of a Suburban Adult?

This charge of Johnson's may seem vindicated in that the Bond brand is used by many companies to merchandise a vast array of items from cars to watches to video games and even underwear. Bond after all had only the best of cars and tailors. But this charge also overlooks the longstanding philosophical stance on proper eating and living (alluded to at the beginning of our chapter) as well as the history of heroes in the Western tradition.

Among the ancient Greeks, treachery and profanity were frequently attributable to disordered or unnatural eating. The most telling cases invariably involved cannibalism. Improper dress was also considered disdainful. One can see a lingering reference to this tradition in the New Testament parable of the wedding (Matthew 22:1–14) in which those who are not properly dressed are exiled. In Greek mythology, sometimes garments would be poisoned to bring about great revenge (for instance in the tragedy *Medea*).

Bond's "snobbery"—his being rightly dressed, eating and drinking well—harkens back to this tradition. Bond may be seen as struggling to reverse or offset the bad behavior, manners, and actions of those who are cruel and inhospitable. Bond's link to this side of the ancient heroic tradition is explicit in the book *Colonel Sun*. Bond teams up with a Greek espionage agent named Ariadne. She is named for the maiden in the story about the Minotaur. She explains the myth to Bond:

> "The original Ariadne was supposed to have been the girlfriend of King Theseus of Athens. She helped him to kill the Minotaur—you know, that guy with the bull's head who lived in the maze. But then Theseus went and dumped her on the island of Noxos so that he could go and . . ."
>
> She stopped speaking so abruptly that Bond gave her a quick glance. "Go and do what?"
>
> "Oh, I forget what came next. I suppose he went off and hunted the Calydonian boar or something. Anyway, Ariadne wasn't on her own for long. The wind-god Dionysus happened to be passing at the time and she latched on to him. Which is a funny coincidence because this restaurant's named after him. Well, what do you think?" (Colonel Sun, p. 53)

The story of Theseus and Ariadne is one of the more famous cases in Greek mythology in which a male lover abandons his beloved—the others include Jason's abandonment of Dido in the *Aeneid* and Jason's treacherous abandonment of Medea in Sophocles's tragedy. The case of Ariadne is especially interesting in thinking through heroic tradition and, we believe, in thinking through Bond's style and character. Let's consider the story more fully and then return to Bond and the charge of snobbery.

A man named Minos sought the throne of the island of Crete. To confirm that he was favored by the gods, he maintained to the people of Crete that the gods would answer *any* of his prayers. So, the Cretans challenged him to call on the god of the seas, Poseidon, to deliver a bull from out of the ocean. Minos prayed to Poseidon for this gift, and promised that should the bull appear he would sacrifice it to the god. The ocean parted and, to everyone's amazement, a magnificent bull appeared. Minos was immediately appointed as King. But he was so taken by the bull that he reneged on his promise to sacrifice it. Because of his failure to revere and render unto Poseidon what he had promised, the sea god cursed Minos and had his wife fall in love with the bull.

In one of the most bizarre episodes in Greek mythology, the wife disguised herself as a cow in order to attract the bull. They mate, and the offspring is a child with the lower body of a man, and the upper body of a bull. Since the Minotaur (as he is called) is fierce and has a taste for human flesh, Minos has him enclosed in a vast labyrinth. Some time later, the King's other son participates in the Olympics, winning all the prizes. Some Athenians, jealous of the son, kill him. To seek vengeance Minos attacks Athens. After conquering the city, he demands that, at regular times, seven maids and seven young men be sent to Crete so he can feed them to the Minotaur. One of these men is Theseus who intends to kill the Minotaur. However, the King's daughter, Ariadne, falls in love with Theseus and gives him a string. As Theseus advances into the labyrinth he lets out the string so that, once he has killed the Minotaur, he can escape. He does kill the Minotaur and escapes with Ariadne but, as noted in *Colonel Sun*, he abandons her on his way home.

Back to Bond: 007 does not willingly abandon Ariadne or other woman in distress in any book or film. When a good deed is done for him by a woman or man, he invariably seeks to make some kind of appropriate recompense. Unlike the Athenians who killed Minos's son out of jealousy at his winning all the games, Bond does not cheat in any of the games he plays unless he is doing so to expose the cheating of a villain (*Moonraker*). In this respect, Bond employs the techniques of cheating to expose a wrongdoer. In addition to all this, Bond conducts himself with scrupulous attention to proper manners, clothes, and habits that distinguish him significantly from Theseus. Theseus, for example, does not attend to the details of his appearance.

After abandoning Ariadne on Noxos, Theseus also forgets a vital detail: he had agreed with his father that if he were successful in killing the Minotaur he would sail home deploying white sails. Instead, he neglects to use the right sails. And when his father sees the black sails, he commits suicide. Bond, ever attentive to nuance would have remembered to change the sails. Recall that in the film *From Russia with Love*, Bond reasoned that Captain Nash was a Soviet assassin because the killer (Red Grant) drank red wine with fish.

Let's review one other connection between Bond and this aspect of the heroic tradition. Consider King Leonidas, who in the fifth century B.C.E. participated in one of the most heroic last stands of recorded history. The Spartan king Leonidas and his guards held off the vastly superior Persian army at the pass of Thermopylae. What did they do before the final Persian assault? They brushed and combed their beards. They were readying themselves to die. But they were not going to die without looking their very best.

It may seem completely irreverent to compare that extraordinary last stand to a Bond film. But the films and books do offer up the picture of someone who is constantly on the edge, forever locked in life and death struggles, yet does so looking his best. Recall the scene in *The World is Not Enough* when Bond is aboard a speedboat on the Thames trying to capture an assassin on a launch. When Bond's boat transforms itself into a submarine and he is now under water, he is seen straightening his tie. This may seem to be a comic act, but it is in fact in keeping with the heroic tradition.

The Comic Hero

In the course of our reply to Paul Johnson's charges laid out in his review "Sex, Snobbery, and Sadism," we have advanced an alternative portrait of Bond; a portrait that paints him as non-sadistic and chivalric in his conduct in everything from sex to his attire. While there are elements of the chivalric tradition that are indefensible, there can be elements that are life-affirming insofar as *eros* is seen as a force for good and a principle emphasis is placed on protecting and rescuing those in peril.

We have aligned Bond with the philosophical and heroic traditions of fighting justly and bravely (as Socrates did) and exercising right manners and avoiding vulgarity (not falling into the faults of Theseus). By way of conclusion, we now propose to round out our view of Bond by sketching his role as a *comic* hero—a complement and counterpoint to his chivalric being.

The image of Bond as a knight is quite explicit in some of the novels. Consider this passage from *Goldfinger:* "Bond sighed wearily. Once more into the breach, dear friends! This time it really was St. George and the dragon. And St. George had better get a move on before the dragon hatched the little dragon's egg he was now nesting so confidently."[7]

But what of the comedy? There are comic elements, sometimes by way of jokes or puns, in almost all the films and books. Of the actors who play Bond, Roger Moore is the best at delivering one-liners. Consider the opening sequence of the film, *The Spy Who Loved Me*, in which Bond's female companion in a moment of ecstasy confesses she cannot find the words to describe her sense of pleasure. To which Moore-Bond responds, "Let me try to enlarge your vocabulary."

But more important than that is the way in which Bond winds up cheating death again and again and doing so with a sense of humor. He survives almost impossible situations in John Gardner's book *Nobody Lives Forever* which, in the cover of the paperback, has a tombstone with the letters 007 written on it. The Bond books, more consistently than the movies, make death out to be savage and brutal. But both the films and the books exhibit the ways in which death may be avoided or rendered the object of a comic joke.

Given that Fleming depicts Bond as an adult at the end of World War II, there is even a suggestion that Bond has, by some unknown process, avoided aging. We suggest this is "comic" in

---

[7] Ian Fleming, *Goldfinger,* (London: Cape, 1958), p. 158.

the sense that it constitutes a victorious celebration of an ordinary man over impossible odds. It may seem peculiar to think of Bond as "ordinary," but as Kingsley Amis has pointed out, Bond is *not* superhuman. When he gets up in the morning he has a regular exercise program. His powers, then, are the outcome of training and commitment, rather than innate superhuman powers owing to some extraordinary physiology. Bond does not die (not yet: *Die Another Day*), but no film or book implies he is immortal. He can be killed and he has certainly been scarred, and by the luck of things (or perhaps even by God's grace, as Gardner sometimes hints), Bond makes it.

This death-defying aspect of the Bond character places him in the general Platonic tradition from the ancients through the medievals in which the soul overcomes even death itself. What Bond accomplishes through the many films and books is clearly impossible for any of us (remaining perpetually youthful or at least at middle age for so long). But Bond remains convincing and attractive as a heroic character because he embodies many enduring values, including a perpetual optimism no matter how impossible the circumstances. In *The Poetics*, Aristotle referred to "a likely impossibility"; Bond is a likeable or even *delightful impossibility*. His feats are impossible for any of us to pull off, but we are delighted to surrender ourselves to this world of films and books which propel us and thrill us with Bond's knightly behavior and feats. And yes, we want to make sure that he makes it through once more.

SECTION III

For England, James?

Bond, Politics, and Law

8

The Moral Status of the Double-0 Agent: Thinking About the License to Kill

MATTHEW TEDESCO

A new neighbor comes over for dinner. You've seen him a few times since the moving trucks pulled up, cruising around the neighborhood in a slick little sports car. You suspect he's single; he always seems to have a different woman accompanying him in the car, each more fetching than the one before. He's a pleasant fellow with dashing good looks; he speaks with a smooth British accent. You ask him if he'd like a drink, and he has strangely specific directions for a martini. And oh yes, over conversation, he happens to mention that he has a license to kill. At that moment you might've heard your spouse drop dinner on the kitchen floor, if you weren't busy spitting out your own drink.

A big part of what makes the James Bond character so intriguing is his license to kill, a license granted by the British government to a very exclusive club: the double-0 agents. It's not clear exactly how many agents have this special license— in Fleming's novel *Moonraker*, there are apparently only three double-0 agents, while the movie *Thunderball* implies that there are nine—but whatever the number, we know that the double-0 designation is extraordinarily rare. Yet taken by itself, the idea of being licensed to kill is a strange and morally troubling one. In our lives, we are routinely licensed for all sorts of behavior: we need a license to drive a car, to marry a spouse, to build an extension on our house, to work as an accountant, to fly a plane. All of these licenses share something in common: they involve engaging in some morally permissible activity, and the license declares your legal eligibility to engage in that activity.

James Bond's license to kill is much different: we typically think it's wrong to kill people. In fact, not only is killing wrong, but we typically think of it as among the most seriously immoral of actions. You would be a lot less troubled if your new neighbor had a license to blackmail, say, or a license to commit adultery. So what does this mean for how we view Bond, morally speaking? Lots of people seem to admire Bond, yet he's got a license to kill, and he uses it—so shouldn't we instead be repulsed by him? Instead of celebrating Bond, shouldn't we be condemning him? Morally speaking, in other words, is Bond really a bad guy? Or can we find a way to somehow vindicate Bond, from a moral point of view? In order to try to answer these tough moral questions about James Bond, we first need to understand exactly what is involved in having a license to kill.

James Bond: Assassin

Philosophers often engage in the project of analyzing concepts. To take one famous example, consider the concept of personhood. Everybody agrees that you and I are persons, and so whatever moral consideration you get, I get too. So, if you have a right to life, so do I—though the right to life is yet another tricky concept! If it's wrong to imprison you without charge, the same goes for me. In this way, calling you a person is to be distinguished from calling you a human, where the former is a moral category, while the latter is merely a biological classification.

But while it may be obvious that you and I are persons, other cases are a lot thornier. Are newborn infants persons? What about a little while earlier, when they were fetuses? Is a permanently comatose human still a person? How about cognitively advanced creatures like whales and chimpanzees—might they count as persons? These kinds of questions impact morally controversial issues like abortion, euthanasia, and animal rights, and they all revolve around one central issue: the concept of personhood. These are philosophical questions that all of us grapple with at times in our lives. So conceptual analysis isn't just a task for philosophers—it's one that we all undertake from time to time. James Bond, were he to exist, clearly would be a person—so we can happily put that concept aside—but his license to kill is a concept we need to think about, if we're going to think meaningfully about the moral questions surrounding the license to kill. Once we figure out what's involved in having a license to kill, we can then think about our moral evaluation of James Bond.

Surprisingly, just like we don't know exactly how many double-0 agents there are, the Bond books and movies tell us very little about precisely what's involved in having a license to kill. We have lots of examples of Bond killing people in self-defense when his own life is threatened—Scaramanga's hunting of Bond for sport in the movie version of *The Man with the Golden Gun* is a clear example of this. But this doesn't help us understand the license to kill; if anyone's life were threatened in this way, we'd probably think it morally permissible to kill in self-defense. So if everyone has the right to kill in self-defense, but very few of us are double-0 agents with a license to kill, the license to kill must extend beyond killing in self-defense.

Another possibility for the content of the license to kill revolves around the notion of "on-the-job" killing. So, in my job as a college professor, there are lots of things that it's perfectly alright for me to do: on any given day, I might prepare a lecture, I might grade a paper, I might do research. But when I'm on the job, it's pretty certain that no situation is going to arise where I might be called upon to kill. The same isn't true for James Bond, though. When Bond is on the job gathering information, or conducting surveillance, or engaging in any number of professional duties, something might come up where he might have to drop a guy into the gears of a printing press (as in the movie *Tomorrow Never Dies*). This isn't true of me, nor is it true of bankers, or lawyers, or real estate agents, or the vast majority of professions. Could this be what's involved in the license to kill—the possibility of on-the-job killing?

While this suggestion is a little bit better, it too breaks down. It's better than the self-defense suggestion—there, *everyone* seemed to have the license to kill. Here, at least, the on-the-job suggestion rules out most of us (which at least makes for a safer workplace). But it's just not exclusive enough. Sure, my colleagues are very happy to know that I don't have the right to kill on the job. But some people do have this right: police officers, for example, or even more clearly, members of the armed forces. Most people think that at least some military actions are morally permissible, and that these actions might involve killing people. These killings are on-the-job killings, yet the soldiers involved don't have a license to kill. If they did, the double-0 section would number in the thousands. Because we know the double-0 section is far more exclusive than this, we must look deeper to figure out the concept of the license to kill.

In the end, maybe the closest we can get to understanding the license to kill is to look at Bond's own actions. It's not enough to talk about killing on the job; we need to look at exactly what kind of killing is involved in the double-0 agent's job. We learn in Ian Fleming's novel *Casino Royale* that Bond earned his double-0 status by carrying out two assassinations. The book version of *The Man with the Golden Gun* introduces a decidedly less debonair Scaramanga than the character in the movie, and Bond is out to assassinate him. Other Bond stories, such as Fleming's short story "For Your Eyes Only," see Bond sent on assassination missions as well. These situations build a cumulative case supporting the idea that the license to kill is in some way tied to being a state-sanctioned assassin. How exactly someone earns a double-0 classification is unclear, but we can say at least this much: more than killing in self-defense or killing while on the job, the license to kill allows Bond and his double-0 cohorts to undertake assassination missions. Assassination, though, is morally a pretty troubling action. So with the concept of the license to kill now a little bit clearer, the more important question once again comes up: if Bond is a state-sponsored assassin who has previously engaged in assassination missions, why do we like him so much? Is James Bond really a bad guy, morally speaking? If not, what does this mean for our views on assassination?

The Ethics of Assassination

Assassination is a special kind of killing. People use the word in a variety of contexts, but it typically involves the murder of a public figure by surprise attack, without any chance for trial or defense. This puts it way out on the far side of morally questionable actions—no matter how bad a person is, one moral ideal we hold to is that they deserve the right to face a fair trial. In *Duncan v. Louisiana* (1967), Justice Byron White affirmed that a trial by jury "is among those principles of liberty and justice which lie at the base of all our civil and political institutions." This sentiment is also echoed in The Universal

Declaration of Human Rights adopted by the General Assembly of the United Nations in 1948, which guarantees to all persons the right to a fair public hearing. This ideal is reflected in the United States' official blanket prohibition on assassination, enacted by President Ford in 1976 under Executive Order 11905 and affirmed by President Reagan in 1981 under Executive Order 12333.

But all of this creates a bit of a pickle for what we think about Bond: if assassination is really this bad, and Bond's double-0 status makes him an assassin, maybe we shouldn't like him so much after all. Sure, he's smooth, handsome, and even kind of funny; but when smooth, handsome, funny people do really bad things, they don't get excused for being smooth, handsome, and funny; they're still bad people.

Lots of people accept this blanket prohibition on assassination because of the very common belief that some acts are just *wrong*. National and international prohibitions against assassination are just one example of this kind of moral view. More generally, the idea that some actions are unconditionally wrong is captured by *deontological* (duty-based) moral theories.

The most famous defender of a deontological theory was Immanuel Kant (1724–1804). Kant believed that the moral quality of an action had nothing to do with the consequences of the action, and everything to do with the action itself. Kant offered several formulations of the single moral law, what he called the Categorical Imperative, which shows us how to discover which actions are wrong in themselves. The most straightforward version of the Categorical Imperative tells us to always treat people as ends in themselves, and never merely as a means to some other end. Perhaps the most famous illustration of the Categorical Imperative is the case of deception. For Kant, lies fail to treat persons with respect; they use the person being deceived as a means to some other end. Lying, therefore, is impermissible, and this holds even when telling a lie is the only way to bring about some great good like the saving of an innocent life. At first glance, this seemingly absolute response to lying also looks as if it applies to killing. If I kill you because I dislike you, I've used you as a means to my own happiness, so my action is wrong. Even if I kill you because you're about to kill me, I've used you as a means to my own self-preservation, so my action is still wrong. Killing, for Kant, must be just *wrong,* always and for everyone . . . right?

Not so fast. Kant himself was actually a defender of capital punishment. On the face of it, this might seem contradictory: when we put a criminal to death, aren't we using that criminal as a means to some other end, and so failing to treat that person with respect? More generally, doesn't *any* punishment have this problem? Kant didn't see it this way. Generally, punishment is justified not because we think the criminal is any less of a person, but rather because the criminal deserves an appropriate response to his conduct. We respect a criminal as a person by responding appropriately to his action. So for Kant, the death penalty, when applied to murderers, *is* in fact treating the murdering criminal with respect. When someone chooses to commit murder, that person is making a certain kind of statement about how people ought to be treated; to kill a killer is to treat that killer with the same respect that he accords to others. For Kant, though killing is morally impermissible in virtually all cases, certain special cases actually do actually allow for morally justifiable killing.

As we think about the moral status of the double-0 agent, where the license to kill is held by state-sponsored assassins like James Bond, we now might wonder: is assassination one of those special cases of killing that Kant allows for? That's a tricky question; one of the key reasons for prohibiting assassination is that a trial is needed to fairly determine a person's guilt. Kant's justification of killing presumes facts about the alleged killer that we can only really know with confidence after a fair trial. And deeper questions remain about Kant's moral theory. Kant's theory is built up from the moral claim that the consequences of actions are morally irrelevant. Think again for a second, though, about Kant's claims about the moral permissibility of lying, set against the following fact: lots of people tell lies all the time. Miss Moneypenny's new hair color might look like a mistake at the crayon factory, but if you tell her it looks nice when she asks, have you done something wrong? Perhaps this kind of lie is permissible; a person might plausibly believe that lies such as these are innocent, while still thinking that lying and saying the brakes on the school bus are just fine when they're not is really, really wrong. To take a more extreme example: what if I lie to save a person's life? Yes, all of these are lies, but the clear difference between them is found in the consequences of the lies. Kant thinks consequences are irrelevant . . . but maybe he's wrong. Generally we approve of Bond, because he makes the world a better place. We like him because of the consequences of what he does.

Consequentialist moral theories are concerned not with actions themselves, but with the consequences of those actions. Is it wrong to lie? For a consequentialist, that all depends on the consequences of the lie. If I lie and say that I fixed the brakes on the school bus, the really bad consequences that follow make the lie wrong. But when a guy knocks on my door and asks for my roommate, explaining that he's planning on killing him, it's probably right to say my roommate has moved to Australia even though he's really cowering in the other room. James Bond is lying to Alec Trevelyan in *Goldeneye* when he claims that Natalya Simonova means nothing to him, but the lie is told in order to save her life, and it sure seems like the right thing to do to the rest of us. For a consequentialist, this distinction makes sense, because consequentialists judge the moral worth of actions based on the likely outcome of those actions. And on the face of it, this theory looks as if it helps Mr. Bond. Sure, 007 may be an assassin, but when he takes down a ruthless drug kingpin like Kananga in *Live and Let Die,* we think this action is morally good because Kananga is a sinister guy who brings nothing but grief and misery to this world. His elimination makes the world a better place, and we should thank our favorite secret agent for ridding us of him.

Is that it? Are we now all consequentialists? It sounds like a good theory so far, but like Kant's theory, this one turns out to be pretty demanding too. If we're always on the hook for bringing about good consequences, we ought to be really careful about going to the movies, or spending a night chatting with friends. There are soup kitchens that need staffing, children that need mentoring, and charities that need funding. And, to adopt a famous example, what does the surgeon do when he has a patient under anesthesia for routine surgery and one of Q's weapons tests nearby goes horribly awry? The victims come rolling in, and as it turns out, one needs a heart, one needs lungs, one needs a kidney; and for every victim that comes in needing an organ to survive, it turns out the only possible donor to save these lives is the one otherwise healthy (but potentially very unlucky) patient already on the table. It's tempting to say that obviously the doctor should leave the anesthetized patient alone, because if word got out that doctors were carving up and harvesting the organs of healthy people under anesthesia, chaos would ensue (or, at least, lots of appointments would be cancelled). But let's say our doctor knows the patient is an unloved hermit who knows nobody, and no one else would ever find out what happened to him. Filling in details like this to our imaginary case, virtually everyone thinks that surely the doctor still should not harvest his patient's organs. But why not, if consequentialism were correct? The answer that's probably striking you now is: there are some things you just can't do, regardless of the consequences. But if that's true, are we pushed towards a deontological (duty-based) ethic once again? And where does that leave the moral status of James Bond?

The Ethics of Torture

A part of the problem we have here is that ordinary morality—the moral standards that people typically hold—has both deontological and consequentialist components. Most people think that some actions are wrong in themselves, yet they also think that consequences matter a lot to the moral status of an action. These two beliefs can clash, and when they do, we're sometimes left in a morally fuzzy place. James Bond is an assassin—he pre-emptively kills public figures without a trial. Currently in the United States, this kind of action is strictly prohibited. But should it be? This policy hasn't always been in place, as the CIA's failed attempts to assassinate Fidel Castro in the 1960s illustrate. Was that policy a good one, morally speaking, and were we wrong to change it, thus prohibiting the possibility of the double-0 agent? Or, morally speaking, is it a good thing that we now have a blanket prohibition on assassination?

This kind of moral puzzle is about James Bond, but it's not only about him; it concerns other important real-world policy questions as well. Besides guaranteeing every person a fair trial, The Universal Declaration of Human Rights also strictly prohibits the use of torture in interrogation. Like the prohibition on assassination, this prohibition on torture is also the current policy of the United States government. But should it be? The Bond books and movies also address the morality of torture. Torture often conjures bad memories for the Bond fan; when torture comes up in the world of Bond, it's often 007 getting the worst of it, and at the hands of some particularly nasty bad guys. In the very first Bond novel *Casino Royale,* Bond is tortured by having his genitals beaten, and the torture continues through the movie *Die Another Day,* where Bond endures months of physical and psychological torture at the hands of North Koreans throughout the title sequence. There's no question that those incidents of torture are morally reprehensible, but other cases of torture might be less clear.

This question has received a lot of attention since the events of September 11th, 2001, because we can imagine a scenario where torture might be the only way to stop another similar event in the future. Imagine that we have very strong evidence that a similar attack is imminent and that, along with this strong evidence, we have very good reason to believe that a recently captured person is the only person with information that could conclusively stop the attack. The clock is ticking, the attack is minutes away, thousands of innocent lives are at grave risk, and the potential informant is saying nothing. What then? Is torture permissible, or is it not? This question is a difficult one, made cloudier by questions about whether or not the torture is likely to yield true information. As hard a question as it is, at least some people out there are open to the idea that, under just the right set of circumstances, torture might be the right thing to do, morally speaking. Others disagree.

This tension was highlighted again following the September 11th attacks, when President George W. Bush authorized the assassination of Osama Bin Laden, given his status as a terrorist and the claim that the United States was at war. And given that James Bond is a British agent, it's worth noting that Britain's Intelligence Services Act of 1994 immunizes MI6 agents from prosecution for crimes committed on foreign soil (thus leaving the door open to assassination). So Britain has never had the blanket prohibition against assassination that the United States has had. With all of these competing considerations, the moral status of assassination seems more elusive than ever before. What ultimately is the right answer?

There's a real danger in saying here that there's no right answer; just because a moral question stirs debate doesn't mean that we give up on trying to answer it. When slavery was legal in the United States, there was lots of passionate debate about it. Obviously this didn't mean that there was no right answer. As opposed to centuries past, nobody is today arguing in favor of slavery; perhaps moral puzzles like assassination and torture will be similarly settled in the future. When we see moral controversies like these, instead of thinking that there is no answer, the better response is to work harder to find an answer. And in the end, when we're wondering about the moral status of torture, it seems like the same question we're asking when we're wondering about the moral status of the double-0 agent. There's no getting around it—James Bond is an assassin. What does this mean for his moral status? The answer to this question probably depends a lot on what we think the moral status of assassination is. We might not have any clear answers here yet, but if we're asking the right questions, we're not just wondering about James Bond—we're wondering about questions that really affect all kinds of moral puzzles out in the world we share.

9

"Just a Stupid Policeman": Bond and the Rule of Law

GREG FORSTER

When one dines with supervillains as often as James Bond does one must be prepared to endure the repetition of certain conversation topics. How tiresome Bond must find it to have yet another discussion at the dinner table on the feasibility of world domination by a private individual! And yet such is his grace and poise that he never betrays even the slightest hint of the crushing boredom from which he must be suffering—one wonders if his hosts even begin to suspect what dull company they are.

One of these regularly repeated topics is the relationship between the kind of work Bond does and the liberal constitutional order his work upholds. The word "liberal" is used here not in the currently popular sense, as the opposite of "conservative," but in the older philosophical sense, describing a political order characterized by ideals of democracy, individual liberty, consent of the governed, the rule of law, and so forth. Bond does what he does in order to defend the liberal political community against would-be tyrants of every stripe—from communists to shadowy global conspiracies to megalomaniacal chrysophiliacs. But the things Bond does to defend the liberal order seem to violate everything that order claims to stand for. He especially seems to negate the rule of law—the very idea of issuing someone a "license to kill" seems to imply placing that person above the law. So, does Bond exemplify the values of liberal democracy and the rule of law because his actions protect the liberal order, or does he represent a failure of the liberal order to live up to its own standards?

The supervillains themselves are divided on the question. Dr. No takes the former view, dismissing Bond as the embodiment of everything he finds repulsive about the liberal order:

> **DR. NO:** I was curious to see what kind of a man you were. I thought there might even be a place for you with SPECTRE.
>
> **BOND:** Well, I'm flattered. I would prefer the revenge department. Of course, my first job would be finding the man who killed Strangways and Quarrel.
>
> **DR. NO:** Unfortunately, I misjudged you. You are just a stupid policeman—whose luck has run out.

For Dr. No, Bond is just the superheroic embodiment of stupid bourgeois moralism. As lawless as his actions may appear to be, underneath it all Bond really believes in Goodness and Order and Freedom and Democracy and, yes, even Law. Scratch the tuxedo and you'll find a police uniform.

On the other hand, when Francisco Scaramanga looks at Bond he doesn't see very much of that goodness-and-freedom stuff at all. He sees . . . well, himself:

> **BOND:** You live well, Scaramanga.
>
> **SCARAMANGA:** At a million dollars a contract, I can afford to, Mr. Bond. You work for peanuts—a hearty "Well done!" from Her Majesty the Queen, and a pittance of a pension. Apart from that, we are the same. To us, Mr. Bond—we are the best.
>
> **BOND:** There's a useful four-letter word, and you're full of it. When I kill, it's on the specific orders of my government. And those I kill are themselves killers.
>
> **SCARAMANGA:** Come, come, Mr. Bond, you disappoint me. You get as much fulfillment out of killing as I do, so why don't you admit it?
>
> **BOND:** I admit killing you would be a pleasure.

By now audiences are jaded with this storytelling cliché. ("You explore the notion that cop and criminal are really two aspects of the same person. See every cop movie ever made for other examples of this.")[1] But it's a cliché because there's some truth in it. There really is a more than superficial similarity between the things lawbreakers do and the things governments do to catch and punish them.

Bond and Current Debates on the Rule of Law

So whom do we believe—the Ming the Merciless ripoff with the world's firmest handshake, or the guy who was doing Antonio Banderas's shtick when Antonio was in diapers? A lot may depend on our answer. At the beginning of the twenty-first century western societies, and particularly the United States, are debating the meaning of the rule of law along lines that correspond to Dr. No and Scaramanga's debate over Bond. Is it consistent with the liberal constitutional order for law enforcers—not every police officer on the street, of course, but a small group of elites at the top of the executive branch—to do whatever they think is necessary to protect the order they serve? Or is that idea itself one of the greatest dangers to the liberal order, because it overturns the rule of law?

For the sake of clarity, we should note that we are not concerning ourselves here with questions about the validity of international law. Bond does not have much respect for national boundaries, and one could draw parallels between his actions and the arguments of those who want the United States and its allies to act more aggressively in areas that have traditionally been understood as being off limits to them due to the sovereignty of other nations. But that's not the question we are asking here. The debate we are interested in is over the nature of the liberal order itself, not the rules that govern what one nation can legitimately do to another.

This debate does not correspond to the political right and left, still less to the Republican and Democratic parties. While much energy was expended to convince us that John Ashcroft was, in fact, the second coming of Dr. No, the No view of the rule of law is as much represented by muscular progressives like Christopher Hitchens as by Ashcroft. And while Ted Kennedy is an obvious Scaramanga figure, Scaramanga's view can be heard

---

[1] Charlie Kaufman and Donald Kaufman, "Adaptation," Columbia Pictures, 2002.

just as clearly in the comments of libertarian-leaning conserva-
tives like Grover Norquist. There is, of course, the manifest difference that Dr. No and Scaramanga are both opposed to the
liberal order and in favor of lawlessness, while today's No and
Scaramanga figures are for the liberal order and against lawlessness. The relevant point is how these figures understand the
relationship between the liberal order and "lawlessness" as they
define it; on that point, there are No figures and Scaramanga figures in both political camps.

But while this debate does not necessarily correspond to the
usual political lines, it is very clearly there, and it is usually easy
to tell who is on which side. So it matters whether we like Bond
only because he's a cool superhero or also because we admire
him for rescuing the law from evil by taking the law into his
own hands. If one side of our current debate is right, Bond is
not just an entertaining showman but a figure to be emulated.

Some of those who favor relaxing legal constraints on what
government can do to protect the liberal order have put Bond
forward as an exemplar of their cause. As David Frum put it in
his defense of the political worldview that prevailed in the 1950s:

> Modern writers with a polemical quarrel with the 1950s like to rep-
> resent those years as a time of moral naïveté, the era of Ozzie and
> Harriet. In fact, Americans of the 1950s made something of a fetish
> of moral complexity. They perceived their country to be locked in
> a shadowy war against a totalitarian enemy. The enemy used dark
> methods—blackmail, propaganda, manipulation, counterfeiting,
> murder—and could only be defeated by an adversary willing to
> use those same methods. . . . The liberalism in vogue in the 1950s
> was a self-consciously tough-minded liberalism. . . . [In their view,]
> bad liberalism was naïve about power, like poor failed Woodrow
> Wilson. Good liberalism knew how to use power, like the glorious
> FDR—or the ruthless but principled James Bond. . . . Bond is
> simultaneously an organization man and an individualist. . . .
> Above all, he can do wrong for a greater good without losing his
> moral bearings.[2]

William F. Buckley wrote a series of spy novels featuring a
Bond-type hero, intending to confront the reader with the moral

---

[2] David Frum, *How We Got Here* (New York: Basic Books, 2000), p. 38.

rightness of protecting the liberal order by means that go beyond the limits of what he calls "conventional morality":

> What is attempted, in the tales of Blackford Oakes, is to make the point, so difficult for the Western mind to comprehend, that counter-intelligence and espionage, conducted under Western auspices, are not exercises in conventional political geometry. They are a moral art. . . .
>
> Scene: Uganda. Colonel Idi Amin has got possession of a nuclear bomb and plans at midnight to dispatch a low-flying plane to drop that bomb on Jerusalem. A CIA agent communicates to Washington that Idi Amin will lie in the cross-hairs of his rifle at the airport before the bomber is dispatched. Should he squeeze the trigger?
>
> There are those, and Blackford Oakes is one of them, who would answer that morally wrenching question by saying two things: (1) As to the particular question, yes: authorize the agent to shoot, in order to abort the destruction of Jerusalem, and all that might then follow. But (2) do not require as a condition of this decision that rules should subsequently be written that attempt to make lapidary statutory distinctions. It is not possible to write such judgments into law.[3]

Are these members of the Dr. No faction right to think that a hero like Bond can be reconciled with the moral foundations of the liberal order?

The Paradoxical "License to Kill"

Bond raises this question about the rule of law in a way that almost no other superhero does. This is partly because his actions are, at least on the surface, so lawless, but that is not the whole reason. The lawless hero is actually a very common literary figure—an old one, too. Consider the moment in Book 21 of the *Iliad* when Achilles kills Lycaon by the river. There are at least three reasons why it was unlawful, by the moral rules governing the Homeric heroes, to kill him: because he had thrown away his spear and shield, because he was kneeling as a suppliant, and because he had been Achilles's guest. None of that did Lycaon any good. Today the lawless hero is a staple of the

---

[3] William F. Buckley, "The Genesis of Blackford Oakes," in *Let Us Talk of Many Things* (New York: Crown Forum, 2000), p. 314–15.

superhero and espionage genres. On the television show *Alias*, the CIA heroes break the law and deceive their superiors for the greater good on a regular basis. Or think about the godlike power wielded by the Men in Black, who rewrite people's memories as casually as a novelist might revise a draft of his book. It has been decades since any of the big-name costumed heroes worked in close co-operation with the police—try to imagine Batman casually chit-chatting with the police commissioner in a movie today the way he used to in the old television show. If he did, we wouldn't take him seriously as a superhero. In the comic books of the 1980s, the lawlessness of the heroes had reached such a ridiculous extreme that when writer Scott McCloud introduced a superhero who was just a decent guy helping the authorities to fight evil, he was hailed by his peers as a bold, radical visionary. Yet though these lawless heroes might frequently raise questions about the rightness of their behavior, just as Achilles has done for millennia, they rarely provoke us to question the liberal constitutional order itself. Something beyond mere lawlessness is needed for that.

It's because of his paradoxical relationship to the liberal order that Bond raises questions about the rule of law that most heroes do not. On the one hand, he seems to be seamlessly integrated with the liberal order. He is under the command of a duly appointed officer of the intelligence bureaucracy, who in turn is accountable to the Prime Minister of a lawfully constituted government. He does take certain liberties in the execution of his orders that make his superiors cringe, particularly when he's offered an opportunity to indulge his hormones. But on the whole, he fundamentally does what he's told. M sends Bond to bring down Goldfinger; he brings him down. M sends Bond to break SPECTRE's diamond smuggling ring; he breaks it. Whatever friction may occur between Bond and his superiors ("Now 007, do please try and return some of this equipment in pristine order"), there is never a moment's doubt that Bond is an appendage of the liberal political system and that his actions, lechery excluded, are its actions.[4]

---

[4] Some readers might object that this was not the case in the movie *Licence to Kill*, when Bond renounced his affiliation with MI6 and went rogue. Fortunately, that movie raises no problem for our argument because it is so hideously bad that all true Bond fans will readily agree with the suggestion that we just ignore it.

But on the other hand, the double-0 section by its very nature appears to fly in the face of what the liberal constitutional order claims to be. The purpose of the double-0 section seems to be to dispense with the constraints of legal procedure and get the results that the liberal order needs by whatever means are necessary. But one of the most important things distinguishing the liberal order from other kinds of political order is precisely the idea that we must have procedural laws of justice in addition to substantive laws of justice. Historically, the substantive laws of justice have been virtually the same everywhere: don't murder, don't steal, don't break contracts, and so forth. One of the glories of liberal constitutionalism is that it elevates procedural laws of justice, such as laws against arbitrary detention and bills of attainder, almost to an equal level with the substantive laws of justice. If the liberal order can't survive without protectors who routinely resort to summary execution, in what sense is it a liberal order?

This paradox is embodied by those three little words every Bond fan loves to hear: licensed to kill. Nowhere in the books or movies are the legal specifics behind this license explained. But clearly it cannot just mean that Bond is legally allowed to kill people when killing is necessary to avert an imminent threat to innocent life, because every private citizen is allowed to do *that*. If someone is about to destroy the world and the only way to stop him is to kill him first, there's no need to call in a double-0 agent or even an ordinary police officer to do the job—any Tom, Dick, or Harry who happens to be on the scene is allowed to pull the trigger. So Bond's license to kill must be a license to kill people in other kinds of situations. Of course, we assume there must be some kind of threat to innocent life before Bond can kill without fear of prosecution—one imagines Bond isn't allowed to just open fire every time the line at the grocery store is too long—but apparently Bond can kill where others can't.

It may not be quite accurate to say that the license to kill gives Bond legal permission to break the law. After all, the law does make distinctions about who is allowed to do what (police officers may do things that others are forbidden to do) and we don't call this "breaking the law." Nonetheless, Bond's situation looks very different from that of the ordinary police officer. In exchange for the additional power we give him, the police officer is subject to a body of regulations, enforced by special oversight agencies, that is large and astonishingly complex—and growing more so every year as the case law piles up. Bond, by contrast, doesn't seem to be subject to much of anything. There will never be a *Drax* decision or a *Zorin* decision hanging over the heads of double-0 agents as they work in the field, the way police officers are constrained by the *Miranda* decision and its numerous offspring. Indeed, just about the only complaint about Bond's work that we never hear from either M or Q is that he failed to respect the bad guys' rights. If Bond doesn't have legal permission to break the law, he has the next best thing: legal permission to work without effective oversight from the legal system.

The question comes down to this: can we have a law like the one granting Bond a license to kill and still say that we live under "the rule of law"? Or does the need for that kind of law prove that the whole idea of "the rule of law" is a sham—that the liberal order cannot possibly be what it claims to be?

Just What Is the Rule of Law?

We can't determine whether Bond is consistent with the rule of law until we have some idea of just what the rule of law is. But when we turn to this question, we quickly discover that we have a deeper problem. For all the talk one hears in political and philosophical circles about the importance of the rule of law, defining that concept turns out to be pretty difficult.

Obviously it would not be satisfactory simply to say that we have the rule of law wherever the laws, whatever they happen to be, are faithfully executed. This might be "the rule of law" in a superficial sense, in that the laws would rule society. But this is not what we mean when we talk about the rule of law. By this definition, Dr. No's island is the epitome of the rule of law—Dr. No makes the laws, and his henchmen faithfully carry them out!

While this point may seem obvious, we have already discovered a glimmer of hope for the rule of law. For if the rule of law does not mean simply that the law is always followed, then it's possible in principle that the rule of law might sometimes be consistent with not following the law. Of course, to actually salvage the rule of law we will need to show exactly what the rule of law consists of, and why specifically the rule of law might be consistent with not following the law in some circumstances. But this first step towards a definition has already shown us that because the rule of law is not simply identical with the enforcement of the law, there is nothing inherently absurd in thinking that the rule of law might be something that would allow for the law to not always be enforced.

We can clarify the problem of defining the rule of law by turning briefly from the world of fiction to the much duller world of fact—the actual British intelligence services. The 1994 Intelligence Services Act says that the Secret Intelligence Service, colloquially known as MI6, exists "(a) to obtain and provide information relating to the actions or intentions of persons outside the British Islands; and (b) to perform other tasks relating to the actions or intentions of such persons." You couldn't ask for a more open-ended mandate than "to perform other tasks." Presumably they don't spend their time bringing the Prime Minister his coffee and picking up his dry cleaning. So how does Britain square this with the rule of law?

Let's compare the way MI6 answers this question with the way Britain's counter-intelligence service, the Security Service or MI5, answers it. Addressing the topic on its website, MI5 doesn't mince words: "It is claimed from time to time that we have been responsible for murdering individuals who have become 'inconvenient' in some way. We do not kill people or arrange their assassination. We are subject to the rule of law in just the same way as other public bodies."[5]

Surfing over to MI6, we get something subtly different: "To maintain their effectiveness the intelligence and security Agencies must be able to operate in secret. However it is also important in a democratic society that there are effective safeguards and means of overseeing their work."[6] There follows a detailed list of official bodies that have oversight authority over MI6, including a bipartisan committee of Members of Parliament and a commission of senior judicial officers.

The two agencies have chosen to describe the way Britain controls its intelligence services in different ways. MI5 explicitly invokes "the rule of law" and gives us something substan-

---

[5] http://www.mi5.gov.uk/output/Page119.html#3
[6] http://www.archive.official-documents.co.uk/document/caboff/nim/natint.htm

tive—a promise to refrain from certain behavior. MI6 invokes "democratic" accountability rather than the rule of law, and gives us something procedural—a set of institutional processes that limit the agency's freedom to act. On the subject of what it actually does or does not do, MI6 remains conspicuously silent.

Democracy is not the same as the rule of law. Everyone acknowledges that you can have a lawless democracy—we call it "mob rule." For a very long time, ancient Athens was held (rightly or wrongly) to be the prime example, with the trial of Socrates being seen as the paradigmatic case of the mob's will trumping the law. The American founders pointed to Athens and other ancient democracies as cautionary examples illustrating the need to bind government to something other than merely the democratic will of the people. The French Revolution, and the Reign of Terror that followed under the revolutionary government, provides an even clearer example. So MI6's claim to be democratically accountable does not necessarily amount to a claim to be under the rule of law—one could argue that when Robespierre was chopping off heads left and right, he was democratically accountable the whole time.

We can now state with more precision the question Bond raises. Is the liberal political order not really constrained effectively by the law, but only by the will of the voters, with the ideal of "the rule of law" serving as a useful fiction (a noble lie, if you will) that conceals the true nature of the system? Or does the liberal order have something other than democratic accountability that it can point to as proof that it does respect "the rule of law"? And if so, can we reconcile that with the apparently lawless standard of expediency that Bond seems to stand for?

Substantive Rule of Law: The Public Good

To unravel the political paradox of James Bond, we naturally turn first to the only political philosopher in history who also doubled as a secret agent. Well, "secret agent" is stretching a bit, but the English philosopher John Locke was undeniably mixed up with *bona fide* conspiracy and espionage. During the English political crisis of the 1680s, Locke was in the employ of Lord Anthony Ashley Cooper, a leading figure in the parliamentary faction who had a personal network of spies to help him keep a leg up in his power struggle with the king. When the king abolished Parliament and set himself up as the sole ruler of England, Lord Ashley's network undertook a five-year campaign of assassination attempts and insurrection movements, complete with coded messages, hand signals, and fake names (though history does not record whether they had any buzzsaw wrist-watches or amphibious sports cars). While the extent of Locke's involvement with the whole assassination end of things is a matter of debate—some historians insist that he was up to his eyeballs in it—we can say with certainty that he used the information the spy network provided, he wrote tracts to support the legitimacy of their political resistance, he had to flee the country due to his association with Lord Ashley, and while hiding in Amsterdam he lived under an assumed name and maintained contact with the underground community of exiled Parliamentarians as they continued their (eventually successful) efforts to overthrow the king. That's a lot closer to "secret agent" than Immanuel Kant ever got.

Locke is the closest thing we have to a founder of liberal political theory, so his views on the rule of law in his *Two Treatises of Government* are a good place to start looking for an answer to our question. Locke takes up a question similar to the one Bond puts before us when he tackles the issue of "prerogative power," the doctrine that kings have the right, at their own discretion, to contravene the law in particular circumstances where the public good requires it. During the political crisis of the 1680s, the king stretched the prerogative power far beyond its previous boundaries in order to operate without legislative sanction. After the Parliamentarians successfully overthrew the king and installed their own man on the throne, Parliament passed and the new king signed a "Bill of Rights" laying down specific new statutory limits on the use of the prerogative.

Despite the abuses to which it had been put during the crisis, Locke endorses the prerogative power. He observes that "many accidents may happen, wherein a strict and rigid observation of the laws may do harm . . . and a man may come sometimes within the reach of the law . . . by an action, that may deserve reward and pardon." For this reason, "'tis fit that the laws themselves should in some cases give way to the executive power, or rather to this fundamental law of nature and government, *viz.* that as much as may be, all the members of the society are to be preserved" (*Two Treatises*, Section II. 159).[7] When the executive uses this power rightly, Locke asserts, the law gives way not to the will of the executive as such, but to the higher rule that the members of the community must be preserved. After all, it was for this purpose that government was created in the first place. So the written law defers to a higher law—what Locke calls the natural law.

The point is that a government does not exist simply to follow its own rules. If government had no purpose beyond enforcing the law, the community would not have created it in the first place, because before there was a government there were no laws to enforce. Bond is not flying around in space to stop Hugo Drax from annihilating the entire human race from orbit simply because Britain has laws against doing that sort of thing. If there were no purpose to it higher than simply enforcing the laws against annihilating the human race from orbit, there could be no rational answer to the question "why did Parliament pass a law against annihilating the human race from orbit in the first place?", or even the question "why does Parliament exist in the first place?" The only way government's existence makes any sense is if laws are needed for a reason that is independent of government. The government exists for a purpose that is higher than itself—to serve the community by preserving its members. Every aspect of government, even the law itself, is good only to the extent that it serves this higher purpose.

To uphold the written law in cases where doing so endangers the community would be self-contradictory. Suppose the Orient Express has a rule that forbids bringing suitcases booby-trapped with tear gas canisters on the train, and suppose you were the conductor and you discovered Bond was carrying just such a suitcase, but you also knew there was a sociopathic hit man on the train intending to kill three of its passengers, and the suitcase was the only available weapon with which Bond could stop him. You would be crazy to confiscate the suitcase, even if the rules don't explicitly delegate to you the authority to make exceptions to the "no booby-trapped suitcases" rule. The rules of the train exist for the benefit of the passengers; the con-

---

[7] John Locke, *Two Treatises of Government* (New York: Everyman, 1993).

ductor is right to suspend them where the good of the passengers requires it. Locke declares: "*Salus populi suprema lex* [the people's safety is the supreme law] is certainly so just and fundamental a rule, that he, who sincerely follows it, cannot dangerously err" (*Two Treatises*, Section II. 158).

For Locke, government is serving its purpose wherever it acts in the public good, defined as the preservation of members of the community. Problems arise only when power is exercised for the sake of someone's private good over the public good. "The end of government being the good of the community, whatsoever alterations are made in it, tending to that end, cannot be an encroachment upon anybody: since nobody in government can have a right tending to any other end" (Section II. 163). Prerogative power, "whilst employed for the benefit of the community, and suitably to the trust and ends of the government . . . is never questioned. For the people are very seldom, or never scrupulous, or nice in the point: they are far from examining prerogative, whilst it is in any tolerable degree employed for the use it was meant; that is, for the good of the people, and not manifestly against it" (Section II. 161).

Here we come back to our question. Though Locke does not use the particular phrase "rule of law," his thought gives us a substantive account of how upholding the rule of law can allow us or even require us to suspend particular laws—because the rule of law does not mean following every letter of the law at all times. The rule of law is the exercise of political power for the public good rather than for anyone's private good.

However, the substantive account is not enough. With it we can justify Bond-like use of power, but only on the assumption that those who exercise this power will not abuse it. But of course that is precisely why we are so worried about giving people Bond-like power—because we fear that they will abuse it, because we know that those who have power are constantly tempted to abuse it. Locke's own case is a perfect example; the subject of prerogative power comes up for him precisely because it was being abused! That's why Locke gives us one fairly straightforward chapter endorsing prerogative power, followed by a long and much more complicated series of chapters on how to handle abuses of power. The problem also comes up in Ian Fleming's short story "For Your Eyes Only," in which M sends Bond to perform an assassination that appears to be motivated by personal revenge rather than Britain's legitimate security needs.

What we need, in addition to the substantive account, is a procedural account of the rule of law—some concrete mechanism for preventing and redressing abuse of the Bond-like power that the substantive account says government must sometimes have. For Locke, given his historical situation, the relevant procedural mechanism was the people's right to rebel against unjust rulers. That's not very helpful for the question before us. We will have to turn elsewhere to find an answer relevant to our own problem.

Procedural Rule of Law: The Separation of Powers

The abuse of power, and the need for procedures to prevent and redress it, was one of the main animating themes in Baron Charles Montesquieu's 1748 masterpiece of political theory *The Spirit of the Laws*. Here we find a procedural counterpart to Locke's substantive account of the rule of law. For Locke, the rule of law is power rightly used; for Montesquieu, the rule of law is institutions designed to promote the right use of power.

Montesquieu begins with the chief threat to liberty: people want to have power over others. Government's job is to protect each person's liberty by providing us with security against others: "Political liberty . . . is that tranquility of spirit which comes from the opinion each one has of his security, and in order for him to have this liberty the government must be such that one citizen cannot fear another citizen" (*Spirit of the Laws*, Section 11.6).[8] Unfortunately, there is a fairly big, obvious problem with this: government's job is to protect us from people, but the government is itself run by people. The reason we needed government in the first place is that people want power over others, and the people who run the government want power just as much as the rest of us. So although the government provides each private citizen with security against other private citizens, we still don't have liberty because we need security against the rulers.

---

[8] Charles Montesquieu, *The Spirit of the Laws* (Cambridge: Cambridge University Press, 1989).

To solve this problem, Montesquieu famously turns to what is now known as "separation of powers." Where all power is in one person or body, "one can fear that the same monarch or senate that makes tyrannical laws will execute them tyrannically." But if government power is divided into multiple departments, no one person can exercise power tyrannically without being opposed. Indeed, the inevitable competition for power among the people running the various departments will naturally cause each branch of government to keep the others in check. Anything that passes muster with all three branches of government can't be seriously tyrannical—or perhaps we should say that if government corruption is so far advanced that all three branches acquiesce in tyranny, there was no hope to protect liberty under that government by any means whatsoever. This mechanism is so crucial, he emphasizes, that we cannot have liberty without it: "When legislative power is united with executive power in a single person or in a single body of the magistracy, there is no liberty. . . . Nor is there liberty if the power of judging is not separate from legislative power and from executive power" (Section 11.6).

This equation of the separation of powers with liberty had a powerful influence on the American founders. Madison calls separation of powers an "essential precaution in favor of liberty. . . . The accumulation of all powers, legislative, executive, and judiciary, in the same hands . . . may justly be pronounced the very definition of tyranny."[9] That the American founders trusted the separation of powers much more than written laws to serve as procedural checks on abuse of power can be seen most clearly in the vague qualifiers with which they watered down the sections of the Bill of Rights applying to law enforcement. The Fourth Amendment prohibits only "unreasonable" search and seizure. The Fifth Amendment guarantees only "due" process of law. The Sixth Amendment applies only to "criminal prosecutions." The Seventh Amendment allows for the overturning of juries' decisions, so long as this is done according to established common-law procedures. The Eighth Amendment forbids only "excessive" bail and fines. Freedom of religion,

---

[9] James Madison, "Federalist #47," in James Madison, Alexander Hamilton, and John Jay, *The Federalist Papers* (East Rutherford: Penguin, 1961), p. 301.

freedom of speech and the press, freedom of petition and assembly, and the right to bear arms are established by blanket provisions containing none of this hesitancy; however, when it came to the government's power to protect the community, the founders obviously balked at laying down firm limits.

At this point the appeal to democratic accountability in the MI6 statement quoted above begins to look less like a cop-out and more like a real affirmation of the rule of law. When it invokes "democratic" oversight it is not really appealing to democracy so much as the separation of powers. The point is not primarily that the executive is accountable to the people, but that the executive is accountable to the legislature and (in a more limited way) to the judicial branch. The thrust of the argument is not that the government can be removed by the voters—the voters are not even mentioned—but rather that *someone other than the executive is watching over the executive's work*. To believe that MI6 is seriously abusing its power, you have to believe that both the parliamentary committee and the judicial commission are permitting this abuse of power, either through failure to watch closely enough or through knowing acquiescence in the abuse. And if you really think things are so bad that all three branches are failing in this way, what grounds do you have for thinking that any other mechanism would have succeeded in preventing the abuse of power from occurring?

Under the current British system the legislative and executive are not as separate as they used to be back in Montesquieu's time, when the executive was an unelected king. Nor are they even as separate as they are in the United States, where Congress and the president are separately elected. Parliament appoints the Prime Minister, and it can remove him at any time. But the branches are still separate enough for Montesquieu's purposes. He requires only that the offices be held by separate people; where this is the case, the inevitable competition for power among different people provides a sufficient safeguard. In fact, he declares that in most European nations in his time, the judiciary branch was adequately separate from the executive branch, even though judicial officers were typically appointed by the crown. And in this particular case the weakening of the separation of powers produces greater constraint, not less, on the exercise of Bond-like powers, since the executive is now under greater legislative control.

The separation of powers is not a perfect solution to the problem of restraining government from abusing power. Abuses of power by the executive may occasionally slip under the radar of the other branches—as is exemplified by M's vendetta in "For Your Eyes Only." But the world does not admit perfect solutions to any serious social problem. Separation of powers is probably as good a solution to the problem of power as we're going to get.

Answering Scaramanga

We can, then, solve the problem of Bond and the rule of law. To Scaramanga's claim that Bond is just as lawless as he is, we can reply that Bond, consistent with the rule of law, is able to 1. give a substantive reason why he should be allowed to have the power he has, and 2. point to institutional procedures other than the traditional legal system that are able to restrain him from abusing that power. Neither of these two aspects of the rule of law would be sufficient without the other; we need both a reason to give Bond power and a reason to think he won't abuse it. But with them both, we can define the rule of law— the use of power for the public good by a government in which each branch is subject to supervision by other branches—in a way that allows Bond to go about his work.

10

"Don't You Men Know Any Other Way?" Punishment Beyond Retributivism and Deterrence

JACOB M. HELD

James Bond films are full of what have now become clichés. Many of these have become obligatory in any Bond film as well as grist for the parody mill. One such cliché is the glib quip following Bond's elimination of some foe. Examples are limitless. In *Goldfinger*, after throwing an assailant into a bath tub full of water Bond throws in an electric heater thus electrocuting him. Bond utters, "Shocking." Likewise, in *Goldeneye*, when Xenia Onatopp is killed after being pulled against a tree by a crashing helicopter Bond says, "She always did enjoy a good squeeze." This is an allusion to her signature method of killing her victims by crushing them between her thighs.

As this example shows, the need to fulfill the demand for this particular Bond cliché can make some efforts appear labored and ridiculous. The formula has been copied throughout the action-adventure genre and has even become prime fodder for parody. In *Austin Powers: International Man of Mystery*, after decapitating an enemy by holding his head under ravenous sea-bass infested water Austin utters phrases to the effect of, "Not a time to lose one's head. That's not a way to get ahead in life . . ." He makes several more strained attempts at Bondesque quips until his partner puts an end to it. However, it's not only James Bond who gets to follow killing with glib witticisms. In the novel *Live and Let Die*, Felix Leiter is fed to sharks. This appeared in the film *Licence to Kill*. Attached to Felix's mutilated body is a note, "He disagreed with something that ate him." Bond is clearly not the only one who has a way with words. Yet, although these instances might appear to be

139

merely comic relief or attempts at humor in the humorless world of espionage I think they are much more. These comments and our enjoyment of them are an expression of our attitude towards criminals and punishment generally. They betray an implicit acceptance in the meting out of just desert and the belief that criminals deserve very little indeed. Bond's behavior betrays utter disrespect for the criminal as a fellow human being.

Consider our respective responses to Felix being eaten versus any of the myriad horrific deaths met with by Bond's adversaries. When the Robber (In the book *Live and Let Die*)/Sanchez (in the movie *Licence to Kill*) responds to Felix's disfigurement with the quip that he disagreed with something that ate him, we respond with disgust. How could he be so cavalier about the pain and suffering of a noble CIA agent? Felix doesn't deserve such treatment. The Robber/Sanchez must be pure evil and inhuman. James Bond ought to kill them, preferably in a similar way or at least in some fashion equally, if not more, gruesome. Yet when Bond responds to the death of a villain with such nonchalance we laugh or giggle and generally take pleasure not only in the death but the way in which Bond responds to it, namely, with such lightheartedness that he might have just flushed a fish down the toilet instead of dropping a defenseless Blofeld wheelchair and all down a smoke stack. In many cases, such as the example from *Goldfinger* above, it is clear that Bond had to kill. It was self-defense, or at least not gratuitous. Yet in the case of dropping Blofeld down a smoke stack as occurs in the opening scene of *For Your Eyes Only*, Bond had the option not to kill.

Bond's behavior towards criminals exemplifies at times a retributive theory of punishment and at other times a deterrent theory of punishment, and both these theories have limitations. Bond's actions illustrate the problems inherent in theories of punishment that do not contain an essential element of respect for human dignity. I will suggest that a moral education theory of punishment is more fitting in this regard even if it fails to quench our blood lust and doesn't offer Bond opportunities to make his famous quips. Let's first look at Bond the retributivist.

"You Earned It, You Keep It": Retribution

The retributive theory of punishment has been defined as, "*very generally* . . . a theory of punishment that seeks to justify punishment, not in terms of social utility, but in terms of *this* cluster of moral concepts: rights, desert, merit, moral responsibility, justice, and respect for moral autonomy."[1] The fundamental claim being: criminals ought to be punished because they deserve to be. That is, criminals ought to get what is coming to them. Of course, there are various ways to determine exactly what criminals deserve. Some argue that punishment ought to function according to the classic principle of *lex talionis*, or an eye for an eye, a tooth for a tooth. Others maintain that the punishment deserved is that which would deprive the criminal of the unfair advantage he acquired through the commission of the crime. And yet others propose that criminals ought to be punished so that their suffering is the effective nullification of the suffering they themselves caused. Regardless, criminals are to get what they deserve for no other reason than that they deserve it, no matter how desert might be determined.

Now consider why we revel in Bond's treatment of his adversaries. It appears to be because we believe Bond to be distributing just desert and that this is an appropriate justification of punishment. Apparently, Blofeld deserves nothing more than to plummet to his death down a smoke stack. Odd Job deserves to be electrocuted. And what could be more befitting for Sanchez than to be burned alive or for Killifer than to be eaten by the very sharks that fed on Felix? But these examples raise serious questions.

Can we determine just desert? It seems impossible to objectively, or even consistently, determine just desert. Simple *lex talionis* has its obvious flaws. Consider Bond's treatment of Killifer in *Licence to Kill*. Killifer was complicit in the feeding of Felix to sharks. Bond finds himself in a position where he can save Killifer or let him suffer the same. Killifer tries to bribe Bond with one half of the two million dollars Sanchez paid him for turning on his former colleague. Bond responds, "You earned it, you keep it, Old Buddy." Bond then tosses the money to Killifer and knocks him into the water where he is eaten by the same sharks that devoured Felix. Bond watches unflinchingly; an eye for an eye and then some. Yet, this seems more cruel than just.

---

[1] Jeffrie G. Murphy, *Retribution Reconsidered: More Essays in the Philosophy of Law* (Dordrecht: Kluwer, 1992), p. 21.

This is the classic problem of the application of *lex talionis*. Nobody can, with any moral authority, truly propose giving a criminal like for like, such as raping rapists. On the face of it, it's as wrong to rape a rapist as it is for the rapist to rape his victims, and for the same reason. But if this is out of the question, how do you mete out just desert?

What about the theory that a punishment ought to nullify the moral wrong of the criminal act?[2] This suggests that punishment is to function as some form of cosmic or karmic justice. Aside from the obvious political questions about whether or not it's the role of the state to function as an agent of karma there is the clear problem of how one could calculate the moral equivalence between an illegal act and the subsequent punishment.[3] Consider any Bond villain. How do we determine and achieve moral parity between Zorin's attempt to destroy Silicon Valley and his punishment? Is death appropriate? Could we do more? What about Hugo Drax and his attempt to destroy the human race? These examples illustrate a real problem. Some acts are so morally repugnant they do not afford an equivalent even if equivalence were determinable. So it doesn't appear as if there's a way to nullify the moral wrongness of a past act.

But this brings us to another proposal: what is deserved is that the criminal be denied the unfair advantage he acquired through his transgression. This presumes that laws protect rights and interests and thus confer on us the benefit of having these interests secured. A criminal act thus gives a criminal an unfair advantage since he does not have to respect the constraints we respect by not infringing on those interests that the law protects. As Shafer-Landau puts it: "This approach is to correct unfair advantages obtained by a criminal through his wrongdoing."[4] But again parity appears impossible. How would this apply to a murderer or rapist? How do you deprive them of whatever unfair advantage they acquired? What would the unfair advantage be in the case of rape? Or consider, again, the case of

---

[2] This notion is most commonly associated with the work of nineteenth-century German philosopher Georg Hegel.

[3] On this point see Russ Shafer-Landau, "Retributivism and Desert," *Pacific Philosophical Quarterly* 81 (2000), pp. 189–214, and Richard L. Lippke, "Victim-Centered Retributivism," *Pacific Philosophical Quarterly* 84 (2003), pp. 127–145.

[4] Shafer-Landau, "Retributivism and Desert," p. 205. For a classic presentation of this view see Herbert Morris, "Persons and Punishment," *The Monist* 52 (1968), pp. 475–501.

Bond's foes. What unfair advantage does Dr. No acquire through the toppling of missiles? It seems that punishment in his case is warranted as a case of national defense. In fact, if interests and their protection is the goal of punishment, as unfair advantage retributivism seems to suggest, then maybe we are looking in the wrong place entirely. Maybe we should be looking at deterrence as the justification for and goal of punishment.

Death Is So Permanent: Deterrence

Jean Hampton states: "I believe we must accept the deterrence theorist's contention that the justification of punishment is connected with the fact that it is a necessary tool for preventing future crime and promoting the public's well-being."[5] I think she's right. Punishment is a subset of law which itself is a subset of political right. Punishment is a function of the state and must be justified according to the goals of the state. One of these goals is the protection of the interests of the citizenry and the promotion of their welfare. This goal can't be met if we do not prevent interests from being violated through crime prevention. Punishment must serve as a deterrent. However, this is not to say that the sole justification of punishment is its deterrent effect, or that the only reason to punish is to dissuade criminals from committing illegal acts. Let's consider why deterrence is problematic as the sole purpose of punishment.

Simply put, James Bond is the ultimate deterrent. The criminals Bond punishes never commit their crimes again. Granted this is because they are dead, but he serves his purpose well. If his goal as an instrument of the legal system is crime prevention, then he is highly effective. But there is a problem with this justification of punishment.

Deterrence is a consequentialist justification of punishment. It maintains that the attainment of the end, prevention, justifies any method that achieves this end. Bond is a highly effective deterrent even if he does have to kill those he punishes. Again, consider Killifer. Killifer is not a threat when Bond has him dangling precariously over a shark tank. Bond could arrest him. But he doesn't. Although his motives are revenge, the end result is

---

[5] Jean Hampton, "The Moral Education Theory of Punishment," *Philosophy and Public Affairs* 13: 3 (Summer 1984), p. 211.

that Killifer will never commit treason again. Likewise, every anonymous henchman that Bond kills is effectively deterred even if they are denied due process and their role in the criminal enterprise might be questionable.

If we justify punishment based on its consequences, then we open ourselves up to the possibility of grave abuses. For example, torture, executions for any variety of crimes, punishment of the innocent or inordinately harsh punishment to "send a message," and so on.[6] There are ways one can attempt to avoid these. One could claim that only punishing the guilty is most effective or that overly harsh punishment tends to back-fire creating more resentment than respect for the law; therefore our punishment ought to be tempered with mercy. However, these limitations are contingent based ultimately on effectiveness and if torture proved effective it would be justified.

The problems associated with retributive and deterrence theories of punishment, even though only briefly discussed, illustrate an important problem with these approaches; there is no inherent upper-bound limit on what can justifiably be done to a criminal because the criminal is never considered as a person. We only think about the act itself, its punishment, and preventing it from occurring again. We never ask about who committed the crime.

What's This All About? The Moral Status of Criminals

What happens to most Bond villains is not punishment. It isn't jail time or even death by lethal injection. Even when they could be captured they are not. Instead these villains are exploded, burned, drowned, electrocuted, eaten, shot (with bullets, harpoons, lasers . . .), or dropped out of planes. Some deaths are more unpleasant than others, but all are celebrated. We never find ourselves saying, "Bond should have followed protocol, he never Mirandized that person, he ought not to have killed that person, Dr. No has rights, there are more effective ways to prevent criminal behavior . . ."

---

[6] For a discussion of this see Richard B. Brandt, "The Utilitarian Theory of Criminal Punishment," in John Arthur and William H. Shaw, eds., *Readings in Philosophy of Law* (Englewood Cliffs: Prentice-Hall, 1984), pp. 189–194.

Our enjoyment of Bond evinces our tacit approval of a quite harsh retributivist theory of punishment, our belief in deterrence as a necessary goal of punishment, and the fact that criminals appear to occupy a different realm in the moral universe than do law abiding people. It appears as though we maintain that criminals do not possess the same rights that we do. Not only should they get what they have coming, but this is usually painful, humiliating, and often lethal. Criminals, apparently, cannot make the same moral demands regarding their treatment that we can.

The act of punishing criminals, in and of itself, is the denial of certain moral rights that we otherwise consider essential. Incarceration is the violation of one's right to liberty. Fines and other forms of torts are violations of the right to property. There is also the example of the denial of convicted felons of the right to vote. This has motivated some to offer an account of right forfeiture. Essentially what is claimed is that the only way punishment can be justified as not violating these rights is if criminals, upon the commission of some criminal act, forfeit these respective rights thus opening up the door for their punishment.[7] If we want to understand why criminals appear to occupy a lower place on the moral ladder than do regular citizens, this seems to be the place to start.

Some state that one loses one's moral rights when one demonstrates an unwillingness to respect the same rights in others.[8] Contained within this theory is the notion that one forfeits a like right to the one they violated. So theft is repaid through a loss of the right to property and one could go so far as to say that murder is repaid with a loss of the right to life. Of course, there will be problems of cases like rape again, not to mention questions about length and breadth of the forfeiture, but these are not my current concern.[9] What I'm concerned with is the claim that criminals can lose their standing as moral agents and

---

[7] There are other ways to justify the violation of normally protected moral rights in the case of criminals, such as protection of the public's welfare, promotion of the public good, and so forth. But I'm concerned with the notion of the criminal's apparent loss of moral worth.

[8] Christopher W. Morris, "Punishment and Loss of Moral Standing," *Canadian Journal of Philosophy* 21 (1991), p. 65.

[9] These are expressed clearly in Richard L. Lippke, "Criminal Offenders and Right Forfeiture," *Journal of Social Philosophy* 32: 1 (Spring 2001), pp. 78–89.

thus be opened up to what might otherwise be morally reprehensible treatment.

If our attitude towards Bond is an indication of our attitude towards punishment in general, then we might claim that we not only believe that criminals forfeit certain moral rights but that they are incapable of making the same demands for respect and humane treatment as the rest of us. We accept the inhumane treatment of the super-villains. Nobody objects to not only Bond killing when he could have just as easily arrested a perpetrator, but his flagrant disregard for decency when it comes to his handling of offenders. Rather, James Bond is extolled as justice personified. We wish there were a James Bond dolling out swift justice in such an unambiguous way.

James Bond's actions and our tacit support of them, betray a belief that criminals occupy a less than human position in our moral universe. Punishment, therefore, is not constrained by demands for respect and often becomes humiliating and dehumanizing. We don't miss the lack of an upper bound limit on retribution and deterrence since we don't believe one to be morally demanded since criminals fail to occupy a position capable of making such a demand. But is this an appropriate attitude to hold regarding criminals and punishment?

I am about to become very unpopular among James Bond fans. I am going to take the side of the villains over Bond and make the following claim: Bond's retributive and consequentialist brand of punishment is morally questionable since it fails to secure a moral minimum as regards the treatment of criminal offenders. Instead, a theory of punishment that does respect this minimum must be applied if we are to guarantee the dignity each human being possesses merely in virtue of existing. A moral education theory of punishment is able to do just this.

Nothing Humiliates Like Humiliation

To begin, let's look at Bond's treatment of criminals and see how this illustrates our own perspective on criminals and their moral status. I want to do this through an examination into the nature of humiliation. Bond's quips are not simply instances of comic relief; they are also attempts on Bond's part to humiliate his adversary. On the face of it this may not seem to be an important or pressing issue. Who really cares if Dr. No is humiliated or embarrassed? But humiliation comes in two varieties: the deflation of pretense and the denial of one's common humanity.[10]

In the first sense, humiliation is merely the experience of embarrassment that occurs when one's pretensions are deflated. That is, one is humiliated when one's claim to an unjustified social position or demand for unjustified respect or admiration is denied in a way that makes one appear foolish. Bond sets up Dr. No is this way when, with reference to Dr. No's unique aquarium he states, "Minnows pretending they're whales. Just like you on this island, Dr. No." Bond here insinuates that Dr. No is demanding an unwarranted status. His subsequent remark at dinner, "Tell me, does the toppling of American missiles really compensate for having no hands," is not simply an insult but an attempt to deflate Dr. No's pretense.

We might also consider the more mundane example of a haughty individual who slips on ice only to find herself falling on her backside in full view of a lot of people. This type of humiliation is trivial, superficial, and usually humorous. It is accompanied by an experience of enjoyment since we see somebody getting what they seemingly deserve, that is, to be taken down a notch. Another prominent example is every occurrence wherein Bond faces his adversary in a game of baccarat. The villain is full of pretense sitting behind a large pile of money and next to a very attractive woman, who will undoubtedly be yet another of Bond's sexual conquests. (If her name is an allusion to a sexual position this is guaranteed.) In these instances, Bond casually takes the seat across from his adversary and proceeds to beat him all the while making not-so-subtle comments about who he is and how much he knows about his adversary. What Bond does in these cases is to remove the aura of respectability from the undeserving and replace it with the ridicule they seemingly deserve. This is the common sense in which we often use the term humiliation. However, we can also use humiliation to describe graver experiences. This is the second sense of humiliation; humiliation with an "H."

Humiliation with an "H" is that form of humiliation often associated with the victim of sexual assault, rape, or torture.

---

[10] This distinction is taken from: William Ian Miller, *Humiliation and Other Essays on Honor, Social Discomfort, and Violence* (Ithaca: Cornell University Press, 1993).

People Humiliated in this way are not brought down from pretension to the level of the rest of us or a more appropriate level of status. Rather, the implicit claim made is that their very claim to humanity is unfounded and pretentious. The rape victim is Humiliated since her status as a human being worthy of respect is denied by her assailant, who through his actions states: "How dare you claim to be worthy of the same respect the rest of us humans enjoy. You are nothing." The same is true of torture victims. Although humiliation of the first sense is harmless, even if malicious, Humiliation of the second type is more insidious since it is predicated on the denial of the victim's status as a human being.[11] Humiliation of this later sort is morally repugnant insofar as it exhibits the denial of the victim's dignity as a human being.

The enjoyment we take in watching Bond humiliate his adversaries betrays our tacit belief that villains deserve no better. The cases of the card game and his insults seem fitting and we do take pleasure in them. But what about cases where Bond Humiliates the villains? Do we really believe that some people deserve to be denied their status as human beings? Can we truly claim that Dr. No's claim to a common humanity is mere pretense?

Aside from the casual killing of countless anonymous henchmen, Bond oftentimes makes statements and treats his villains in a way that indicates he views them as less than human. He makes several degrading comments regarding Jaws. The books are less "politically correct" and here we get degrading comments about Odd Job being Korean, the Japanese in general, the Turkish, and Mr. Big insofar as he is a "negro." At first blush, these might appear to be cases of gleeful humiliation, however they mask the dehumanization of the villain. Consider how Bond's villains always appear, whether in the novels or films.

Bond's villains are usually disfigured or "other." Blofeld is bald, disfigured, and disabled, Dr. No is racially mixed (German and Chinese) and has mechanical hands, Scaramanga has a superfluous third nipple, Mr. Big is African-American and has quite a large head, Jaws is extremely tall with metal teeth, Renard can't feel pain, Zorin is the result of Nazi eugenic exper-

---

[11] For an extended discussion of Humiliation see Miller, *Humiliation*, Chapter 4.

iments, and so on. Here we have a descriptive account of Bond's own perspective; the criminal is "other," he is not human and therefore need not be treated as such. Not only is our enjoyment in their humiliation demonstrative of our lack of fellow feeling, but our acceptance of Bond's Humiliation indicates our belief that they do not occupy a similar space in the ethical realm as do other human beings. When Bond nonchalantly kills them and makes a quip about it he is effectively denying them their pretense to human standing. They deserve inhumane treatment since they are not human. And we revel in it. Bond is not an isolated instance of this attitude. Prison rape is more often the punch-line of a joke than the topic of an ethical discussion; it is more comic than tragic. People believe rape is almost a part of punishment. Criminals deserve no better. But one's status as a moral being, as human, is not something that can be lost.

You Have Not Been Recognized, Dr. No: Recognition's Demand

The implicit claim in our attitude towards super-villains and even pettier criminals seems to betray an attitude that they forfeit their status as humans deserving of basic respect and human rights. The theory of rights forfeiture maintains that criminals can lose rights, namely, the rights afforded them that are equivalent to the rights of their victim. But one's standing as a human being is not derived through some social contract. Humanity is not a convention of justice or a fabrication of the liberal democratic state. Humanity is inherent in our existence. One way of understanding this is through the notion of recognition.

First and foremost, recognition is the foundation to ethical relations between free and equal human beings. It presupposes that human beings require each other in order to actualize their latent potentialities and that the only proper way for human beings to interact is through mutual recognition where the relationship is one of mutual cooperation and not one of domination and servitude. We are each the condition for the possibility of the actualization of both our and the other's humanity. We are not fully or properly human until we treat others in a mutually respectful way and are thusly treated.

There's a vast amount of literature on how exactly this falls out and what specifically is required for mutual recognition in the political, legal, and moral realm.[12] These accounts begin from the claim that recognition as mutual respect is a necessary condition for proper psychological development and the development of a healthy attitude of self-respect and respect for others. To fail to provide the conditions necessary to secure mutual recognition and instead to create an environment of Humiliation and disrespect or domination fosters the creation of psychological maladies and prohibits the appropriate development of the individual.

We can see that Bond does not afford his adversaries mutual recognition. Instead, just like retributivism and deterrence theories of punishment, Bond disregards his adversaries as moral agents, specifically their psychological frailty and demands for recognition. Thus, Bond doesn't merely behave in an ethically repugnant way but he also forecloses the possibility of rehabilitation and possibly a much more effective way of dealing with crime and criminal behavior itself.

Consider another common cliché in Bond films and novels, the inevitable encounter between Bond and his nemesis. The villain lays out his plans to Bond for appreciation. Bond insults him usually claiming he is insane or otherwise impaired. The villain is peeved and throws Bond into a cell or some equivalent with the intent of killing him. But Bond will of course escape and save the day. These encounters are examples of the classic demand for recognition. The villain sees Bond as an equal and demands of him that he recognize his genius and thus himself as a human being worthy of consideration. Bond denies him this.

The movies are much less articulate about the origins of the villains than are the books. But the books present a more, even if still limited, picture of the villain as a flawed human being, much as Bond is quite flawed through out the books. The villains are the disenfranchised, dispossessed, and orphaned members of society. Dr. No is a mixed-race pariah rebelling against authority, as he states the adoption of his last name indicates. Mr. Big is attempting to gain recognition as the first black super criminal. He comes from a historically disenfranchised group

---

[12] The best contemporary discussion of this occurs in: Axel Honneth, *The Struggle for Recognition: The Moral Grammar of Social Conflict* (Cambridge: Polity Press, 1995) especially Chapters 5 and 6.

and is demanding his recognition through his criminal endeavors. Hugo Drax is a proud German attempting to reclaim the respect his country lost in World War II. (The book is very different from the movie.) In *On Her Majesty's Secret Service*, Blofeld is trying to claim royal heritage to get the prestige that comes with it. There is no other motive than this.

Each of these villains is attempting to gain recognition from a recalcitrant world. Granted they try and force the issue through violent, immoral, and unethical means, but the demand is there. Bond's response fails to take this into account. Bond responds with more Humiliation compounding the psychic damage and perpetuating the cycle of violence. Some criminal activities and violent behavior can be accounted for as responses to Humiliation and other perceived attacks on one's moral worth. Rage and violence is, in these cases, the perceived last resort for the attainment of the recognition denied.[13] There is a link between Humiliation, rage, and criminal behavior.

The Humiliating effect of punishment on the criminal may not be a problem for those who believe that punishment is simply about just desert or deterrence, but what if punishment is about more than that? What if we actually want to rehabilitate criminals? Then, it might be beneficial to start treating them as though they were actually people capable of redemption and who could possibly function as laudable moral agents.

Live and Let Learn: Moral Education and Punishment

We have seen that deterrence must be a necessary component to any theory of punishment even if it fails to be adequate as the sole justification. But what could be a better way to prevent crime then to have criminals genuinely decide that they don't want to commit crimes? There is no better way to regulate behavior than internally. External coercion is limited and only functional when feared or undesirable, conspicuous, and inevitable. But internal sanctions, that is, moral beliefs causing one to decide for oneself that one will not commit a criminal act are infinitely more effective. An approach to punishment from

---

[13] See Jack Katz, *Seductions of Crime: Moral and Sensual Attractions in Doing Evil* (New York: Basic Books, 1988), pp. 22–29.

this perspective will be not only an effective preventative measure, it will have the added bonus of recognizing criminals as though they actually were moral agents.

> The moral education theory of punishment: maintains that punishment is intended as a way of teaching the wrongdoer that the action she did (or wants to do) is forbidden because it is morally wrong and should not be done for that reason. The theory also regards the lesson as public, and thus as directed to the rest of society. When the state makes its criminal law and its enforcement practices known, it conveys an educative message not only to the convicted criminal but also to anyone else in the society who might be tempted to do what she did. (Hampton, p. 212).

There's a fundamental shift in perspective from the classic retributive and deterrent theories to the moral education theory. Classic retributive and deterrent theories operate from the premise that punishment is the commission of harm and should either make sure the harm is equal to the original harm caused by the crime or it should be undesirable enough that people obey laws to avoid having that harm imposed on them. But both operate from the belief that punishment is to be harmful to the criminal. The moral education theory begins from a different premise. Let's assume that criminals are moral agents and our behavior towards them is to respect this fact. Then we must acknowledge that as moral agents they are not simply to be trained like dogs or harmed for the sake of some cosmic sense of just desert. Rather, we should educate them as to why they are being punished so that they are afforded the opportunity, as moral agents, to later make the right choice for the right reason. I can't explain to my dog why he should not bite the neighbor child, so I negatively reinforce the behavior. I can explain to a child why he should not hit another child. Doing so fosters his development as a moral agent. The punishment of criminals, I contend, is similar. Although we can punish harshly in an attempt to make prison undesirable enough to be motive enough for not committing crimes this has proven to be less than successful. Likewise, we can pay like with like and harm criminals for the simple reason that they deserve it. But if the criminal's harming of his victim is morally repugnant, then how can the same action be morally laudable when done by the state? I guess it is a question of why someone would believe that we should harm anybody as opposed to helping them become better people and even protecting ourselves in the process.

When children hurt one another we don't harm them back because they deserve it. At least good parents don't. Instead, we make sure that our punishment is instructive and *this is its primary goal.* Criminals, if they are to be respected as moral agents, must be afforded similar treatment. We must operate from the belief that criminals are moral agents capable of reform. From this foundation, education is the appropriate goal of punishment.

Of course there are many who would view this theory as naïve, overly optimistic, or exceedingly charitable to those we are not disposed to afford much charity. Consider Zorin, Dr. No, or Hugo Drax. They are probably not going to turn their lives around. They will not repent and they probably are insane so education is pointless, although treatment is a possibility. They appear to be cases of hopelessly corrupted individuals. But can we, *with certainty*, determine who is hopeless and who is not? If we truly respect human beings as moral agents, then we must acknowledge the capacity for redemption and the demand that this always be considered an option, regardless of how improbable it might appear. After all, if Jaws can find redemption at the end of the film *Moonraker* by assisting Bond, it just might be possible for others.

SECTION IV

Oh, Don't Be an Idiot, 007

Knowledge and Technology

11

The Epistemology of James Bond: The Logic of Abduction

JEROLD J. ABRAMS

Abduction is, after all, nothing but guessing.
—Charles S. Peirce[1]

James Bond is a spy, an assassin, and a Commander in the Royal British Navy—but above all, he's a detective, one in a long line of fictional detectives going all the way back to Voltaire's *Zadig*. And like all good detectives, Bond seems to have special powers: somehow he's always able to figure things out in a hurry . . . always able to discover whodunit and why.

But what exactly *are* these "special powers"? Why is Bond's mind so impressive? In philosophy this question belongs to a distinct branch known as "epistemology" (or, the "theory of knowledge"). Epistemology is concerned with all of the various "problems of knowledge," each of which can be put into the form of a question: for example, "What exactly is knowledge?" and "Is it possible to be deceived about everything, as Neo is (at first) in *The Matrix*?" Our particular question here—with regard to Bond—is this: "How does the mind formulate guesses (and, more particularly, *good* guesses)?" In the history of philosophy, this question is, in fact, relatively new. Before the nineteenth century, frankly, it didn't really get much airplay (. . . just a few light skirmishes here and there). Most philosophers simply contented themselves with the notion that guessing was just a

---

[1] C.S. Peirce, "On the Logic of Drawing History from Ancient Documents," in *The Essential Peirce*, Volume 2 (Bloomington: Indiana University Press, 1998), p. 107.

chaotic process and (perhaps) somewhat "artistic"—but hardly anything with a distinct *form*, hardly anything "logical."

All of that changed, however, with the pioneering work of America's greatest philosopher, Charles S. Peirce (1839–1914). There is, in fact, a logical way in which the mind makes guesses. Peirce called it "the logic of abduction," and showed this to be precisely the logic by which all detective work operates. Indeed, Peirce was quite right—for we see this distinct logic played out in all great detective fiction—and, as we will soon see, 007 is certainly no different.

The Logic of Abduction

According to Peirce, abduction is one of three distinct forms of logic (abduction, induction, and deduction), which work as follows:

Deduction

[Assume: Premise 1]		*Rule.*—All spies have multiple aliases.
[Assume: Premise 2]		*Case.*—This man is a spy.
[Therefore:]	∴	*Result.*—This man has multiple aliases.

Induction

[Assume: Premise 1]		*Case.*—This man is a spy.
[Assume: Premise 2]		*Result.*—This man has multiple aliases.
[Therefore:]	∴	*Rule.*—All spies have multiple aliases.

Abduction

[Assume: Premise 1]		*Rule.*—All spies have multiple aliases.
[Assume: Premise 2]		*Result.*—This man has multiple aliases.
[Therefore:]	∴	*Case.*— This man is a spy.[2]

---

[2] C.S. Peirce, *The Essential Peirce,* Volume 1 (Bloomington: Indiana University Press, 1992), p. 188. I have substituted out Peirce's own example of the bean bags (induction: these beans are white and from this bag, therefore all the beans in this bag are white), for an example of spies and their aliases. But the basic logical forms are the same.

In the first form, deduction, we begin by assuming a rule, that all spies have aliases, *and* we also know (as a given) that this particular person is a spy. So, of course, it's just automatic that we know he has multiple aliases—for *that* is part of the very definition of a spy.

With induction, by contrast, we begin with a sample, maybe one spy (or perhaps three or four . . . it doesn't really matter, as long as it's not *all* of them), *and* a result of that sample, namely, that he has (or they have) multiple aliases. From here, we make a generalization: that is, we reason *beyond* our given sample to the idea that *all* spies have multiple aliases.

Now, with *abduction*, in even further contrast, we reason from a rule and a result (although typically the result comes first) to a case—that is to say, we reason to whodunit. Here's how Peirce usually puts the form of abduction (which is more helpful than the form above):

The surprising fact, C, is observed;
But if A were true, C would be a matter of course;
Hence, there is reason to suspect that A is true.[3]

So, for example, let's say I know someone (but only vaguely)—and maybe I discover he has multiple aliases. Naturally, I'm going to find this a little surprising. Immediately my abductive gears are turning; and it's not long before I guess that this guy might just be a spy. Of course, I could easily be wrong: maybe he's *not* a spy . . . maybe he's a musician, and happens to use different stage names (though, then again, maybe I'm *right* . . . and maybe he's *both,* and the "musician gig" is just a cover for throwing people "off the scent" when they discover his multiple aliases).

This is the downside of abduction: it's not exactly super-reliable (like deduction)—it's really just a guess, a "maybe." As Peirce puts it, "Deduction proves that something *must* be; Induction shows that something *actually is* operative; Abduction

---

[3] Peirce, "Pragmatism as the Logic of Abduction" (*Essential Peirce*, Volume 2, p. 231). Actually the original sources for abduction, as Peirce points out, come from Aristotle, *Prior Analytics*, Book II, Chapter 25, in *The Basic Works of Aristotle* (New York: Random House, 1941), pp. 103–04. Peirce discusses Aristotle's passage in "The Three Normative Sciences" (*Essential Peirce*, Volume 2, p. 205).

merely suggests that something *may be*." That is, as sure as a detective might appear, all he ever really has is a pretty strong "*may be*" ("The Nature of Meaning," p. 216). So I'll have to do some more investigating if I want to get to the bottom of the matter. But the initial process by which I reason to the case (that this guy may be a spy)—*this* is precisely what Bond does, and does very well . . . for, while occasionally he goes wrong, more often he is right.

Bond's Abductions in *The World Is Not Enough*

One of the best sets of abductions in the entire series of Bond films takes place in *The World Is Not Enough*—though, it's easy to miss because it happens so fast. Here Bond (Pierce Brosnan) visits a Swiss banker (in Bilbao, Spain) to obtain information and retrieve Sir Robert King's (David Calder) money. After a fight breaks out, Bond is held at gunpoint by a last remaining banker—who is then killed by a hidden sniper (allowing Bond to escape). Upon returning to MI6 Headquarters, Bond greets M (Judi Dench) and a very grateful King (who soon leaves to collect his money, which is being kept in a safe-room). Bond and M have a drink to celebrate (presumably bourbon, as that is M's drink—we know from *Goldeneye*), and discuss what happened. M is relatively satisfied with how things turned out. But Bond is still bothered by his odd getaway: by all accounts, he should be dead. Only half-listening to M, Bond says, "Interesting. But it doesn't exactly explain why someone would want me out of their office alive." Bond then begins to take a drink of his bourbon (with rocks, which he has retrieved from M's ice container). But something is wrong, and he begins to make the following series of abductions:

- First startling surprise: Bond has escaped a near-death experience—but *why?*
- Second startling surprise (three parts): Bond's drink smells funny. There is a foam in his drink, and some on his fingers.

(1) First abduction:
   a. Second startling surprise: three physical signs don't belong.

    b. But if it were true that a chemical reaction had been triggered, then the new material would be a matter of course.

    c. Hence there is reason to suspect that a chemical reaction has begun.

(2) Second abduction:

    a. New oddity: conclusion of first abduction (the chemicals are on his fingers).

    b. But if it were true that the money, which Bond handled, contained a certain chemical, then its presence on his fingers would be a matter of course.

    c. Hence there is reason to suspect that the money contains certain chemicals.

(3) Third abduction:

    a. New oddity: conclusion of second abduction (certain reactive chemicals, which foam, are currently on the money).

    b. But if it were true that urea were on the money (and reacted with the melted ice on Bond's fingers), then a foam could be matter of course.

    c. Therefore, there is reason to suspect that the money is coated in urea.

(4) Fourth abduction:

    a. New oddity: conclusion of third abduction (presence of urea on the money).

    b. But if it were true that the money is actually a compact fertilizer bomb, then the presence of urea on the money would be a matter of course.

    c. Therefore, there is reason to suspect Bond delivered a fertilizer bomb.

(5) Fifth abduction:

    a. New oddity: conclusion of fourth abduction (Bond delivered the bomb).

    b. But if it were true that someone set Bond up (as a pawn) to deliver the money (which is also a bomb), then his ignorance of the contents of his own delivery would be a matter of course.

    c. Therefore, there is reason for Bond to suspect he is being used.

(6) Sixth abduction:

    a. Return to the initial first surprise: Bond's all-too-easy Swiss bank escape.

    b. But if it were true that the sniper and bomber are one-and-the-same, then his safety would be a matter of course (the sniper keeping his own bomb in play).

    c. Hence there is reason to suspect the sniper (bomber) saved him (Bond).

The whole series of abductions (all six of them) takes Bond but a few seconds, and suddenly . . . *he's got it!* He knows why he's still alive; and he knows a bomb is in play to kill King (*now*). Bond snaps into action . . . "King! The money!" he says urgently (but coolly) to M, and takes off running after King. M hits a button on the speaker phone: "Moneypenny, stop King!" But Bond is too late. The bomb explodes and kills King. Now, Bond and M suspect King's daughter Elektra (Sophie Marceau) may be next. Of course, Bond has been badly injured, dropping from an exploding hot-air balloon, while chasing a female assassin who works for Renard (Robert Carlyle); nevertheless—charming devil that he is—he "persuades" the medical doctor at MI6 to give him a "clean bill of health" (and is allowed to investigate). M sends Bond to meet and protect Elektra, and warns him not to sleep with her . . . but, of course, *it's Bond* (and soon they are intimate).

Shortly thereafter Bond goes undercover, stealing the identity of the Russian atomic physicist Dr. Mikhail Arkov (Jeff Nuttall) to meet Elektra's kidnapper, Renard. Bond catches Renard off-guard, and holds him at gunpoint.

BOND: (*affixing a silencer to his gun*) I usually hate killing an unarmed man. Cold-blooded murder is a filthy business.
RENARD: A man tires of being executed.
BOND: But in your case, I feel nothing, just like you.
RENARD: But then again, there's no point living, if you can't feel alive.
BOND: *Huh?*

Bond is startled by Renard's last comment because he heard the exact same thing from Elektra in Valentin Zukovsky's (Robbie Coltrane) casino, where Elektra (purposefully as a pay-off) lost one million dollars on a single card. Turning to Bond (unshaken by the loss) she says all-too-casually, "There's no point in living, if you can't feel alive." *Now*—cut back to Bond (gun still pointed at Renard): *this* is why he's startled, and indeed suspicious of Elektra. But, alas, Bond has lost too much time listening to Renard: the lead physicist at the nuclear site, Christmas Jones (Denise Richards) has found him out, and led the Russians underground to take Bond into custody. Suddenly the tables have turned: *now* it is Renard who has the upper-hand—and he gloats in his reversal of fortune: "You *had* me . . . But I knew you couldn't [grabbing Bond's left shoulder, which has been badly injured] *shoulder* the responsibility." Renard (somehow) knows exactly where to hurt Bond. So, after escaping, Bond makes the following abductions:

(7) Seventh abduction:
   a. Surprises: (i) Renard and Elektra share a life motto; and (ii) Renard (like Elektra) knows of Bond's injury.
   b. But if it were true that Elektra and Renard were (and are) allies, then (i) and (ii) would be a matter of course.
   c. Hence there is reason to suspect an alliance between Elektra and Renard.

(8) Eighth abduction:
   a. Further oddity: conclusion of the seventh abduction (Elektra is allied with her kidnapper).
   b. But if it were true that Elektra has Stockholm Syndrome (a psychological break with reality, wherein a victim begins to empathize with a kidnapper), then the alliance could be a matter of course.
   c. Hence there is reason to suspect Stockholm Syndrome in Elektra.

So, Bond confronts Elektra—after breaking into her villa:

ELEKTRA: What's wrong with you? Are you crazy?
BOND: Maybe. Maybe I should ask you. After all there's no point in *living* if you can't feel alive. Isn't that right, Elektra? Isn't that your motto?

ELEKTRA: What are you talking about?

BOND: Or did you steal it from your old friend Renard?

ELEKTRA: What?

BOND: He and I had a little chat this morning—he knew all about *us*, knew about my shoulder, knew exactly where to hurt me.

Elektra (not missing a beat) quickly explains away Bond's abduction (by giving him an alternative cause for Renard's knowledge of Bond's injury). Bond had, indeed—as Elektra adeptly points out—attended King's rather high-profile funeral, wearing his arm in a sling. His injury was right there out in the open for all to see. But Bond continues to press her: "He used your exact words." Now Elektra abruptly changes the subject, and accuses Bond of using her as bait, all the while passing the time by having sex with her at his pleasure, while Renard is still hunting her. Bond is guilty enough of *that*—her accusations are correct; and a glimmer of bad feeling crosses his brow. But 007 is no fool: he knows only too well that she changed the subject because she *really is* in league with Renard . . . she *really does* have Stockholm Syndrome . . . and she *really did* kill King. Here's how Bond's abduction works:

(9) Ninth abduction:
   a. New startling surprise: Elektra changes the subject (failing to answer).
   b. But if Elektra were guilty, her lack of account would be a matter of course.
   c. Hence there is reason to suspect Elektra is guilty of killing King.

Essential to Bond's set of abductions about Elektra is his belief that it's simply too coincidental that Elektra and Renard share merely by chance the exact same (and somewhat rare) life motto. In philosophy this idea goes back to Noam Chomsky's early work in linguistics, and is still very much in play today. For example, Robert Brandom in his recent essay, "Vocabularies of Pragmatism," writes as follows:

Forty years ago Chomsky made the epochal observation that novelty is the rule, rather than the exception, in human languages. In fact, almost every sentence uttered by an adult native speaker is new—not only in the sense that that speaker has never uttered it before, but more surprisingly, also in the sense that *no one* has ever uttered it before. A relatively few hackneyed sentences may get a lot of play: "Have a nice day," "I'm hungry," "You'll be sorry," and so on. But it is exceptionally unlikely that an unquoted sentence chosen at random from an essay such as this one will ever have been uttered before.[4]

This is precisely the rule Bond uses to explain the sameness of mottos in Renard and Elektra. For, Bond knows what Chomsky knows—and he knows what Brandom is saying here: and because he knows it, now, finally, he's solved the case.

False Clues and Misguided Abductions: Bond versus Villain

So far we've considered only *one side* of 007's abductive methodology. We might call this the *positive* side of 007's method—his ability to discover whodunit. But there's also a *negative* side: for, as good as he is at making positive abductions, he is *also* quite adept at causing the villain to make bad (or, false) abductions by scattering clues and leading him on a wild-goose-chase. It is on this negative side of 007's detective methodology that we find the distinct advantage of Q . . . though, in fact, Q actually fulfills *two* basic functions for 007. First, his gadgets always provide Bond with an escape route. But second—and equally important—Q's gadgets also allow Bond to re-code the external environment, in order to force the villain to discover "false clues" and throw him (or her) off the scent (. . . and it is this second function which is related to the "negative" dimension of Bond's abductive methodology).

For example, in *Tomorrow Never Dies* Bond uses a portable fingerprint scanner, which digitally reads a fingerprint (already left behind) on a fingerprint "reader"—the reader basically serves as a kind of electronic "keyhole," and admits people with the correct fingerprints. After scanning the print off the

---

[4] Robert Brandom, "Vocabularies of Pragmatism: Naturalism, and Historicism," in Brandom, ed., *Rorty and His Critics* (New York: Blackwell, 2000), p. 175.

reader, Bond saves and then projects that print back onto the reader, and quickly gets inside. The villain is thus tricked into thinking that whoever is entering the secure site, *ought* to be entering it. Or, take *The Man with the Golden Gun.* Here Bond wears an artificial third nipple in order to make others think he is, in fact, Scaramanga (who is known for this trait). Again, Bond is using technology in order to cause his opponent to make false abductions. Of course, these are fairly simple examples. But consider a much more elaborate technique of deception, namely, Bond's car in *Die Another Day*, which R (John Cleese in the role of Q's assistant and successor) proudly "unveils": "Aston Martin call it the [V 12] Vanquish, we call it the Vanish." R continues: "Adaptive camouflage. Tiny cameras on all sides project the image they see onto a light-emitting polymer skin on the opposite side. To the casual eye it's as good as invisible." Certainly Q branch has outdone itself—for in the world of detective work, nothing cloaks a spy better than the illusion of absence . . . that is, nothing cloaks a spy better than "nothingness" (Bond's own apparent non-existence).

Nevertheless, as good as Bond is at discovering clues and laying false evidence, Bond and the villain are always pretty evenly matched. And they both use very similar techniques: they both manipulate the trail of clues they leave behind, in order to cause one another to make false abductions. Consider the following example of head-to-head negative abductive methods in *The World Is Not Enough.* Bond and Jones realize a bomb is in play within Elektra's (empty) oil pipeline. They enter the pipeline and ride a jet sled through the line, to chase and defuse the bomb, which itself is riding a jet sled within the pipeline. Once Jones realizes the bomb is non-nuclear, Bond tells her to let it explode—which she does, but does not understand Bond's plan. (Meanwhile, M and Elektra are watching via satellite, and believe that Bond and Jones are killed in the explosion.)

JONES: Do you want to explain why you did that? I could've stopped that bomb. You almost killed us.

BOND: I *did* kill us. She thinks we're dead, and she thinks she got away with it.

JONES: Do you want to put that in English for those of us who don't speak 'Spy'?

Elektra blows up her own pipeline because, as Bond puts it, "it makes her look innocent. The explosion covers up the theft of the plutonium. And they make it look like a terrorist attack." So, Elektra is trying to force MI6 to make a false abduction—that *someone else* blew up her pipeline, which puts to rest any doubt that she is innocent (doubts Bond has now formally voiced to Elektra and M). But Bond counters Elektra by making *her* abduct that he, Bond (M's best spy), is dead—and *this* now affords him the element of surprise. Once again he is cloaked inside the illusion of non-being.

We find the same sort of standoff in *Tomorrow Never Dies* where Elliot Carver (Jonathan Pryce) uses a secret encoder to cause a satellite to give false signals to a British naval warship, the HMS Devonshire. The crew think they are safe in international waters—contrary to the Chinese MiG's (correct) warnings that the Devonshire is actually in Chinese waters (only eleven miles off the Chinese coast). Meanwhile, the Carver Media Group, using a stealthboat, launches a "seadrill" (a form of torpedo) to drill a hole into the hull of the Devonshire, sinking it. Being in a stealthboat, moreover, the Carver Group escapes radar (once again, and like Bond, cloaked in "absence"), which makes it look like the Chinese MiGs (who now have a perfectly good motive) dropped a torpedo into the water, sinking the Devonshire. "The British will think it's a Chinese aerial torpedo." So, the Carver group has caused the Chinese to make the (false) abduction that the British Devonshire has hostile intent (being in Chinese waters)—and the British to make the (false) abduction that the Chinese *attacked* the Devonshire. Having caused all of this, the Carver Media Group (based out of Hamburg) has *also* created the perfect breaking story to launch its new satellite network. That is, Elliot Carver has caused the public to make the (false) abduction that (the newspaper) *Tomorrow* is simply honestly reporting the story—rather than also (dishonestly) creating it. Indeed, Carver recognizes his power to manipulate the external environment—seeing it for what it is: information to be decoded, yes, but more importantly, material to be *recoded* (again and again). According to Carver, *that* is the real power of the modern world: "Words are the new weapons, satellites, the new artillery."

Nevertheless, Carver makes a critical mistake when he sinks the Devonshire, and then turns around and advertises it.

BOND: There is one strange thing. When I called our contact in Saigon, he said the Vietnamese only found our sailors three hours ago.

CHARLES ROBINSON (Colin Salmon): How'd they get the paper out so fast?

BOND: Somebody at *Tomorrow* knew before the Vietnamese government did.

M: How much do you know about Elliot Carver, 007.

Here, Bond and M are making the abduction at the same time. They begin with a startling event: the newspaper, *Tomorrow*, printed a story about the Devonshire even before MI6 knew about it—and *that* is virtually impossible . . . *unless* . . . it were true that Carver, who runs *Tomorrow*, were linked to the sinking of the Devonshire. And now M and Bond are hot on the trail of clues.

The Bond Advantage: Games of Chance and the Play of Musement

Of course, it was only a matter of time before Bond figured out whodunit. The basic plot is always the same: Carver, Elektra, Renard, Scaramanga—they simply cannot win . . . we know *that* for sure (even before seeing the film). But, then again, that is not why we watch 007 do what he does. For, rather than *that* Bond will win, we watch 007 films because we want to know just *how* he will win . . . *how* he will discover whodunit . . . which clues will give the game away, and why. In other words, we want to know why Bond is simply *better* (at a methodological level) than the villain. For, in a game of spy versus spy, where the two are close to evenly matched, there must be *something* about Bond's mind that always seems to give him the edge.

There are, I think, two distinct advantages that give Bond the edge. First, Bond is excellent at both causing false abductions and making correct abductions, while the villain's method is lopsided: his talent lies mainly in causing false abductions. Second, Bond's mind excels at positive abductions precisely because it is more agile, more plastic—in a word, more "playful." With regard to the first point, think of it this way. It's pretty obvious the villain's method is to lay false clues. But when it comes to making his own abductions, very often he simply doesn't have the skills. Take for example, *Tomorrow Never Dies*, when Carver is trying to figure out who Bond is, but can't. So he relies on his techno-terrorist, Mr. Gupta (Ricky Jay), who researches Bond's record:

> **GUPTA:** Bond's got a perfect employment record. Ten years. He's crossed every T. He's dotted every I.
> **CARVER:** Which means?
> **GUPTA:** Government agent. I call it Gupta's Law of Creative Anomalies. If it sounds too good to be true, it always is.

Carver doesn't see the problem with Bond's squeaky clean record—so, there's no anomaly, and hence no abduction. But Mr. Gupta is used to this sort of thing, and has even invented his own rule for handling such surprises. Indeed, there's a pretty good reason why Carver (and Bond villains, more generally) aren't very good at making positive abductions. Carver's basic role isn't really about *discovering* new clues—his job isn't to figure out whodunit, because *he's* the one whodunit.

Umberto Eco calls the kind of thing Mr. Gupta does here "creative abduction." Eco distinguishes creative abduction (wherein the detective invents the rule) from "overcoded" and "undercoded abductions." Overcoded abductions occur when the abduction is obvious: it's easy to infer from a footprint that someone stepped there. Undercoded abductions are harder: other options are possible. We must select one from among the possible rules . . . for example, the one I gave above: we may infer from multiple aliases that the individual is a spy, or perhaps a musician, or perhaps an actor, or some combination of these.[5]

Bond, however, is a master of both ends of abduction—discovering true clues, and laying false ones: so, his method is more internally diverse. And this diversity of understanding and control allows him to keep more possibilities in play at all times. He's able to crawl quickly inside the villain's mind—whereas the villain can't do the same (not nearly as well anyway) with Bond. Put very simply, Bond has a far richer—far more playful—abductive imagination. And here (in making this point about "play") I draw considerably on Eco's insightful

---

[5] See Eco, "Horns, Hooves, Insteps," in *The Sign of Three: Dupin, Holmes, Peirce*, edited by Eco and Thomas Sebeok (Bloomington: Indiana University Press, 1983), pp. 206–07.

analysis of the structure of the Bond story, in his book, *The Role of the Reader* (Chapter 6, "Narrative Structures in Fleming").[6] Here Eco analyzes the basic structure of the 007 story, and highlights the importance of "Play Situations and the Story as a 'Game'" (*Role of the Reader*, pp. 156–161). The point is this: a Bond film (or Bond novel) is—at its most fundamental level— *not* really a story about good versus evil, *nor* one of East versus West, nor *even* one of capitalism versus socialism . . . but is, in fact, a game of chance and strategy. As Eco puts it, "This interpretation of the story in terms of a game is not accidental. The books of Fleming are dominated by situations that we call 'play situations'" (*Role of the Reader*, p. 155). Eco continues further on: "Bond always gambles and wins, against the Villain or some vicarious figure. . . . here it must be said that, if these games occupy a prominent space, it is because they form a reduced and formalized model of the more general play situation that is the novel. The novel . . . is fixed as a sequence of 'moves' inspired by the code and constituted according to a perfectly prearranged scheme" (*Role of the Reader*, p. 156).

I certainly agree with Eco on this point, but I also think the analysis of play should be extended a little further—for, just as Bond is a better player than the villain in the casino, so too is he a better player in the detective's "game of abduction." Indeed, *this* is the distinctly 007 advantage—his ability to play the game that Peirce (in his analysis of abduction) calls "musement" . . . and defines as the "pure play" of consciousness (which occurs *just before* the "flash" of an abduction) (*Essential Peirce*, Volume 2, p. 436). In the simplest terms, according to Peirce, good guesses come from good play: the better we are at allowing the material of the mind to play freely, the better our abductions will be. So, Bond must be able to play with the elements of perception and memory, continually placing them in alternate orders (always looking for the right fit)—all the while maintaining a (vague) focus on the problem at hand ... (patiently, quietly, calmly) ... until suddenly . . . *voilà! He's got it!*

This is no easy process, and it takes a great deal of practice to master—playing with all the elements of thought. And just as hard is the amassing of so much information and so many

---

[6] Umberto Eco, "Narrative Structures in Fleming," in *The Role of the Reader: Explorations in the Semiotics of Texts* (Bloomington: Indiana University Press, 1984).

concepts, which Bond can somehow summon up even at a moment's notice. It's no accident that Bond's mind is incredibly "encyclopedic" (highly detailed and highly organized)—for, the more comprehensive his mind, the more concepts he can apply to a clue. In the case of Bond, this knowledge comes from two sources: the Ivory Tower and the criminal underground. With regard to the first source, Bond is extremely well educated. In *You Only Live Twice* he says he studied Oriental Languages at Cambridge. And in *The World Is Not Enough* he also says he studied at Oxford. This allows him to make the (above) abductions about the urea bomb and Stockholm Syndrome (having knowledge of chemistry, electricity, psychology, and terrorism).

The second source is Bond's distinctly hands-on style of investigation, which directly contrasts with the typical Bond-villain who performs much of his work through others. Remember in *Tomorrow Never Dies* that it is Dr. Kaufman (Vincent Schiavelli)—*not* Carver—who murders Paris (Teri Hatcher) and plans to make it look as if Bond killed her; and (again) it is Mr. Gupta who makes the abduction that Bond is a government agent. Bond, however, works alone: he is always on the scene, examining the evidence himself, always close to the clues. And, really, there is no environment he does not understand or control: he is at home on land, underwater, underground, in the air, in the desert, even in outer space in *Moonraker*. So, he is better than the villain at reading (and, indeed, manipulating) different kinds of signs—and, as a consequence, has a much richer abductive imagination.

To be sure, Bond's mind is no pedantic catalog of bits of data, all haphazardly shuffled about on a whim—not at all: 007 has that unique detective ability to draw from a vast array of possibilities the right rule to explain the case in the flash of an instant. And this process, like his manner, in general, is handled with the remarkable admixture of art and strategy that defines his very character as a great "player" in a grand game of sex, crime, and rationality. *That* is his advantage . . . and *that* is why he always wins.[7]

---

[7] I am very grateful to James B. South, Jacob M. Held, Bill Irwin, and Elizabeth Cooke for reading and commenting on an earlier version of this chapter, and for many helpful conversations on James Bond. Of course, any mistakes which remain are my own.

12

James Bond and Q: Heidegger's Technology, or "You're Not a Sportsman, Mr. Bond"

STEVEN ZANI

One of the most enduring aspects of the James Bond legacy is his relationship to technology. A typical Bond movie contains at least one extended scene with Bond receiving a tutorial from Q, his technological mentor and supply source, on the virtues and limitations of the most recent spy equipment.[1] The effectiveness of the scene, and the subsequent use of equipment later in the film, has struck a chord with audiences. Bond's "gadgets" are recognized as one of the functional characteristics of heroism, and have been duplicated by many other films—most recently, for example, where the scene is carbon copied in *Van Helsing*, and in *XXX*, or less directly in movies like *Blade* and its sequels. Perhaps the best proof of the essential quality of technology in Bond is that it appears in parodies such as *Spy Hard* and the *Austin Powers* series. Bond's use of machinery has clearly passed into cinematic function, or stereotype.

A number of investigations of Bond stereotypes have been undertaken over the years. One of the earliest and most noteworthy is a 1966 article by Umberto Eco, "The Narrative Structure in Fleming," where he suggested that the Bond narratives have a consistent pattern like that of a Fairy Tale, which results in a number of observations, such as "Bond is the Cavalier and the Villain is the Dragon."[2] This early struc-

---

[1] Q is not quite as definitive a character in all of Ian Fleming's novels, though the emphasis on technology is still generally present.

[2] "The Narrative Structure in Fleming" appeared in English originally in *The Bond Affair*, edited by Umberto Eco and Oreste Del Buono (London: MacDonald, 1966), though it

turalist approach to Bond offered a great deal to readers in terms of revealing patterns, but it ignores the contemporary technological elements that are so clearly a major part of Bond's enduring popularity. If the Bond films and books offer consistent messages and patterns, where technology can be seen as one of many repetitive structural elements involved in the works, then what do those repetitive elements mean? How does technology function in the James Bond films, and what can James Bond tell us about our own relationship to technology? If Bond films relate to machinery in a particular way, what does that say about humanity, and how we should use our own machines? What does it mean that Bond is defined by technology?

Heidegger's View of Technology

The answer to these questions can be found by looking at technology through the lens of twentieth-century German philosopher Martin Heidegger. Throughout his career, Heidegger emphasized that the nature of human beings was connected significantly to the technological. Technology is essential to understanding how people may be differentiated from animals. While it is arguable that some animals employ technology on a limited scale—monkeys use rocks for digging, gulls drop shellfish onto rocks to open their shells—no animal invokes technology so systematically or completely as an element of life as the human being. As Heidegger puts it succinctly, "Technology is a human activity."[3]

Why is technology so important to us? Heidegger argues that technology *is* us. Technology is not simply the use of tools, or the building of machines. On its most fundamental level, it is *Techné*, a Greek term he relied on in order to remind his readers that technology should be, as it was in the classical era, associated with craftsmanship and artistic endeavor. More comprehensive than simply using tools, for Heidegger, technol-

---

has been reprinted a number of times since. This quotation is taken from a reprint of the article in *Popular Culture: Past and Present*, edited by Bernard Waites (London: Routledge, 1989), p. 260.

[3] "The Question Concerning Technology" from *Basic Writings* (New York: Harper and Row, 1977), p. 288.

ogy is very closely related to *Wissen*, wisdom.[4] Technology is the concrete form of any application of human intelligence. Not only a mark of difference between us and animals, it is the "ins-Werk-setzen," the "setting to work" of life itself. For Heidegger, *techne* is a word that describes man's relationship to the world, and technology is employed in some basic sense every time a human thinks. When one looks at a rock and sees that it is not just a rock, rather something that could be grasped and used, that is technology in operation. Take, for example, *You Only Live Twice*, where an ordinary piece of stone statuary, artwork in the room, is picked up by Bond and used to bash the skull of his opponent in combat. For Heidegger, such an action can be extremely profound, for taking up and using the things around us, we engage both in revealing the world (for example, seeing the statue, in Bond's case), but also in creating it, making it into something it wasn't before (such as a weapon). The rock, or statue, becomes something new, and this is technology in operation, namely, a project that forges not only new objects but an entirely new universe.

Disagreeing with the Greeks

For Heidegger, taking up the technological—when one understands a rock or any other object as more than "just" a rock—is a creative as well as a perceptive act. While many of the Greek philosophers from Plato onward argued that there is an eternal world of Forms, or Ideas, that our real world only imitates (the way that a shadow is only the imitation of the more substantial object that produced it), Heidegger disagreed with Plato and argued that the Platonic philosophers misunderstood how language functions in actually producing reality ("The Question," p. 312).

For Heidegger, the work of technology is not just humanity recognizing the world, but rather a process of shaping and

---

[4] A more elaborate explanation of the connection between technology and thinking can be found in Philippe Lacoue-Labarthe's *Heidegger, Art, and Politics* (Cambridge, Massachusetts: Blackwell, 1990), particularly his chapter "Techne," pp. 53–59, which is the source of the material in quotation marks in the remainder of this paragraph. Lacoue-Labarthe's book is a systematic look at the relationship of Heidegger's work to fascist politics.

framing that changes the very nature of what it works upon. Think of the large collection of items that Bond uses in his fight with a henchman at the health farm in *Never Say Never Again*. In various moments of the fight, Bond uses weights, a door, a blanket, and even his own urine specimen as a weapon to attack his assailant. Each of these instances is the same as the actions that occurred the first time prehistoric man picked up a rock to smash open a walnut. The rock was not seen for what it was, some kind of eternal "form" of the rock as Plato would suggest, but rather the rock was made into something it wasn't before. What was once only rock is now also a device for procuring food, what was once a blanket for warmth becomes a net to wrap around Bond's opponent, and for Heidegger these newly created tools don't just mimic the eternal, Platonic "form" of the tools, rather their very use is what brings them into existence.

The implications of this understanding of technology, beyond the usefulness for what we can do with rocks, can be seen more clearly in Heidegger's later argument that technology isn't just what we use to produce a better world. Technology doesn't just help humanity; on some fundamental level it *is* humanity; it's the way that humanity reveals and becomes itself. For Heidegger, the simple act of basic craftsmanship, or manipulating things around us (what many would not consider particularly creative, or innovative), is a creating and enframing of life. When each of us ties a shoe, uses a screwdriver, or writes a sentence, we are entering into a relationship where we both define and make the world (we create knots, boxes, and books that did not previously exist), and even more importantly we create ourselves (as shoe wearers, builders, pencil users, etc.). The important questions of life, what is a human being and what is the place of humanity in the world, can be answered by reference to technology.

Think again of Bond, this time in *Die Another Day*. When he sees a pair of binoculars in an office, he immediately procures them, not just because they'll help him as typical spy gear for surveillance—which he does use them for—but also because they can become one element of his newly invented disguise as an ornithologist. In the same film, during a fight scene in a hospital, Bond turns on the Magnetic Resonance Imagery (MRI) machine, not because he needs a scan, but because he knows it will magnetize the room, and disarm his opponent. Bond is representative of the quintessential human in relationship to technology. In these examples he accomplishes his purposes, but in doing so he reveals an understanding of the dynamic nature of reality, and the importance of maintaining an open relationship to the world.

If technology is so important, then, the question for Heidegger is whether this *Technê*, all of our collective creative endeavor, will always be positive. There is, he argues, a possibility of danger in technology, particularly in how it has developed in the modern era, the danger of turning the world into something fit only for use value. If people further technologize the world, they may enact a process of appropriation and domination, and in that transformation from one world to another, humanity could lose something valuable that might otherwise be retained.

Technology in the Movies

For a concrete example of how technology can function either as a specific danger or as salvation, we need to look no farther than the world of the movies. Countless films and books represent technology in either a positive or negative light, and the specific agenda of any number of films is to argue about technology on one side or the other. Think of the many anti-technology films[5] of the past decades. Contemporary film heroes frequently achieve victory by rejecting guns and machines in favor of direct physical combat. Stallone, Schwarzenegger, and countless other cinematic icons have fought the robotic or technologized enemies of the world with their "natural" bows and arrows (*Rambo: First Blood II*) or wooden forest snares (*Predator*), and many recent films similarly play on fears of cloning and genetic experimentation (*6th Day*, *Replicant*). On the other side of this equation are the multiple films that glorify technology, using it to enact positive encounters in space (*Contact*), overcome illnesses and disabilities (*At First Sight*) or embrace freedom and democracy (*I, Robot*).

---

[5] A tradition that began in film at least as early as Fritz Lang's 1927 masterpiece *Metropolis*, though *Metropolis* owes its themes to a long literary history, such as the beautiful but unsatisfying female robot of E.T.A. Hoffmann's 1817 short story "The Sandman."

Where does James Bond fit within the technology paradigm? Is Bond for or against technology? Rather than providing a simple answer to that question, Bond movies play out the relationship of humanity and technology on many levels. These movies present Bond as the ultimate representative of our technological selves. Any look at the books already dedicated to the Bond phenomenon will reveal Bond's status as a kind of archetypal human, which people see as forceful, decisive, and capable of mastering any situation.[6] But there's much more going on in a typical James Bond movie than the glorification of either humanity or technology. In Bond movies, both the hero and enemies are skillful, and both can be described as technological. Bond may use spy equipment constantly, but think of the hidden fortresses of the many Bond villains, or the metallic teeth of the recurring character Jaws. Since villains use technology just like Bond, what's the difference?

The answer can be seen in how each character uses that technology, and there is a lesson here in the way that Bond films differ from the typical techno-oriented films that saturate the market. Bond films draw out a distinction that Heidegger made, revealing the problem of living as technological selves. For Heidegger, when people have an incorrect relationship to technology, they relate to the world only in a way that turns everything into a stockpile, a "standing-reserve" that serves no purpose but consumption and control. As a result, people themselves are reduced to nothing but property holders. Heidegger explains that this danger is two-fold.

> As soon as what is unconcealed no longer concerns man even as object, but exclusively as standing-reserve, and man in the midst of objectlessness is nothing but the orderer of the standing-reserve, then he comes to the very brink of a precipitous fall, that is, he comes to the point where he himself will have to be taken as standing-reserve. Meanwhile, man, precisely as the one so threatened, exalts himself to the posture of the lord of the earth. In this way the illusion comes to prevail that everything man encounters exists only insofar as it is his construct. ("The Question," p. 308)

---

[6] Most people do not immediately describe Bond with the negative characteristics that Fleming himself had also originally intended for his hero, such as the description "brutal and cold" from the opening chapter of the first Bond novel, *Casino Royale* (New York: Macmillan, 1953), p. 15.

Technology has progressed in just such a dangerous fashion. With each machine we build, we continue to increase our power and capacity for manipulating the world. With each era we move more earth, dive deeper into the oceans, and peer farther into the heavens. But in accomplishing our ends, every mountain becomes an ore mine, every forest a lumberyard, and every planet a potential colony. In the process, we transform ourselves into nothing but owners and stockholders. We become the things we own, and we have no life outside of them.

In taking more and more of the world as our own, we transform it to our purpose, either by using it, or simply by observing it and fitting it into our perceptive categories. But these categories and transformations bear consequences. Take, for example, gold. While an animal might ignore a yellow rock on the ground, for people in our culture that simple rock has become worth killing over, or spending a lifetime accumulating. Virtually every Bond villain is an example of the negative consequences of technology gone awry, but Auric Goldfinger is perhaps the best Bond example of the attempt to appropriate the world through gold in particular.

Goldfinger demonstrates a technological relationship that is domineering and static. His use of gold is always controlling, and always ends in death, including the death of his beautiful assistant Jill Masterson (memorably suffocated by gold body paint), and eventually even his own. With Goldfinger, then, we can see the attendant problems that come from something as simple as recognizing gold as different from the rocks that surround it. Through technology, we organize our world, and assume mastery over our universe, but that mastery is only an illusion. We transform the world with our tools, but Heidegger warns us that we can also make ourselves into nothing but tools in the process. We sacrifice our lives to the objects we create, and in the process we can become nothing but static placeholders of land and space, the keepers of the objects. While we assume that we rule what we hold, the reverse is true—all of our actions are controlled by the necessity of maintaining what we have, and getting more.

The World Is Not Enough

Heidegger argued that this dangerous use of technology began with the philosophers Plato and Aristotle, whose methods of thinking have dominated the world from Ancient Greece to the present day. If the goal in a Platonic-Aristotelian world is to recognize eternal forms in the things of this world, and more clearly understand them, then human beings, in such a world, can be nothing but mere tools, like hammers or screwdrivers. They become objects devoted to a singular task, forever seeking more knowledge, forever taking and holding more property in their grasp, in an attempt to come closer to Truth. Perhaps it's no coincidence that one of the world's greatest conquerors, Alexander, was a student of Aristotle, whose approach to examining and categorizing the natural world became the foundation of the modern scientific method. Science and Philosophy, and the grasp they take upon the natural world, are the intellectual version of Alexander's conquering armies.

But it is exactly here, in relation to technology and its potential to conquer the world, where Bond films play out their plot lines, and where Bond and his enemies reveal their differences. Bond villains routinely use their technology in the dangerous fashion that Heidegger warns of. In scene after scene, scheme after scheme, they reveal aggression, a drive for domination and a need for complete control. With an antagonistic relationship to the world, they murder for pleasure (Hugo Drax in *Moonraker*), revenge (Franz Sanchez in *Licence to Kill*) or to eliminate competition (Max Zorin in *A View to a Kill*). In short, they use their intellect and technology in an expansionist, oppressive fashion, and one that is the opposite of Bond's reaction in the same situations.

The film *Moonraker* is exemplary in demonstrating what makes a Bond villain. In *Moonraker*, Hugo Drax hatches a plan to kill the earth's entire population from the safety of his hidden base, orbiting high above the planet. As Bond is flown in for his preliminary meeting with Drax on Earth, he quizzes the voluptuous pilot about the man and his estate. The pilot looks out over Drax's property and smugly explains, "What he doesn't own he doesn't want." With this description, Drax takes his place amongst the stable of Bond villains who reveal their maniacal self-interest in appropriating the world around them.

Drax later invites Bond outdoors to join him hunting. As servants flush birds from the surrounding territory, Drax announces the pleasure he takes in the outdoors, proclaiming that shooting is a "really good sport." Bond replies "unless you're a pheasant."

When Bond finally takes the gun, he deliberately misses the birds in flight and kills an assassin hiding in the tree line. The message is clear in terms of differentiating Bond from Drax. Drax is a hunter, who kills for the sake of amusement. Bond also takes up the rifle—he uses technology—but his relationship is different. He refuses to hunt for mere sport because he acknowledges the effect upon the target, the pheasant. Bond has a different understanding of his relationship to the world around him, and when he does finally shoot his target, it is a gesture of preservation and defense.

Later in the film, the same gesture is taken again when Bond is vaulted into a pool of water by Drax's machinery. The pool, a natural-looking stone depression that is actually constructed by Drax, contains a large python, which Bond dispatches with a poison pen borrowed from his CIA counterpart.

> **DRAX:** Mr. Bond, you defy all my attempts to plan an amusing death for you. You're not a sportsman, Mr. Bond. Why did you break off your encounter with my pet python?
> **BOND:** I discovered he had a crush on me.

Bond is again defensive in his use of technology. If Drax's sole agenda in planning Bond's death is his own amusement, the same goal of selfish amusement can be used to describe his plan to destroy the world and remake it in his own image. With Bond, by contrast, we have the perfect relationship to technology, the man whose aggression (and perhaps sexuality—he acquired the poison pen from lover-compatriot Dr. Goodhead) allow him to take up technology to accomplish his ends, but unlike Drax he does not do it at the expense of the material he oversees, nor does he allow the world to appropriate him in return. In a cinematic oeuvre where both hero and villain are technologized, Bond's relationship is one of necessity rather than sport.

That's Détente

Bond's different, less oppressive, relationship to the world explains, as well, why he's popular with audiences and readers despite being a figure that is traditionally hated and feared, an assassin. *For Your Eyes Only* systematically reveals how Bond can be an assassin but not a murderer, precisely because he relates to the world differently than the villains around him. The Bond girl of the film, Melina Havelock, tries to take revenge upon the villain Kristatos for killing her parents. Bond convinces her not to kill him in cold blood by repeating a Chinese aphorism, "Before setting out on revenge, you first dig two graves." The danger of technology—in Heidegger's sense of the interactions we have when we take up a relation to the world—is that we will always become that which we do. Those who enact revenge become nothing but revenge itself. In killing their object, they become death.

For Your Eyes Only explains the appropriate relationship to the world in even more technological terms, however, throughout its plot. Early in the film, Bond and Melina flee an assassin's henchmen. As they approach Bond's Lotus Esprit, they watch as two men smash open the "Burglar Protected" window, which explodes the car and kills the men in the process. Bond is blasé about the loss, and quickly switches focus to another avenue of escape (Melina's less glamorous Citroen 2CV). The scene demonstrates the use of technology—in the car itself, and in the overly exacting alarm system—but it also demonstrates Bond's willingness to abandon the objects and devices of his world when necessary. As Fleming remarks in the novel *Thunderball*, "Bond refused to be owned by any car. A car, however, splendid, was a means of locomotion . . ."[7] This comment can apply equally to all of the gadgets in Bond's life.

Later in *For Your Eyes Only*, Bond will even push a car off a cliff in order to kill an assassin known as "The Dove." But it is Bond's willingness to relinquish any technology, not simply cars, which marks him as different from the obsessive villains around him. The movie ends when Bond finally manages to wrest the ATAC away from Kristatos. Although now in possession of the long-desired machine, his success is not timely enough to prevent the arrival of Soviet General Gogol, who also holds claim to the device. Instead of relinquishing the ATAC to Gogol, Bond hurls it off the mountainside, where it disintegrates upon hitting the rocks below. "That's *détente*," proclaims Bond, and he and Gogol both smile. Technology, when it would lead

---

[7] In *Bonded Fleming* (New York: Viking Press, 1965), p. 49.

to absolute control or domination, is refused.[8] For all of the reliance on technology, a repetitive characteristic in these films is his refusal to cling to it, even technology like the ATAC that provides enormous power and control. Bond demonstrates instead a capacity to relinquish that which is no longer useful to him, or that which would only result in an escalation of conflict. In Bond films, the goal is not control, or the collection of artifacts, but rather the easing of tension between opposing parties, or tension between oneself and one's environment. Bond's relationship to technology is both a willingness to use it when it accomplishes that purpose, but to allow it to recede when it does not.

From Russia with Love

A closer look at Bond villains reveals the technological relationship further. A common misconception held by casual Bond viewers is that the movies only represent the politics of the Cold War; that they focus on a Western spy's struggle against Soviet spies and Soviet aggression. In fact, any systematic look at Bond movies reveals the opposite. Soviet spies are usually not the aggressors in Bond films. Rather, they are shown as cautious and reasonable adversaries with an agenda not considerably different from their British counterparts. The central villains in Bond films are usually ambitious despots who use the Cold War political situation, or any political situation, in order to manipulate others for their own gain. Greed and control are their primary characteristics. Many Bond plots involve an attempt either to decimate the world's population outright, or to accomplish the same thing by pitting superpowers against one another and goading them into an accidental World War through deception. However, it is not the Soviets who are the monsters of the films, but rather individuals who pervert the resources of the world in an attempt to hold everything as their own personal stockpile.

This particularity of Bond villains is telling, for it demonstrates the technological agenda of Bond films. Governments

---

[8] Both Bond and Gogol participate in this refusal, for even if Gogol was present in order to claim the device, he is not particularly saddened at its loss, nor does he exact revenge upon Bond for its destruction. The Soviets in Bond films may also participate in a correct relationship to the technology.

and political enemies are not, in and of themselves, evil in nature, and villains are not defined by virtue of politics or nationality—Bond villains are multiple in national and racial origins. *From Russia with Love*, a movie where some Russians are villains and some are heroes, easily reveals that the Bond agenda is not a nationalist one, but the movie also contains a casual scene that succinctly explains the appropriate relation to technology. Early in the film, Bond meets his driver at the airport and asks for help with his cigarette.

> **BOND:** Can I borrow a match?
> **DRIVER:** I use a lighter.
> **BOND:** That's better still.
> **DRIVER:** Until they go wrong.
> **BOND:** Exactly.

Later in the film, we discover that the scene is not as casual as it seems, because it's repeated, word for word, when Bond meets other people in other locations. What is happening in these scenes in terms of plot is that the agents are exchanging passwords with one another, identifying themselves and ensuring that some other agent has not sabotaged their meeting with a replacement. Metaphorically, however, the words are the epitome of the Bond relationship to the technological. Bond favors the lighter over the match when available, but he also knows the limitations that come with using it. The agents around him reveal their status as agents not because they belong to one country or another, or share in some announced political agenda, but because, by repeating the phrase, they reveal that they share in the same Bond philosophy and agree with the metaphor.

Bond villains, on the other hand, do not share this agenda, and it is inevitably their downfall. Red Grant, the central antagonist of *From Russia with Love*, reveals his technological expertise early in the film, as he kills a man with a garrote-device attached to his watch, but ultimately it is his greed for the sovereigns in Bond's suitcase that turn the tables and allow Bond's victory.[9] Whether they use technology or not, the primary goal

---

[9] There are many occasions where Bond, by contrast, shows his completely indifferent attitude about money, for example in *Octopussy*, when he throws a large collection of

of Bond villains is greed and control. Bond obviously also uses technology, his victory over Grant is accomplished with his briefcase, but he is satisfied with whatever object will help him in the moment. In the film's end, Bond defeats the final villain, Rosa Klebb. Klebb employs technology, with a poison-tipped dagger in her shoe, but Bond defeats her with what he finds in his immediate area, namely, a chair.

Perhaps the World Is Enough

Bond, then, is our hero not just because he uses technology, but because he has a particular relation to it. Comfortable in virtually every setting, Bond employs technology not in opposition to the world around him. All the Bond movies take place in multiple settings: cities, mountains, skies, deserts, and oceans. In each case we have Bond using cars, skis, planes, parachutes, and boats to navigate them. As he glibly and successfully flies, drives, skis, and sails, we see that the world is something to be enjoyed, no matter what the setting, with technology always both a complement and supplement. Think of the Bond villains, who are defined by how they take the natural world and mold it into their own image. They occupy volcanoes (*You Only Live Twice*), mountaintop fortresses (*For Your Eyes Only*), arctic ice palaces (*Die Another Day*), or remote island paradises (*The Man with the Golden Gun*). By contrast, Bond travels throughout multiple settings without distorting them into versions of himself. He doesn't destroy or control what he oversees. And as we watch the nefarious schemes of multiple villains crumble to the ground (along with their isolated fortresses, no longer tainting the natural world they infringed upon) we can see the hope of a relationship to technology that pre-dates Plato and Aristotle. In Bond, we see freedom rather than control, and a world where nature and technology help to define humanity, instead of consuming it.

We might all be better served if our own relationship to the world, and the technology we use to mediate that world, were just as Bond's. But that, then, is exactly the fantasy that makes the films so popular. And if none of us has the capacity to be

---

currency into the air behind his vehicle, in order to impede those chasing him, remarking "Easy come, easy go."

James Bond, perhaps learning to have the proper relationship to technology is the beginning step towards becoming the agent who meets Bond at the airport. If we can learn to recite the encoded mantra, if we can realize and share in Bond's non-oppressive relation to the world, then humanity itself will change. We may then begin to dwell in a world of enjoyment, where we use our tools when necessary, rather than having our tools use us. In such a world, Bond would hear our code words, hand us our lighters, and say "Exactly."

13

James Bond and the Philosophy of Technology: It's More than Just the Gadgets of Q Branch

WILLIAM J. McKINNEY

"Secret agent man, they've given you a number, and taken away your name." This popular Johnny Rivers line from his 1966 song, "Secret Agent Man," (made popular again in the Bond-esque spoofs of the Mike Myers *Austin Powers* series) points to a philosophically important notion. The act of naming something gives the party granting the name a significant power over the object being named. This act sets that "something" in a context which makes it a means to an end. In effect, it becomes a tool. When the "secret agent man" had his name taken away, he effectively became a tool, a piece of technology.

Looking at the distinction between the names "James Bond," and of course, "007" we will find that by distinguishing between James Bond and 007, we have James Bond the man and 007, a weapon used by the British government. We will take a look at Bond's interactions with Miss Moneypenny, his enemies, Q, and, most importantly, M, in the films *Dr. No, Goldfinger, Live and Let Die,* and *Die Another Day* in order to demonstrate that while James Bond is very much a human being, 007 is a technological construction, used by the British to achieve their ends around the world.

Pay Attention, 007: The Technology of Bond

While our most commonly used connotation of "technology" is that of devices or tools, an expanded notion defines "technology" as also referring to techniques and skills. Finally, "technology" is expanded to include any means to an end, making it possible for us to see how both James Bond the man, and 007 the agent of the British government, exist simultaneously.

To talk of James Bond and technology seems almost too obvious. Technological gadgets have become one of the highlights of the film series. In *Dr. No*, we see Bond's introduction to his most familiar technological device, his handgun. Consider this exchange, the first that we would ever see with M and Major Boothroyd (who would later become Q).

> **M:** Take off your jacket. Give me your gun. Yes, I thought so, this damn Beretta again. I've told you about this before. You tell him, for the last time.
>
> **MAJOR BOOTHROYD:** Nice and light . . . in a lady's handbag. No stopping power.
>
> **M:** Any comment, 007?
>
> **JAMES BOND:** I disagree, Sir. I have used the Beretta for ten years. I've never missed with it yet.
>
> **M:** Maybe not, but it jammed on you last job and you spent six months in the hospital in consequence. If you carry a double-0 number, it means you're licensed to kill, not get killed. And another thing, since I've been head of MI6 there's been a forty percent drop in double-0 operative casualties, and I want it to stay that way. You'll carry the Walther, unless of course you'd prefer to go back to standard intelligence duties.
>
> **JAMES BOND:** No, Sir. I would not.
>
> **M:** Then from now on you carry a different gun. Show him, Armorer.
>
> **MAJOR BOOTHROYD:** Walther PPK, 7.65 mil with a delivery like a brick through a plate glass window.

So begins a series of introductions to Bond's technology that we would see as a constant in all of the Bond films. Homing devices, ejector seats and an array of devices all the way to and including the invisibly cloaked Aston Martin in *Die Another Day*. This is what most of us think of when we hear the phrase "technology and James Bond." They are tools, built by humans to solve problems. They are means to an end.

Let's delve a bit deeper into the meaning of technology. An important facet of technology is that it is designed with a purpose. That purpose frames the context within which the technology exists. That context makes some things possible, and others impossible. However, it's often difficult to know the purpose of an object with which you have no familiarity. Philosophers of technology refer to this phenomenon as "technological embodiment." Don Ihde asks a very important question about technology that is central to our discussion about 007.

> What is there about the artifacts we employ? The human-technology juncture displays a puzzling ambiguity. Imagine there to be, lying on my coffee table, a symmetrically shaped stone. It is ovaloid in form with one end more pointed than the other, flattened by chipping and flaking such that a sharp edge runs around the entire circumference. My guests arrive, and after the first round of drinks, someone picks up the stone and asks, "What is it?" The artist at the party takes it and pronounces that is an *objet trouvé*. It is a kind of art object. A writer, noticing that the breeze is now ruffling the pages of the magazine on which the stone had been placed, counters that the stone is merely a paperweight, a practical object. But the anthropologist scoffs, and with Sherlockean deductions delivers the assertion that it is, *in reality*, an Acheulean hand axe. He notes that not only is it shaped right but that objects of this sort are familiar parts of the Stone Age tool kit, found from the banks of the St. Acheul River in France to the Vaal River in South Africa. The difficulty under this party game is genuine. What *is* the object?[1]

What is the object, indeed? What we are asking here is precisely the question, what is the difference between James Bond and 007. Depending on perspective, the artist, writer, and anthropologist above each see the carved oval stone in a different way, declaring it to be a uniquely different thing—a work of art, a practical paper weight, a prehistoric tool. Ihde's central point here is to maintain that the way in which one perceives an object determines its utility.

This is what philosophers would call a "pragmatic" definition of reality. No one in Ihde's discussion denies that the oval stone object is actually on the table, so it does exist in that sense. The disagreement surrounds the nature of the object, its use, and its purpose. An exploration of definitions is important here.

---

[1] Don Ihde, *Instrumental Realism* (Bloomington: Indiana University Press, 1990), pp. 68–69.

Technology before Q

What of this term, "technology?" Where does it come from? What are its roots? The Greek word *technê* actually denoted a kind of knowledge. This was a knowledge derived in the manner of an artisan, through the use of the hands in an interaction with his surroundings. It was knowledge derived through action, and through manipulation.

The American pragmatic philosopher John Dewey spent much time discussing technology as knowledge, and arrived at the conclusion that as tools, technological artifacts can be more than just hammers, levers, jet packs, and exploding attaché cases. Technological artifacts could be techniques as well, ranging from abstract mathematical theorems to the way in which one prefers a drink to be made. Consider this exchange from *Dr. No.*

> **DR. NO:** A medium dry martini, lemon peel, shaken not stirred.
> **JAMES BOND:** Vodka?
> **DR. NO:** Of course.

If you were to ask a martini drinker about technology and that particular libation, he or she might respond by listing the cocktail shaker (or the pitcher and stirrer, if so inclined), and maybe the means by which the vodka was distilled, the glass manufactured, and so forth. What of the actual technique of mixing a proper martini? Any good bartender will tell you that this is not a trivial matter. Techniques are means to ends, just as technological devices. Not surprisingly, "technique" and "technology" share "*technê*" as a root. A preference for shaken, as opposed to stirred, martinis marks a preference for a particular technique which is, like all technological artifacts, a means to an end. Thus, shaking one's martinis, as a technique, is every bit as technological as using a laser beam for either cutting metal or dispatching one's nemesis.

Martin Heidegger pushes our understanding of the term "technology" even further. In a conceptually challenging 1954 essay entitled "The Question Concerning Technology," Heidegger takes his audience on a journey that includes the ancient Greek *technê* and pushes it to its limits in what he sees as the modern world. In addition to technology as a means to an end, Heidegger argues that technology is that which "brings forth" or "reveals," much as the artisan brings forth a chalice from raw silver. In our terms, a good bartender brings forth a perfectly mixed martini from vodka, vermouth, ice, and a lemon peel. Without those materials, the bartender's know-how, and of course the cocktail shaker and glass, there would be no martini, or at least not the kind that James Bond prefers. Technology, it would appear, is the capacity to create and make things real through this "bringing forth."

This is not mere philosophy-speak. In his essay, Heidegger asks us to consider the work of modern science. He asks us to consider whether modern science is so successful because it has captured the way in which the world really works, or whether modern science is so successful because of the ways in which it has represented the world. As he notes, "Because physics, already as pure theory, sets nature up to exhibit itself as a coherence of forces calculable in advance, it therefore orders its experiments precisely for the purpose of asking whether and how nature reports itself when set up in that way."[2] Modern science succeeds, at least in part, because it has set itself up to succeed. If you conceive of nature, indeed name nature, in terms of forces and particles, then when you set up experiments to measure forces and particles, you will see nature behaving as forces and particles. The capacity to name something thus creates a contextual reality around it. Just as Adam's naming of the plants and animals of Creation in Genesis gave him divine license for dominion over them, so too reasons Heidegger. Naming nature as a calculable collection of forces and particles gives us power over nature as forces and particles. Likewise, naming James Bond "007" gives M power over him as an intelligence operative with a license to kill.

008 Can Replace You

As a tool, 007 is a resource to be used at M's will. In spite of Bond's occasionally reckless behavior and frequent late-night socializing, 007 must respond whenever M calls him to duty. We have seen this throughout the series. Many of the Bond films

---

[2] Martin Heidegger, *The Question Concerning Technology and Other Essays* (New York: Harper and Row, 1977), p. 21.

have early scenes wherein he is interrupted by M's call. His gambling winnings and initial flirtations with Sylvia Trench are interrupted in *Dr. No.* In *Live and Let Die*, M and Moneypenny appear in the wee hours at Bond's apartment, interrupting his date with a mysteriously missing Italian agent. Bond's personal activities mean nothing to M, except perhaps as an annoyance. 007 is much like a machine to be activated when necessary, and it is M, and M alone, who decides that necessity. He is, as Heidegger would note, "standing reserve."

Furthermore, 007 is a commodity, even to the point of being disposable in *Die Another Day*, whereas James Bond is as human as you and me, complete with fears, desires, and flaws. Miss Moneypenny refers to him as "James" or "Mr. Bond," denoting at least respect, if not a friendly familiarity. Villains present a very interesting interaction, as they tend to use both "Mr. Bond" and "007." The former indicating the respect granted a worthy adversary and the latter, the impersonal reference to an enemy you wish to liquidate. Finally, both Q and M refer to Bond exclusively as "007." There is no interest in Bond as a person in these exchanges. In fact, there is at times contempt, where he is seen as a flawed but necessary tool, one that they would gladly discard if a better one came along.

Consider our introduction to Miss Moneypenny in *Dr. No.* As Bond walks into the outer office at Universal Exports, she exclaims, "James! Where on earth have you been? I have been searching London for you." Then, on the intercom to M, she says, "007 is here, Sir." When speaking directly to Bond, she uses his first name, but in notifying M of his arrival, she uses "007." In *Goldfinger*, we see a similar interaction, this time with Bond and M (via the intercom) in on the conversation.

JAMES BOND: And what do you know about gold, Moneypenny?

MONEYPENNY: Oh, the only gold I know about is the kind you wear. You know, on the third finger of your left hand?

JAMES BOND: One of these days we really must look into that.

MONEYPENNY: Well what about tonight? You come around for dinner, and I'll cook you a beautiful angel cake.

JAMES BOND: Well, nothing would give me greater pleasure, but unfortunately I do have a business appointment.

MONEYPENNY: That's the flimsiest excuse you've ever given me. Oh well, some girls have all the luck. Who is she James?

M: (via the intercom) She is me, Miss Moneypenny. Now kindly omit the customary by-play with 007. He's dining with me and I don't want him to be late.

Contrast this behavior with the way in which 007 is expected to behave in the preceding dialogue with M.

M: Gold?

JAMES BOND: She died of skin suffocation. It happens to cabaret dancers. It's alright so long as you leave a bare patch at the base of the spine.

M: Someone obviously didn't.

JAMES BOND: And I know who.

M: This isn't a personal vendetta, 007. It's an assignment like any other. But if you can't treat it as such, coolly and objectively, then 008 can replace you.

James Bond is horrified at Jill Masterson's gold-clad murder at the hands of Goldfinger, and no doubt feels to some extent personally responsible. This doesn't matter to M. M's sole concern is to investigate Goldfinger, and 007 is the tool by which he will achieve this. This is not the only time in the series where M has been disgusted with how Bond's behavior interferes with 007's function.

Timothy Dalton's portrayal of the vengeful Bond in *License to Kill* is a most telling example. When drug lord Franz Sanchez brutally maims Felix Leiter by dangling him, legs first, into a shark tank and murders his wife, Bond seeks vengeance for his long-time CIA partner and dear friend. When M warns him that such actions would cost him his double-0 designation, Bond actually leaves Her Majesty's Secret Service, albeit temporarily, to seek his revenge on Sanchez. As 007, he was powerless to avenge his friends. As James Bond, he was a free agent. Furthermore, there is the handgun passage from *Dr. No*, where M threatens returning Bond to standard intelligence duty. Intelligence officers do not carry the double-0 license to kill, and in fact, M actually refers to them, as in the case of intelligence officer Strangways in *Dr. No*, by name. In *Goldfinger*, he threatens to replace Bond with 008. Quite clearly, 007 is replaceable, even expendable.

Bond is obviously expendable to his enemies. Yet, his interactions with those enemies demonstrate that they treat him both as James Bond and as 007. There is obviously respect when Bond demonstrates himself to be a thoroughly worthy adversary. Yet, when they refer to him as 007, they realize that he is intent on disrupting their evil plans. Consider this exchange from *Dr. No*.

> **DR. NO:** You persist in trying to provoke me, Mr. Bond. I could have had you killed in the swamp.
> **JAMES BOND:** And why didn't you?
> **DR. NO:** I thought you less stupid. Usually when a man gets in my way. . . . (he crushes the metal table decoration) But you were different. You cost me time, money, effort. You damaged my organization and my pride. I was curious to see what kind of man you were. I thought there might even be a place for you with SPECTRE.

The contrasting behavior among the villains is also clear in the famous laser scene from *Goldfinger*. We all remember this exchange:

> **JAMES BOND:** Do you expect me to talk?
> **GOLDFINGER:** No, Mr. Bond, I expect you to die!

What precedes it, however, is most telling, and draws the sharp distinction between Bond and 007.

> **GOLDFINGER:** Good evening, 007.
> **JAMES BOND:** My name is James Bond.
> **GOLDFINGER:** And members of your curious profession are few in number. You have been recognized.

That curious profession is, of course, the agents who have that special distinction of not only the license to kill but also the status of being so secret as to be perfectly expendable. In short, he is a commodity.

Make Yourself Useful . . .

The preceding passages demonstrate the extent to which the act of naming creates a context. M, Moneypenny, Dr. No, and Goldfinger all view James Bond differently, much as Ihde's artist, writer, and anthropologist had different perceptions of the same stone object. Yet, in order to fully understand the extent to which 007 is a technological creation, one must fully understand the extent to which 007 is an expendable commodity; one that is at once useful but, when that utility is questioned, easily disposed. There are two important meetings with M in *Die Another Day*, each illustrating how 007 can be conceived of as a means to an end.

M: Welcome back.

James Bond: Such hospitality. You don't seem too pleased to see me.

M: If I had my way, you'd still be in North Korea. Your freedom came at too high a price.

James Bond: Zao?

M: He tried to blow up a summit between South Korea and China. Took out three Chinese agents before he was caught. And now he's free.

James Bond: I never asked to be traded. I'd rather die in prison than let him loose.

M: You had your cyanide.

James Bond: Threw it away years ago. What the hell is this about?

M: The top American agent in North Korean high command was executed a week ago. The Americans intercepted a signal from your prison naming him.

James Bond: And they think it's me.

M: You were the only inmate. They concluded you cracked under torture and were hemorrhaging information. We had to get you out.

James Bond: And what do you think?

M: With the drugs they were giving you, you wouldn't know what you did or didn't say.

James Bond: I know the rules, and number one is no deals. Get caught, and you're given up. The mission was compromised. Moon got a call exposing me. He had a partner in the West, even his father knew about it.

M: Whether that's true or not, it's irrelevant.

JAMES BOND: No it isn't. The same person who set me up has just set me up again to get Zao out, so I'm going after him.

M: The only place you're going is our evaluation center in the Falklands. Double-0 status rescinded!

JAMES BOND: Along with my freedom?

M: For as long as I deem necessary, yes. You are no use to anyone now.

007 the technological device is no longer useful to M. This is the clearest example of 007 as artifact, and the clearest illustration within the Bond films of technological embodiment. The entity 007 is something quite different from the human James Bond. James Bond is recovering in a secret British hospital, while 007 is merely a heap of damaged goods. The central points about technology discussed above now become clear. Perception, according to Ihde, determines an objects pragmatic existence. In this case, M perceives James Bond as 007, an object whose costs now outweigh its benefits. In a Heideggerian sense, James Bond can be nothing other than 007 for M, for that is the only way in which she relates to him. The second exchange with M, this time in the London Underground, emphasizes these points.

JAMES BOND: I heard of this place. I never thought I'd find myself here.

M: Some things are better kept underground.

JAMES BOND: Abandoned station for abandoned agents. . . .

M: So what have you got on Graves?

JAMES BOND: You burned me! And now you want my help. . . .

M: What did you expect, an apology?

JAMES BOND: No. I know you'll do whatever it takes to get the job done.

M: Just like you.

JAMES BOND: The difference is, I won't compromise.

M: Well, I don't have the luxury of seeing things as black and white. While you were away, the world changed.

JAMES BOND: Not for me. . . .

M: Well, it seems you've become useful again.

Many moral philosophers will argue, with good reason, that persons should never be regarded as mere means to an end. They are, as Immanuel Kant maintained, "ends unto themselves." While that may very well be the case for James Bond the man, stripped of his name and given the number 007, he is purely a means to an end. Such is the central point of the philosophy of technology above. Technological artifacts are not necessarily devices, they can be ideas, techniques and, in this case, a name. A name which, as it would appear, M finds to be useful again.

The act of naming an object creates a context around it, and in part, that context is determined by the purpose of that name. We can see through interactions between James Bond, M, Moneypenny, Dr. No, and Goldfinger, that this context can be usefully interpreted technologically, so long as one is willing to expand his definition of the term "technology." When an object is named, it takes on many of the characteristics of technological artifacts, including utility, especially for the party that named the object. In this case, the object was James Bond, an English gentleman, Cambridge graduate, and Royal Navy Commander. As 007, he becomes precisely that which MI6 demands of its double-0 agents—a weapon to be used, or discarded, as his superiors see fit.

SECTION V

Why Do Chinese Girls Taste Different from All Other Girls?

Multiculturalism, Women, and a More Sensitive Bond

14

"That Fatal Kiss": Bond, Ethics, and the Objectification of Women

ROBERT ARP and KEVIN S. DECKER

> In the relationship with *woman*, as the *prey* and handmaiden of communal lust, is expressed the infinite degradation in which man exists for himself . . .
>
> —Karl Marx[1]

It's night. Bond makes a surreptitious underwater entry into a quiet Latin American port town; midnight works in his favor as he scales a wall, knocks out a guard, then slips to the base of a very special refinery tower. He opens a secret panel, then locates and deploys explosives on the nitro tanks in the hidden opium-processing lab. Stripping off his wetsuit to reveal an impeccable white dinner jacket and tie beneath, he retires to the local cantina and awaits the inevitable explosion. Bond informs his contact that he has "some unfinished business to attend to," namely an intimate encounter with the cantina dancing girl that begins just after the refinery goes up in flames. As Bond strips off his jacket and sets aside his sidearm in her upstairs room, he moves in for a passionate kiss. But 007's keen sense for danger is never switched off. He opens his eyes during the embrace, only to see the reflection of an attacker behind him in his lover's eyes! Timing his movement precisely, he swings the girl around to take the brutal blackjack blow to the head intended for him, then wrestles with the attacker as she slumps to the floor.

---

[1] Karl Marx, *Economic and Philosophical Manuscripts*, in *Early Writings* (New York: Vintage, 1975), p. 347.

Finally, he dispatches the other man by throwing an electric heater into a bathtub where the assassin has landed as the result of their struggles.

Shocking.

Now, whether Bond is justified in the ruthless and often fatal tactics he uses against thugs, enemy spies, and megalomaniacal madmen is the subject of other chapters in this book. But what about the way that he treats women? When it comes to them, Bond's seductive charm has its dark side: he uses violence, intimidation, and lies to obtain sexual pleasure and get his job done. Whatever good Bond does by completing his missions successfully, these behaviors and Bond's nonchalant attitude toward them seem intuitively wrong to many of us. What's important to make clear is, first, that these intuitions can be supported by reason, and second, that Bond's misogynistic tactics are not necessary to his work. We can prove both these points by examining Bond's "objectification" of women through the lens of a variety of moral theories—Kantianism, utilitarianism, and virtue ethics. We'll also demonstrate that a moral stance based on *virtue* is preferable to the others in this regard, and that Bond actually becomes *more virtuous* in his relationships with women in the films since the early 1980s.

"Who Will He Bang? We Shall See . . .": Bond and the "Male Gaze"

Objectification is everywhere in the James Bond film series: Bond constantly uses others to gain information, the upper hand, or sex. What precisely is "objectification?" The word "object" traditionally applies to lifeless, inanimate things like bottles of Dom Perignon, Aston Martins, and Walther PPKs. These things can be used or manipulated as means to fulfill our needs and wants, and if they have any value at all, it's because they serve in these roles. But in western philosophy, "object" gets its meaning by contrast with "subjects"—typically living, breathing human beings who *have* the needs and wants and *do* the using or manipulating of things. If "objectification" has a clear meaning, then it must refer to acts in which a subject is treated as an object in a person's thoughts or in their behaviors: it is a form of dehumanization. If objectification is morally problematic, it is because dehumanizing thoughts or behaviors are morally impermissible, not merely because we find them distasteful or "different."

Bond's treatment of women is a glaring case of objectification. For example, in Bond's initial sexual encounters with Sylvia Trench in *Dr. No* and Miss Caruso in *Live and Let Die*, his sole purpose is a quick romp in the sack before he rushes off to his next important mission. In both cases, Bond seems to view these women as valuable only to the extent that they are capable of bringing him sexual pleasure. Sexual objectification, however, is not a vice merely confined to Bond's escapades. When it occurs in Fleming's stories and novels and MGM/UA's wildly popular films, sexual objectification is merely a pop culture reflection of the more general "Male Gaze," a deeply unjust perspective that feminists from Mary Wollstonecraft (the eighteenth-century author of *A Vindication of the Rights of Women*) down to the present have been concerned with. The "Male Gaze" is a perspective that sees women as "other"—that is, inferior physically, mentally, and socially—and perhaps even as inherently wicked. According to feminist Sarah Bromberg, the prevalence of this perspective "allows men to unconscionably oppress and coerce women in order to satisfy their fantasies," while reinforcing a wider male dominance and affirming to men and women alike that what men want, they will eventually get.[2]

Moral theory, though, provides a number of grounds for "talking to the gaze" and we will examine three approaches out of many. First, there's the view inspired by the great Enlightenment philosopher, Immanuel Kant (1724–1804). He would say that objectification, *especially* sexual objectification (Kant was chaste his entire life) is wrong because it denies the inner worth of a person, reducing the person to a tool for sexual pleasure. Second, there's the view refined and popularized by John Stuart Mill (1806–1873) commonly called utilitarianism: actions are morally good when they carry the least cost and greatest benefit for the most people affected by them. Mill would likely say that although sexual objectification might bring extraordinary pleasure to his fellow Brit James Bond, it

---

[2] Sarah Bromberg, "Feminist Issues in Prostitution," online at http://www.feministissues.com; also in *Prostitution: On Whores, Hustlers, and Johns* (Buffalo: Prometheus, 1998).

has obviously harmful consequences to women in society and so it's morally impermissible.[3] Third, there is the view inspired by the ancient Greeks, most prominently Aristotle (384–322 B.C.E.), called virtue ethics. Aristotle held that morally right action is dependent upon, and issues from a good character. For someone who thinks in virtue terms, objectification would likely be considered immoral because it's not the sort of thing a virtuous person would do.

"Any Woman He Wants, He'll Get": A Kantian Puzzle

At first glance, Kant's moral views give us the strongest case against objectification. For him, every adult person, women included, has inner worth and dignity and must not be treated as a means to an end. Objects or things have *instrumental* value only for Kant—they are good or bad only so far as they are good or bad *for something*. But persons aren't *for* anything, for Kant—they are "ends in themselves."[4] Certain outspoken feminists use and extend this idea to highlight precisely what is wrong with the sexual objectification of women—that male acts of dominance regarding women are "aggressive intrusions on those with less power," and that, to be blunt, heterosexuality itself is "constructed" on a violent framework of "visual appropriation, then forced sex, finally in sexual murder."[5]

Yet powerful characters in the Bond films, 007 included, are constantly treating others as means to their ends. In *Moonraker*, Hugo Drax decides that the loyal, hulking Jaws has finally outlived his usefulness and abandons him to die on an exploding space station with his girlfriend Dolly. And despite the milestone marked by the ascension of Judi Dench as the first female M, she gives Bond orders ruthless enough to impress Drax in telling Bond how he is to treat ex-lover Paris Carver in *Tomorrow*

---

[3] Mill and his wife, Harriet Taylor Mill, were prominent early supporters of the rights of women in their co-written book *The Subjection of Women* (1869).

[4] Immanuel Kant, *Foundations of the Metaphysics of Morals* (Upper Saddle River: Prentice Hall, 1989); see also Onora O'Neill, *Constructions of Reason: Explorations of Kant's Practical Philosophy* (Cambridge: Cambridge University Press, 1990).

[5] Catherine MacKinnon, *Toward a Feminist Theory of the State* (Cambridge, Massachusetts: Harvard University Press, 1989), p. 127.

Never Dies: "Pump her for information." But this is the height of immorality, for Kant.

Is there any case *for* the permissibility of objectification from the Kantian point of view? Well, another way of putting this point about not using force or fraud against others is that no person deserves this kind of manipulation because every person is *autonomous* (from the Greek word *auto*, or "self," and *nomos*, or "law"), and therefore can and should "rule himself or herself." Their own informed decisions should be respected, and in most cases, we should not interfere with the life decisions of others, although we can certainly offer them advice and arguments. The interesting implication of Kantian autonomy is that when a rational adult chooses to engage in an action that does not harm anyone else, then that person is fully justified in making her decision. This is so *even if the decision-maker puts himself or herself in the position of being used by another person or group of persons.* It is the voluntary, informed character of the decision that puts it beyond moral reproach. In *On Her Majesty's Secret Service*, Bond is removed from pursuit of Blofeld and decides to resign from MI6; in doing so, he might have been legally obligated to stay on, but could not, on Kant's view, have strictly been *morally* obligated.[6] Similarly, evil henchmen from the tarantula-wielding Professor Dent (*Dr. No*), to Odd Job (*Goldfinger*), Nick Nack (*The Man with the Golden Gun*), and General Zao (*Die Another Day*) know full well the risks they assume, as well as the rewards for working for their masters. But the mere fact that their job entails their being in the ultimate "hazardous workplace" is not enough to question their free and autonomous decision!

If we put the stress on personal autonomy, then there would be nothing immoral about 007 seducing a female spy from "the other side" to gain information or for a sexual dalliance. Freely chosen, reciprocal sexual objectification like this occurs in *The Spy Who Loved Me* between Bond and Anya Amasova and in Bond's hot-tub party with Pola Ivanova in *A View to a Kill*. All parties have freely and autonomously agreed to engage in these behaviors, knowing that they are in some degree being used. As

---

[6] Fortunately for his fans, Bond was given temporary leave by M rather than a permanent vacation. Miss Moneypenny, what *would* we do without you?

one writer argues, "if one decouples Kant's repulsion for sexual acts from his overall contractual emphasis, a strong case can be made in favor of reciprocity in sexual relations, outside of a marriage contract."[7] That is if one ignores the chaste Kant's own personal view of sexuality as inherently degrading and accepts sexuality as a natural and even desirable aspect of life, then consensual and non-violent sex, even outside of marriage or a sustained relationship, can fulfill an important human need.

Obviously, there is a conflict in Kant's description of the moral decision-making process between two ideas. On the one hand, we ought never to use another person as an instrument, but on the other, autonomous persons may make their own well-informed decisions, even those that voluntarily submit them to being used by others. At best, this is a moral stalemate, since the same idea of "rational autonomy" implies *both* the condemnation and the justification of the objectification of women.

"His Lies Can't Disguise What You Fear": A Utilitarian Dilemma

Something similar happens in the context of utilitarian thinking. Remember that for the utilitarian, consequences count, so an action is morally good to the extent to which its actual consequences have the greatest benefit or pay-off in terms of pleasure or freedom from pain for the most persons affected by the action. As opposed to the Kantian view that persons can never be used as a means to some end, the utilitarian position can justify the treatment of persons as means to a greater good, achieving some benefit for the majority. So if the consequence of Bond's saving the whole world from Blofeld requires the death of one, two, or even a hundred henchmen in the process, then for utilitarian reasons, the killing is morally correct even if regrettable. In fact, it seems clear that 007 has a "license to kill" on the purely utilitarian ground that his work for Her Majesty's Secret Service protects the world from SMERSH, SPECTRE, rogue Soviet agents, and psychopaths of all flavors.

---

[7] Timothy J. Madigan, "The Discarded Lemon: Kant, Prostitution, and Respect for Persons," *Philosophy Now* 21 (1998); also available online at www.philosophynow .org/archive/articles/ 21madigan.htm.

As utilitarians then, we have to ask the question: does the objectification of women affect the happiness or pleasure of enough members of society to make it wrong? The lesson of the past has been that dire consequences follow when whole groups of persons are systematically treated as objects. Think of all the instances of majority enslavement of minorities through-out human history. Or think of totalitarian regimes, like the USSR under Josef Stalin or Hitler's Third Reich, in which peo-ple were tortured, tormented, displaced from their homes, experimented upon, and murdered in the name of some "greater good." More to the point, think of the consequences to individuals and communities in the contemporary Western world when people, particularly women, are treated as sex objects every day in advertising, music and music videos, tele-vision shows, and the cinema—Bond movies included. Such objectification has been linked to violence against women, date rape, eating disorders, and an erosion of respect for the sanc-tity of intimate relationships.[8]

Now, not one utilitarian, Mill included, thinks that we ought to favor short-term consequences (such as the titillation of voyeuristically watching Jinx Jordan rise from the water on a Cuban beach like some latter-day Venus) over long-term conse-quences to Jinx, women, and social relationships in general, for many of these consequences may be negative. Mill himself was concerned about the "tyranny of the majority" over minorities, a tyranny behind history's dominant pattern of male authority over women's identities, their sexuality and control over their own bodies.[9] On utilitarian grounds, one can confidently argue that these forms of objectification are immoral and should be condemned.

Unfortunately, that confidence can be shaken by the real-ization that a moral stalemate also arises from within utilitari-anism. We can ask if any *positive* consequences arise from these practices and attitudes of objectification? For example, if we're

---

[8] See the resources, videos and articles at www.vawnet.org; also, Lisa Tessman, "Critical Virtue Ethics: Understanding Oppression as Morally Damaging," in *Feminists Doing Ethics,* edited by Peggy DesAutels and Joanne Waugh (Lanham: Rowman and Littlefield, 2001), pp. 79–99; Kathleen Barry, *The Prostitution of Sexuality* (New York: New York University Press, 1995); Susan Dwyer, *The Problems of Pornography* (Belmont: Wadsworth, 1995).

[9] John Stuart Mill, *On Liberty.* Norton Critical Edition. (New York: Norton, 1975), p. 6.

willing to extend our look at consequences far enough into the future of troubling or tragic events, then it is correct to say that even horrors such as slavery, Stalin's gulags, and Hitler's atrocities have yielded some good consequences for their survivors and those who ended them: moral advancement and consensus, human rights regimes, soul-making, and other benefits. Unfortunately, these benefits seldom outweigh the original immoral acts, and certainly do not justify them.

More to the point, there may be benefit to the sexually charged roles that women like Xenia Onatopp and Elektra King play in Bond films. It is a matter of fact that men tend to be more sexually active, even more aggressive than women. When we take into account the fact that more men than women watch Bond movies, it may be a good thing that men can act out some of their fantasies in a "safe" way rather than involving others. In other words, Bond's sexual escapades could have the positive consequence of acting like the release valve on a pressure cooker even as men struggle for a better understanding of *themselves* as sexual creatures. Some forms of objectification may also be of benefit to women. In this respect, Wendy McElroy, a contemporary "pro-sex" feminist, argues that experience of erotic scenes of men and women in sexual situations can, for interested adults, be good therapy for lonely individuals and for couples looking to enhance their relationship. She also points out that a woman's ability to use her sexuality for money, power, or control over her own life is just as much of a legitimate consequence of sexual freedom as are feminism and worries about objectification.[10]

At this point, you may be as confused as Bond entering Scaramanga's funhouse. It seems as though we have a duty not to treat others and ourselves as objects, but also a duty to allow a person to exercise control over her own life, even if that entails making herself a sex object. We want to try and balance the positive and negative consequences that objectification entails, but we cannot. Since you only live twice, what's a moral person supposed to *do?*

---

[10] Wendy McElroy, "A Feminist Defense of Pornography," *Free Inquiry* 17 (4); available online at www.secularhumanism.org/library/fj/mcelroy_17_4.html.

"It's Murder on Our Love Affair": The Virtue of Being Bond

If you can argue equally well for and against the objectification of women from a perspective like utilitarianism or Kant's view, then there may be good reason to leave behind these moral theories when trying to justify what many of us intuitively think to be wrong with such treatment.[11] One of the things these two moral perspectives have in common is that they are based on a *rule* that separates morally permissible from impermissible acts. When that rule is up to multiple interpretations, it produces contradictory results. Yet there is another option, based in the thought of the ancient Greeks—and particularly Aristotle—that places emphasis on the *moral character* of the agent. To have a good character and act on it is to be virtuous. Furthermore, in being virtuous, we will not only do the right thing, but ultimately our actions will have good consequences as well.[12] In the current context, virtue ethics is preferable because we can avoid falling into the familiar stalemate trap about objectification from the previous section. But—as strange as this question sounds—*which* virtue ethics?

Aristotle and contemporary virtue ethicists see virtue in terms of good habits through which we foster a balance in our psychological dispositions, or *character*. Moderation is key: when considering how to react in a situation, we ought to aim between the extremes of "too much" and "too little" for an appropriate response. When our actions and emotional states hit (after much trial and error) what's "just right," the *mean* between extremes, then the virtuous person has begun to cultivate the kind of character that aids her in future moral dilemmas. Think of Bond in Q's virtual reality training exercise in *Die Another Day*, where success involved not merely firing at any and every potential target nor hiding from the virtual invaders

---

[11] The other possibility, of course, is that we, the authors, haven't pursued a conclusive resolution to the Kantian and utilitarian dilemmas. We admit this is partially true because of the limitations of space, and so we invite the interested reader to pursue these arguments further by taking a look at *Feminist Interpretations of Immanuel Kant*, edited by Robin May Schott (University Park: Pennsylvania State University Press, 1997) and Susan L. Brown, *The Politics of Liberal Individualism: Liberalism, Liberal Feminism, and Anarchism* (New York: Black Rose, 1993).

[12] Aristotle, *Nicomachean Ethics* (Upper Saddle River: Prentice-Hall, 1962).

of headquarters. His "measured response"—a matter of *skill* in terms of physical prowess, sensory acuteness, and familiarity with a firearm—in that scenario can be applied, for Aristotle, to understand morality. "The mean" also applies across the general list of virtues: honesty, courage, prudence, generosity, integrity, affability, and respect, just to name a few. Virtue ethics, with its emphasis on sound judgment in difficult and complex life situations, is the moral approach that fits Bond's dangerous and unusual lifestyle best; it is certainly the one in which the goal of human flourishing—that is, achieving the best that one is capable of in all respects—is most significant. We know that Bond typically sets his standards for achievement in terms of personal best, although competition from other agents such as Wai Lin in *Tomorrow Never Dies* and Alec Trevelyan in *Goldeneye* may inspire him to new heights. From this perspective, *my* objectification of another person, man or woman, would stand in the way not only of *my* becoming virtuous but also be an obstacle to *their* virtuous development. It would be morally impermissible to do so, in short.

This Aristotelian view of virtue has not been uncontested, however. Some thinkers in the virtue ethics camp have argued for a different set of virtues and for a great deal of selectivity about who is best suited to become virtuous. Philosophers like Niccolò Machiavelli (1469–1527), Thomas Hobbes (1588–1679), and Friedrich Nietzsche (1844–1900) have, for different reasons, argued that *power* is the consequence of the properly cultivated character, and is the reason for being virtuous. For each of them, power is maintained through master/slave relationships between the virtuous and the non-virtuous. This relationship is founded in the basic recognition (going back to Plato's *Republic*) that different people are born with, and have to live with, different psychological dispositions. There's little or no possibility for change of disposition for most people. Some have the natural disposition to handle power wisely, but the greater number of people are and will remain powerless and need to be controlled by others . . . for their own good, of course. Most Bond supervillains seem to believe that subjugating, destroying, or restarting the human race is *good* because they are *virtuous* in this sense. Hugo Drax and Stromberg think they are *born* to make the difficult decisions no one else can. But is this a correct description of Bond as a virtuous agent of Her Majesty's Secret Service? If we adopted this view of virtue, then objectification would be morally *permissible*—contrary to our intuitions about it—because Bond would be fulfilling his natural station in life, while the women he uses and throws away would be acting naturally as slaves or playthings.

Do we have another stalemate? Which virtue-ethics perspective is better? It may seem sensible, from a practical perspective, to say that we all ought to fulfill whatever our natural-born predispositions are. The way Machiavelli and company might put it, if you don't have the skills to become a secret agent, then don't bother beating yourself up—you'll never make it to the ranks of the double-0's and you'll only find misery in your constant disappointments. However, this perspective may be too limited because it puts the emphasis too much upon what *is* the case—that some people are unequal to others in important ways—and not what *ought* to be the case—that all people ought to be treated equally in some respects. One vital element of the Aristotelian virtue ethics picture is missing from a view that emphasizes virtue as a means to power. This element is *respect.*

Respect is a key virtue. Part of our process of becoming virtuous is recognizing that others are also on the path to virtue, and that they deserve, if not our active encouragement, at least breathing room to develop their capacities. It is obvious that the perspective shared by Machiavelli, Hobbes, and Nietzsche doesn't extend respect to unequals, however. Respect is not a virtue that can easily and authentically coexist with unequal relations of power between masters and slaves or men and women. Some virtue ethicists have argued that objectification as a practice or an attitude stems from a disordered or unbalanced psychological state. If this is true, then people who consistently fail to show respect are more like the ill and less like moral paradigms: they *need our help*, not our admiration. The person who has cultivated respect for others as a part of his or her character will not, though, objectify other persons, or if they do so, they will feel appropriate guilt and take measures to see that they don't do it again. And this is precisely what James Bond has done in the course of his long career as the protagonist of twenty films: he has become progressively more virtuous.

"I Feel Safe, I Feel Scared. I Feel Ready, Yet Unprepared": Bond's Progress

Bond has come a long way since the scene from *Goldfinger* depicted at the beginning of this chapter. He has become more virtuous in the course of refining his own sensibilities and skills as an agent, and by adapting to a social and political world more complicated than that of the Cold War. In *For Your Eyes Only*, Bond began confounding expectations by refusing to sleep with nubile young ice-skating champion Bibi despite her willingness. In the Timothy Dalton installments, a conscious effort was made by producers Albert R. Broccoli and Michael G. Wilson to "modernize" Bond by making him more or less a "one woman man" in his relationships. In *The Living Daylights*, for instance, Bond feels sympathy when Czechoslovakian cellist Kara Milovy is manipulated by her defecting lover, Soviet General Georgi Koskov, and develops a close relationship with her.[13] And despite dangerous advances from drug kingpin Sanchez's girlfriend Lupe in *Licence to Kill*, Bond falls for ex-CIA pilot Pam Bouvier, revealing a virtuous reciprocity in their relationship. As Bond moves in for a kiss at the end of the film, Pam asks, "Why don't you wait until you're asked?" Bond replies, "Why don't you ask me?"

Pierce Brosnan's Bond, in many ways a return to the grittiness and unpredictability of Connery's portrayal, has a mixture of both objectifying and sensitive relationships with women, but new dimensions of respect and reciprocal sexual tension have emerged in his relationships with Wai Lin and Jinx Jordan. Intriguingly, the (razor-tipped) shoe was even on the other foot when the beguiling Elektra King toyed with this Bond's emotions, sexually using and discarding him to get to M in *The World Is Not Enough*. Far from merely being a case of the *objectification of men*, though, this plot element ably put some male viewers in the uncomfortable position shared by most "Bond women" in earlier movies.

---

[13] Film historians Lee Pfeiffer and Philip Lisa write: "Some speculated this [one-woman Bond] was to promote the 'Safe Sex' environment of today. But, more probably, the script called for a return to Fleming's concept of [Bond] involved with but a single love interest in each story. Which also legitimizes the lead female character beyond the level of an impersonal sexual plaything for 007." In *The Incredible World of James Bond* (Secaucus: Citadel, 1992), p. 127.

How virtuous can Bond become in the twenty-first century without losing his edge, and his audience? The writers and film-makers who give him life should continue to search for an answer to this question. But to make Bond more of a sympa-thetic and believable to character to his audience, they have to continue to respond to feminism and changing cultural concepts of virtue. This means creatively spicing up Bond's relationships without relying on the objectification of women.[14]

---

[14] This chapter's title and section headings were taken from several James Bond film themes. In order, they are: "A View to a Kill," sung by Duran Duran, written by Duran Duran and John Barry (1985); "The Man with the Golden Gun," sung by Lulu, written by Don Black (1974); "Thunderball," sung by Tom Jones, lyrics by Don Black and John Barry (1965); "Goldfinger" (1964), sung by Shirley Bassey, lyrics by Lesley Bricusse and Anthony Newley; "Tomorrow Never Dies," sung by Sheryl Crow, written by Sheryl Crow and Mitchell Froom (1997); and "The World Is Not Enough," sung by Garbage, lyrics by Don Black (1999).

15

The New Millennium Bond and *Yin-Yang* Chinese Cosmology

DEAN A. KOWALSKI

The end of the Cold War signaled hope for world peace, but despair for many James Bond fans. What would become of the most famed action-adventure-spy-hero of all time? At a more practical level, the situation was even worse. The last Bond, Timothy Dalton, had left the role to pursue other interests. But the extremely devoted—the Bond fanatics—knew the situation was graver yet due to the unrest at United Artists and Metro-Golden-Mayer.

All of this seemed like a well-conceived plot by Blofeld to bring about the final demise of our hero. Much like the end of a Bond film, however, the day was saved. Danjaq/Eon Productions worked a new deal with UA and MGM. They also found (or found again) Pierce Brosnan to play their lead man. With the addition of new writer, Bruce Feirstein, and his elegant choice to pen scripts where "the world has changed, but Bond hasn't," the scenario ended exactly the way we wanted—with the phrase "James Bond will return in a new feature."[1] Blofeld had been foiled again.

Bond did return, of course, with a vengeance. The next four pictures did amazingly well at the box office. Brosnan seemed uncannily suited (pun intended) to play Bond. In fact, Roger Moore, visiting the set of *Goldeneye*, once said, "Both Sean Connery and I will be forgotten after everybody sees Pierce"

---

[1] John Cork and Bruce Scivally, *James Bond: The Legacy* (New York: Abrams, 2002), p. 245.

(*James Bond: The Legacy*, p. 242). While that's probably a bit of an overstatement, Brosnan is eerily a perfect combination of the two famed Bonds: He has Connery's stage presence and Moore's dry wit. Thus, Bond didn't change at all. He got better.

The Bond films were improved by improving the movie around Bond. The writing, especially the character development, was more intricate. Bond became more interesting by being placed in more fascinating situations and surrounding him by more complex characters. Thus the Bond films began to have more substance, facilitating more interesting interpretations of themes and elements associated with the films. As such, a careful analysis of the post–Cold War Bond films—the new millennium Bond—surprisingly uncovers affinities to certain elements of ancient Chinese thought, especially *yin* and *yang* cosmology. Cosmology is the study of the fundamental workings of the universe. The recent Bond films have been improved by bolstering *yin*, thereby achieving a better harmony with the already present *yang*.

The Meanings of *Yin* and *Yang*

The ideas of *yin* and *yang* are not completely foreign to western culture, of course. Most of us are familiar with the symbol:

What is less clear, however, is what exactly this familiar symbol represents. The ideas involved go back roughly three thousand years. The outer circle encompassing the two interior, interlocking shapes originally symbolized nature, or perhaps, the universe. The two interior, interlocking shapes represent the two universal forces within nature. The one on the left and bottom represents *yang*. This symbol typically appears as white, but sometimes red.

Yang literally means light, or perhaps, originally, sun or sunshine. It could also be interpreted as summer. Not surprisingly, then, this symbol over time also came to mean heat and activity. These derivations seemingly led to the further meanings of hardness, dominance, and masculinity. The symbol on the right and top represents *yin*. It invariably appears black. *Yin* literally means darkness, or perhaps, originally, moon. It could also be interpreted as winter. Not surprisingly, then, this symbol over time also came to mean coldness and passivity. These derivations seemingly led to the further meanings of softness, submission, and femininity.

How *yang* pertains to the Bond films is obvious. Bond flies jet packs, jumps out of airplanes, and drives tanks while struggling mightily to prevent some incredibly wealthy, masculine evil genius from taking over the world. Both typically dress well, drink well and ooze with machismo. And, except for a few noteworthy exceptions, all of this hasn't really changed over the forty-year span of the series. It is the *yin* element of the series that has changed. Beginning with Honey Rider (Ursula Andress), the series over-emphasized the softness, submission, and femininity of the *yin* element to the extreme. In doing so, the filmmakers distorted the true sense of *yin*. But with the choice to have Judi Dench play "M" and characters like Elektra King (Sophie Marceau), the series has approached a more genuine sense of *yin*. These changes, in fact, capture the very essence of the proper *yin-yang* relationship, as we will see.

Returning to the *yin-yang* symbol, note the way that the two shapes envelop each other. This signifies motion, or the constant dynamic between these two forces. It is tempting to interpret this as a struggle for dominance between the two forces. Although the forces are opposites in important ways, this temptation must be resisted. The relationship is more like a dance between two equal partners. It is sometimes described as the relationship between positive and negative electrical charges, or energy and entropy. For example, note how summer, although dominant for a few months, always eventually makes way for winter, but winter, although dominant for a few months, eventually makes way for summer. (This observation might indeed have been the impetus for *yin* and *yang* cosmology.) Thus summer is affected by winter and vice versa, accounting for the changing of the seasons.

More dramatically, if *yang* represents the active parts of nature that result in the violent upheaval of a mountain range or an explosive volcano eruption, then *yin* represents nature as the eventual receding of the mountain ranges through erosion or the containing of the lava flow in valleys and the cooling of the lava into rock, thus stopping its flow and resulting destruction.[2] To apply *yin* and *yang* to human activities, if *yang* is like man and *yin* like woman, then we could say that *yang* would not grow without *yin* and *yin* would not give birth without *yang*. Even if male activity begins a specific birth process, female nurturing energy is required to sustain the process, which eventually results in the birth of new children, which begins the process anew.

Reality as Dynamic and Harmony

These examples are not unique. Seemingly, all observed changes can be understood as a constant but natural (or regular) interplay of opposing forces. As a result, it was believed that *yin* and *yang* described all phenomena. All events are affected by and ultimately change into their opposites in an everlasting cycle of reversal. Consequently, all phenomena have within them the "seeds" of their opposite state.

Returning again to the original analogy, the summer solstice can be understood as the height of summer, but also as the birth of winter. And the winter solstice can be understood as the height of winter, but also the birth of summer. This is represented in *Goldeneye* when Bond's closest ally and friend, Alec Trevelyan (Sean Bean), turns on him to become his gravest enemy, seeking the financial ruin of Great Britain. The change is also represented by the opposite depictions of the Soviet Union. In the earlier films, it was often a great enemy that must be overcome, but in the later films, Russia becomes a most important ally.

Thus, the small light circle in the *yin* symbol and the small dark symbol in the *yang* symbol are sometimes called the

---

[2] Patrick Bresnan, *Awakening: An Introduction to the History of Eastern Thought* (Upper Saddle River: Prentice Hall, 2003), p. 169.

"Seeds of Change." These small circles represent the ideas that everything has the potential to change its direction and given enough time this potential will eventually be realized when it is sufficiently affected by its opposing force. There are times such that one opposite dominates and is experienced for a time, say summer or health, but, again, this is temporary. Soon enough the other opposite will dominate and winter or sickness will be experienced. Too much of either extreme is to be avoided. Excessive *yang* influences like volcanoes, tornadoes, and torrential rains often bring destruction and loss of life. Excessive *yin* influences like a long, harsh winter do the same. The ideal state of nature, then, is when *yin* and *yang* are in harmony, as with the regular turning of the seasons.

This provides us a glimpse into Chinese thought about what ought and ought not to be. A proper understanding of the natural order of things leads to insights into how things ought to be. Consider the following passage from the classic text *Yi Ching*:

> When the sun goes the moon comes; when the moon goes, the sun comes. The sun and the moon give way to each other and their brightness is produced. When the cold goes the heat comes; when the heat goes the cold comes. The cold and heat give way to each other and the round of the year is completed. That which goes wanes, and that which comes waxes. The waning and waxing affect each other and benefits are produced.[3]

The benefits here are left a bit vague, but the basic idea is clear enough. When there is co-operative harmony between opposing forces, mutual advantage occurs, which is desirable. To risk an empty platitude: Too much of one thing is bad. Or at the very least, too much of one thing without its opposite is bad. Perhaps Bond's taste for Russian vodka is an example of the first. Blofeld's blinding thirst for world domination is certainly an example of the second.

This insight was extended to human action. Consider another ancient Chinese source, the *Shu Ching*:

> The several kinds of evidence are rain, sunshine, heat, cold, wind and their seasonableness. When all five of these come in due

---

[3] Laurence Thompson, *Chinese Religion: An Introduction* (Belmont: Wadsworth, 1996), p. 2.

amount and order vegetation thrives luxuriantly. When one of them is too much it is bad, and when one is too little it is [likewise] bad. What we call the auspicious evidences are solemnity, to which seasonable rain is the correlate; good order, to which seasonable sunshine is the correlate; wisdom, to which seasonable heat is the correlate; good planning, to which seasonable cold is the correlate; saintliness, to which seasonable wind is the correlate. What we call the inauspicious evidences are violence, to which constant rain is the correlate; arrogance, to which constant sunshine is the correlate; dissipation, to which constant heat is the correlate; rashness, to which constant cold is the correlate; stupidity, to which constant wind is the correlate. (*Chinese Religion*, p. 6)

Seemingly, the evidence about how we ought to act comes from nature. The ideal is seasonableness. Thus, the ethically desirable states of affairs—solemnity, good order, wisdom, good planning, and saintliness—are correlated with harmonious or regular weather patterns; however, ethically undesirable states of affairs—violence, arrogance, dissipation, rashness, and stupidity—are correlated with unbalanced or extreme weather patterns. We should turn to the regular workings of nature for the guide on how we should behave. Since nature is understood as the *yin* and *yang* dynamic, this, too, can provide a model for how we should behave.

The *Yin* and *Yang* of Bond and Wai Lin

The *yin* and *yang* dynamic is effectively portrayed in the Brosnan Bond films at two different levels. The first is a specific example from one scene in *Tomorrow Never Dies*. In this installment, Bond is sent to investigate British media mogul Elliot Carver (Jonathan Pryce). Carver is launching his brand new global cable news network in grand fashion. His network will be the first to cover an emerging conflict between Britain and China in the China Sea. His network will break the story because Carver's henchmen, with the help of some cutting-edge technology, have caused the development by sinking a British battleship and downing two Chinese fighter jets. Due to the proximity of the events, both governments are led to believe that the other was the aggressor, leading the world to the brink of nuclear war. Carver then intends to finance a civil war in China and install a puppet government, where he will have exclusive broadcasting rights in the country for ninety-nine years.

Scene 20 demonstrates the specific example of the *yin* and *yang* dynamic. This is the exciting motorcycle and helicopter chase sequence. By this time in the film, Bond makes a somewhat reluctant alliance with Wai Lin (Michelle Yeoh), a Red Chinese agent of the People's External Security Force. She, too, was sent by her government to investigate Carver. Carver eventually apprehends both agents, and instructs his chief henchman, Mr. Stamper, to dispose of them both. Bond and Wai Lin escape, but in the meantime have been handcuffed to each other by Stamper. Joined at the wrist, the two agents flee to a busy Vietnamese street and commandeer a motorcycle, only to be chased by Carver's crew in cars and a helicopter. At first, both face forward, with Wai Lin seated behind Bond. Bond has one arm across the opposite shoulder. Bond immediately chides, "Stop fidgeting back there!" The two begin to struggle for control of the bike and disagree about their escape route. Soon, the two begin to work together. Bond calls out "clutch," and Wai Lin immediately presses the lever, one that Bond cannot reach because his only free hand is steering the bike. She then advises a left hand turn, knowing the area better than Bond. Now co-operating more easily, Bond asks, "How many back there?" Wai Lin informs him that she cannot see, but she climbs to the front of the bike so that she is facing Bond and can look over his shoulders at their pursuers. She then performs different maneuvers to aid their escape from her new vantage point, those that she couldn't have accomplished from her original position on the bike. While Bond focuses on the road ahead of them, Wai Lin focuses on the road behind them, increasing their chances of escape.

The two agents, one male and one female, one looking forward and one looking backward are acting like the intertwined dynamic of two opposing forces as represented in the *yin-yang* symbol. Neither is the overly dominant force. Furthermore, one gets the distinct impression that this is how it is supposed to be (at least if they are to escape). Were they not to act as a harmonious dynamic—because one or the other was excessively dominant—it seems unlikely that they would succeed in eluding Carver's henchmen. Their final maneuver to down the helicopter clearly demonstrates this point. Bond races the bike toward the helicopter and then slides the bike on its side under the helicopter. As they slide under and past the helicopter, Wai Lin throws a wire cable and hook into the propeller. These moves seem impossible if Bond and Wai Lin weren't in perfect balance and harmony. Their harmonious arrangement indeed leads to mutual advantage.

Also noteworthy from *Tomorrow Never Dies* is Wai Lin's overall prowess as a secret agent. In every way, she is Bond's professional equal. The same can be said about Jinx (Halle Berry) from *Die Another Day*. In some ways, Jinx mirrors Bond more closely than does Wai Lin, with her well planned, dramatically narrow escapes from danger and sexual appetite. (Recall Jinx's dangerous but elegant cliff dive to safety and the fact that she was the aggressor in the rendezvous with Bond.) Interestingly, the only time Jinx finds herself in any real danger in the film is when she follows Bond's orders to look for MI6 agent Miranda Frost. Because Frost is working as a double agent, but Bond and Jinx are unaware of this, following Bond's order here is tantamount to falling into a deadly trap.

The New M and the Old Bond

The insights pertaining to Wai Lin and Jinx lead to the second level at which the *yin* and *yang* dynamic applies to the recent Bond films, namely the development of their female characters. Perhaps the most notable example of this is casting Judi Dench as M. Utilizing her extensive acting talents, the writers made it immediately clear that Bond's new supervisor did not appreciate his proclivities or unbridled bravado. In a memorable exchange in *Goldeneye*, the first of the new-millennium Bond films, M chides Bond as a "sexist, misogynist dinosaur—a relic from the Cold War." Brosnan's view of his new boss is not all that flattering either. Bond complains that she is not suited for the position, because she is little more than a number-crunching bureaucrat. Thus the stage is set to understand M and Bond as opposing but equal forces, even if commonly allied in British intelligence.

A similar example of opposing *yin-yang* forces in the later Bond films can be found in *Tomorrow Never Dies*. The opening, pre-credit sequence depicts a black-market technology bazaar. We see (via British surveillance satellites) planes, tanks, missiles, and other military paraphernalia. We also see many of the world's most wanted terrorists. Admiral Roebuck hastily orders a missile launch that would, in effect, rid the world of these threats. Subsequent to the launch, we discover that among the black market missiles are volatile Soviet nuclear warheads. The missile ordered by Roebuck will detonate these, causing a nuclear disaster. Although Bond averts disaster, occasioning another exciting, classic opening action-sequence, the point for our purposes is this: Roebuck's choice to launch the missile was akin to a violent volcanic eruption and, thus, represents the undesirable dominance of the active *yang* force.

The opening scene sets the stage for Scene 5. Roebuck, as the ranking military official, and M, as the ranking intelligence official, meet with other high-ranking British governmental officials. They are discussing how to respond to an apparently unprovoked act of aggression by the Chinese. Roebuck, not surprisingly, recommends sending the entire British fleet, swiftly repaying aggression with more aggression. M, on the other hand, advises caution. She recommends gathering more information about the situation and sending Bond to get it before mobilizing the fleet. Roebuck looks her sternly in the eye and says, "With all due respect, M, sometimes I believe you don't have the balls for this job." Disdainfully, M looks him in the eye and says, "Perhaps. But the advantage is that I don't always have to think with them." I suspect the filmmakers were hoping for a laugh with this exchange. But, again, it can be interpreted as much more. M can be seen as an example of *yin*, while that of Roebuck can be seen as *yang*. In the opening action sequence, Roebuck's choice was seen as unfortunate because the *yang* associated with it excessively dominated. However, in Scene 5, we immediately get the impression that M's influence is a corrective to Roebuck's overly aggressive nature, and perhaps that of men generally. As a result of the interplay of these two suggestions, the group decides to follow M's advice, but with the caveat that the fleet be sent in only after Bond investigates and that they reevaluate the situation accordingly. Thus the group of British officials seemed to find harmony among opposing forces. This is representative of the proper *yin-yang* dynamic and thus seems like the proper (or best) course of action.

Elektra as *Yin*, Bond as *Yang*

Another manifestation of the enhanced *yin* force in the new Bond films is the presence of a female villain in *The World Is Not Enough*. Elektra King is the daughter of oil baron Sir Robert King. Elektra was kidnapped and held for ransom by the anarchist Renard (Robert Carlyle). Taking the advice of British intelligence, particularly M, King refused to pay. Elektra eventually escapes, but soon after her father is killed, presumably by Renard. Elektra inherits his fortune, including his oil holdings and interests. However, we soon discover that Elektra and Renard are now partners. She turned Renard into an ally once it became clear to her that the elder King would not pay the ransom. Together Elektra and Renard plotted to kill the elder King. Elektra also intends revenge upon everyone else associated with her kidnapping, especially M.

Before Elektra's plans were discovered, M sent Bond to protect her after the elder King was murdered. M worried that Renard was again out to get the King family. Bond uncharacteristically falls in love with Elektra. We also learn that the oil holdings were originally in Elektra's mother's family, and were so for generations. Thus Robert King married into the oil business. Elektra believes that her father stole the company away from her mother. She has two incentives for murdering her father: revenge for not paying the ransom and regaining her maternal family's fortune. We are led to believe that the second motivation is stronger than the first. In one scene, Elektra assures a group of religious believers that a holy place will not have to be demolished because it lies in the path of the proposed King pipeline. Elektra's father had authorized its desecration. She is rescinding that order, presumably because her family has religious roots in the area. This is just one instance in which the elder King put his own selfish interests ahead of those around him, especially Elektra's family's religious roots and convictions.

At first, we are led to believe that Renard is the main villain of the film and Elektra is the distressed damsel—a "Bond girl" in the classic (or infamous) sense of the term. This simply isn't so. Rather, Renard is merely the muscle. He is Carver's Mr. Stamper, or more nostalgically, Goldfinger's Oddjob. Furthermore, he is a self-proclaimed anarchist. His business is violent upheaval of existing order. As such, Renard is clearly the *yang* force of the

King-Renard operation. Elektra is the brains and the evil heart of the operation. However, she isn't driven merely by greed or world domination, like so many of the villains before her. She is much more complex. She wishes to restore her family's reputation and station in her native land, counterbalancing the *yang*-driven, self-serving actions of her father. Rather than buy her allies or beat them into submission, she seduces them—first Renard, perhaps out of self-preservation, and then, later, Bond. She took advantage of Bond's bravado in order to further her long-term goals. Elektra's attitude and behavior are reminiscent of the *yin* force, and exactly what we would expect from a strong (even if misguided) female character.

The End of the "Bond Girl" and the New Bond

The forces of *yin* and *yang* manifest in two other ways in the recent Bond films at this second level. The first way is that Bond falls in love. While this plot device was initially explored in *On Her Majesty's Secret Service* (Bond was married for a short time), it really hasn't been revisited since. But Brosnan's Bond has two loves in two consecutive movies. We become privy to the first when Paris Carver (Teri Hatcher) re-enters his life in *Tomorrow Never Dies*. Similar to *On Her Majesty's Secret Service*, Bond's love is murdered. Brosnan's Bond is visibly shaken (an entirely new character wrinkle) to discover that Elliot Carver has murdered Paris, as Elliot discovered that she betrayed him to aid Bond. Bond's second love develops from the aforementioned tryst with Elektra King. We see a more vulnerable side to Bond in these scenarios, which makes the character more interesting. The second way is that the notorious "Bond girl" character has all but disappeared from the movies.[4] The female characters are now invariably complex and no longer merely window dressing as they so often were in the earlier films. They are high-ranking British intelligence supervisors, fellow agents, and villains worthy of Bond. This, it seems to me, has made for more enjoyable and more interesting Bond films.

---

[4] Arguably, Christmas Jones played by Denise Richards in *The World Is Not Enough* is a throwback, but even this is controversial. She is a nuclear physicist, even if an unconvincing one due to her age. Perhaps the Cigar girl in *The World Is Not Enough* might be another counterexample, but she is a deadly assassin, reminding us more of Pussy Galore from *Goldfinger* than Honey Rider from *Dr. No*.

We might say, then, that according to *yin* and *yang* cosmology, things are as they should be when the two opposing forces are in harmony with each other. When one of the forces excessively dominates, things are not as good as they could be. Until very recently, the Bond films emphasized the *yang* forces at the expense of the *yin* forces. Thus it seems that the films were not as good as they could have been. Now that the Bond filmmakers have achieved more balance between *yin* and *yang*—in the ways described in this chapter—the Bond films have become better. The fact that this change for the better, resulting from the increased *yin* element, seems so natural only confirms *yin-yang* cosmology. The further apparent fact that Ian Fleming intended both elements to be more equally portrayed in the Bond series lends even more credence to it: The *yin* element began strong in the novels, then waned in the earlier films, and has waxed in the recent films.

One theme of this chapter has been to rely on something most of us are familiar with—the Bond films—to learn about something new, namely *yin* and *yang* cosmology. Another theme is to share ancient Chinese wisdom about how we ought to conduct ourselves: the forces of *yin* and *yang* should be in harmony in our lives, just as they tend to be in nature. Some philosophers, however, led by Scottish philosopher David Hume, believe that we cannot logically justify our moral claims by grounding them in how things are, and not even how things naturally are. Perhaps they are correct. After all, one could say that the existence of viruses is part of the natural order, but it's not clear that we do something immoral by developing and taking anti-viral medication. If so, perhaps *yin* and *yang* cosmology can only tell us so much about how we ought to conduct our lives. Nevertheless, the basic idea—we should strive to live a balanced life and avoid extreme behavior when possible—seems like good advice. Simply as a matter of prudence, it seems that seeking harmony among opposing forces in life is advisable. This advice is well taken in the new millennium Bond films. Thus, learning about ancient Chinese wisdom can also help us better understand that which we already knew, the Bond films; this is a third theme of the essay. Counterbalancing the machismo driven

James Bond films with substantial female characters has improved the series, and has done so without really changing Bond himself. He's pretty much the same (although not completely immune to the amplified *yin* forces). But his movies are better and, for Bond fans, this is as it should be.

James Bond Will Return
MOVIE GUIDE

Sean Connery as James Bond

Title	Year	Director	Screenwriters
Dr. No	1962	Terence Young	Richard Maibaum, Johanna Harwood, and Berkely Mather
From Russia, With Love	1963	Terence Young	Richard Maibaum
Goldfinger	1964	Guy Hamilton	Richard Maibaum and Paul Dehn
Thunderball	1965	Terence Young	Richard Maibaum and John Hopkins
You Only Live Twice	1967	Lewis Gilbert	Roald Dahl
Diamonds are Forever	1971	Guy Hamilton	Richard Maibaum and Tom Mankiewicz
Never Say Never Again	1983	Irvin Kershner	Lorenzo Semple, Jr.

George Lazenby as James Bond

On Her Majesty's Secret Service	1969	Peter R. Hunt	Richard Maibaum

Roger Moore as James Bond

Title	Year	Director	Screenwriters
Live and Let Die	1973	Guy Hamilton	Tom Mankiewicz
The Man with the Golden Gun	1974	Guy Hamilton and Tom	Richard Maibaum Mankiewicz
The Spy Who Loved Me	1977	Lewis Gilbert	Christopher Wood and Richard Maibaum
Moonraker	1979	Lewis Gilbert	Christopher Wood
For Your Eyes Only	1981	John Glen	Richard Maibaum and Michael G. Wilson
Octopussy	1983	John Glen	George MacDonald Fraser, Richard Maibaum and Michael G. Wilson
A View to a Kill	1985	John Glen	Richard Maibaum and Michael G. Wilson

Timothy Dalton as James Bond

The Living Daylights	1987	John Glen	Richard Maibaum and Michael G. Wilson
Licence to Kill	1989	John Glen	Richard Maibaum and Michael G. Wilson

Pierce Brosnan as James Bond

Goldeneye	1995	Martin Campbell	Jeffrey Caine and Bruce Feirstein
Tomorrow Never Dies	1997	Roger Spottiswoode	Bruce Feirstein
The World Is Not Enough	1999	Michael Apted	Neal Purvis, Robert Wade, and Bruce Feirstein
Die Another Day	2002	Lee Tamahori	Neal Purvis and Robert Wade

Daniel Craig as James Bond

Casino Royale	2006	Martin Campbell	Neal Purvis and Robert Wade

For Your Eyes Only—
Authors' Dossiers

JEROLD J. ABRAMS is Assistant Professor of Philosophy and Director of the Program in Health Administration at Creighton University. In addition to publishing regularly on the philosophy of popular culture, Abrams is also a sophisticated secret agent with a license to kill, or be killed, or perform a transcendental deduction of the spontaneous unity of pure apperceptive consciousness. And, of course, he takes his abductive inferences and dicent indexical sinsigns shaken . . . not stirred.

ROBERT ARP is Assistant Professor of Philosophy at Southwest Minnesota State University where it's so cold everybody has their own "License to Chill."

BETH BUTTERFIELD is Assistant Professor of Philosophy at Salem State College in Massachusetts. She has published articles on ethics and political philosophy, feminism and multiculturalism, and Sartre. She regularly teaches existentialism and ponders who truly is "simply the best." Sean Connery, Pierce Brosnan . . . or Pussy Galore?

KEVIN S. DECKER teaches ethics, modern philosophy, and American and Continental thought at Eastern Washington University. He is considering offering an upper-level seminar in care and maintenance of the Walther PPK, and trained his dog using Oddjob's grunts.

GREG FORSTER is a senior fellow at the Milton and Rose D. Friedman Foundation, where he conducts statistical studies and other research on school choice. When they proposed to give vouchers to Louisiana kids displaced by Hurricane Katrina, he responded that Louisiana schools are the one system that clearly doesn't need any reform, since they produced globetrotting spy and international law enforcer J.W. Pepper, whose brilliance and keen insight are matched only by his multicultural relations skills.

MAHLETE-TSIGÉ GETACHEW was born in Ethiopia and grew up in London. She read PPE at Somerville College, Oxford and philosophy at King's College, Cambridge, and is currently a Ph.D. candidate at the University of York. Allegations that she is wanted by Interpol and several state governments are simply not true. In her spare time, Mahlete enjoys diamonds and renovating bunkers in a palatial yet militaristic style.

SUZIE GIBSON is a Lecturer in the School of English, Communication, and Theatre at the University of New England, Australia. Her teaching and research activities are multi-disciplinary and she has published articles in the areas of film, literature, and philosophy. She used to have ambitions of being a "Bond girl" but her true alter-ego is that of Agent 99. She refuses to own or use a cell phone until a shoe version is made available.

JACOB M. HELD is Assistant Professor in the Department of Philosophy and Religion at the University of Central Arkansas in Conway, Arkansas. His research interests include Social and Political Philosophy, nineteen-century German philosophy, and the philosophy of law. He has published on postmodernism, natural law ethics, and punishment and is currently working on problems in Marx and Marxism. He would have concluded with a very witty remark about Pussy Galore but decency got in the way.

DEAN KOWALSKI is currently an Assistant Professor of Philosophy at the University of Wisconsin-Waukesha. He is the author of *Classic Questions and Contemporary Film* (2005) and has published several articles on freedom and foreknowledge. When he isn't teaching, doing research, or spending time with his wife and two precocious children he enjoys his favorite adult beverage neither shaken nor stirred. In fact, it's scotch, and ice is rarely involved.

ISHAY LANDA has published articles on popular culture and Nietzsche's philosophy. He teaches history at Ben-Gurion University in Israel where he tries to instill in his students the realization that although diamonds may be forever, empires are not. He received his Ph.D. in 2004 and is the author of *The Overman in the Marketplace: Nietzschean Heroism in Popular Culture* (forthcoming). Next, a license to kill.

MICHEL LE GALL was trained as an Ottoman historian and lived for a year in Istanbul in the mid 1980s doing archival research and traveling across the Bosphorous on a steamship. A college professor for over a decade, for his sins, Le Gall now serves as a corporate speechwriter. Although not a spitting image of Bond, he does enjoy black coffee, yogurt, and figs. He also owns a Rolleiflex camera although his model does not have a hidden tape recorder.

Sue Matheson has published articles on stereotypes, archetypes, and popular culture. After earning her Ph.D. at the University of Manitoba she is working undercover as Assistant Professor at the University College of the North in Thompson, Manitoba, where she teaches classes in herd dynamics and satisfies an occasional mania for goldeye.

William J. McKinney is a philosopher of science who has published numerous articles on the nature of scientific experimentation and the relationship between ethics, science, and technology. He has held positions as Professor and Chairperson of Philosophy and Religion at Southeast Missouri State University and Visiting Professor of History at Bucknell University. He is currently Dean of the College of Humanities, Fine and Performing Arts at Slippery Rock University of Pennsylvania, a clear sign that he has fallen prey to the specter of academic administration.

South, James South is Associate Professor and Chair of the Philosophy Department at Marquette University. He edited *Buffy the Vampire Slayer and Philosophy* (2003) and has published articles on both popular culture and late medieval and Renaissance philosophy. Being licensed to think about serious matters, James probably doesn't *need* two double bourbons to prompt him to ruminate on life and death, but since it works for 007, he's not inclined to argue with success.

Charles Taliaferro is Professor of Philosophy as St. Olaf College and the author or editor of seven books, most recently *Evidence and Faith* (2005) and *Love, Love, Love, and Other Essays* (2006). His favorite James Bond story is "For Your Eyes Only." Officially, he denies that he has served as an espionage agent on Her Majesty's Secret Service.

Matthew Tedesco is Assistant Professor of Philosophy and Religious Studies at Beloit College. He was previously employed at Universal Exports, though the terms of his employment remain unclear. The managing director could not be reached for comment prior to this volume going to press.

Steven J. Zani is Associate Professor of English and Modern Languages at Lamar University. He has recently published in *The Byron Journal*, *The Journal of Popular Film and Television*, and *Lovecraft Studies*. A government assassin in his former life, since joining academia he has changed his personal credo to "Live and Let Publish."

Index Provided Courtesy
of Universal Exports